OCRICULUM

OCRICULUM (OTRICOLI, UMBRIA): AN ARCHAEOLOGICAL SURVEY OF THE ROMAN TOWN

by
SOPHIE HAY, SIMON KEAY AND MARTIN MILLETT

with
contributions by
LUANA CENCIAIOLI, SOPHY DOWNES, ROSE FERRABY, ENRICO FLORIDI,
SHAWN GRAHAM, SALVATORE PIRO, TIM SLY, LACEY M. WALLACE,
ANDREW WALLACE-HADRILL AND SABRINA ZAMPINI

and illustrations by
SOPHIE HAY, LEONIE PETT AND LACEY M. WALLACE

22
ARCHAEOLOGICAL MONOGRAPHS *OF*
THE BRITISH SCHOOL *AT* ROME

The British School at Rome, London
2013

www.bsr.ac.uk

Registered Charity No. 314176

ISBN 978-0-904152-67-8

Cover illustration
Geoff Uglow, *Fall* (oil on linen, 170 × 200 cm, 2005–6).

Typeset by ACADEMIC + TECHNICAL TYPESETTING, BRISTOL, GREAT BRITAIN
Printed by SHORT RUN PRESS LIMITED, EXETER, GREAT BRITAIN

C O N T E N T S

LIST OF FIGURES

LIST OF TABLES

Foreword [1]

Its remarkable extent, state of preservation and monuments make Ocriculum one of the most important archaeological sites, not only within present-day Umbria, but also in ancient Italy as a whole. It is located within a natural landscape of remarkable beauty due to the variety of vegetation and the proximity to the river Tiber, thus forming a unified — and perhaps unique — blend of the historical, archaeological and environmental heritage that must be preserved and protected. Many travellers, some very notable, were drawn to Otricoli and its landscape. Lured by such beauty, Johann Wolfgang von Goethe described it with great passion and naturalistic competence in his *Italian Journey 1786–1788*:[2] 'Otricoli lies on an alluvial mound, formed in an early epoch, and is built of lava taken there from the other side of the river'. In order to convey to a wider audience the appeal that the monuments of ancient Otricoli had exerted on him, in 1985 Antonio Cederna wrote: 'The spectacle is stimulating and dramatic, as always with ancient ruins: the balance between the desire to understand and the burden of ignorance evokes a sense of well-being, it makes us feel alive' (*La Repubblica,* 5 October 1985).[3] And so many others have written similarly. The natural features that we still admire today as advocates for Otricoli's landscape are the same as those that in the past have both limited and fostered its human settlement and use.

The ancient Umbrian centre, bordering Faliscan territory to the west and the Sabina Tiberina to the south, is located on a hill of volcanic tuff at 208 m above sea level, which is now occupied by the modern town. It dominated the Tiber valley at a point where populations with different languages and cultures met: Umbrians and Sabines along the western bank, Etruscans and Faliscans on the eastern. The name might have been derived from the Greek word *ocris* (mountain), which had eventually found its way into the Umbrian (*ocar*) and Etruscan (*ukar*) languages — much like the Latin word *arx*. The site was surrounded by a wall, about 700 m long, built of large tuff blocks, coursed neither vertically nor horizontally, and not bonded with mortar, which Mafalda Cipollone and Enzo Lippolis (1979) dated to the fourth–early third centuries BC and Paul Fontaine (1990) to the fifth–fourth centuries BC. The site was settled during the Roman period too, as attested by archaeological features within the town. At the end of the Republican period it expanded to include the plain below, where there was a large bend in the course of the Tiber: a fluvial port was built there (at the so-called Porto dell'Olio) in an area that, due to a change in the course of the river, is now occupied by agricultural land. A pre-Roman phase is also attested in the archaeological evidence recovered from the landscape: iron age settlements, Orientalizing–Archaic necropolises (Lupacchini, on the modern farms at Cerqua Cupa and Crepafico) and Archaic–Hellenistic cult places.

Allied with Rome in 308 BC, following the battle of Mevania it acquired a strategic function as a frontier town between Umbria and the Sabina, and was an important link between the river and the Via Flaminia, which had been opened in 220 BC and passed through the town. At the time of the Social War (91–90 BC), Ocriculum sided with the Italian communities that rebelled against Rome, and it was destroyed. Awarded the status of municipium, it was rebuilt downslope towards the Tiber. Ascribed to the Arnensis tribe, it was included by Augustus in Regio VI, thus constituting its southernmost centre towards the Sabina. The beauty of its hinterland made it a suitable place for élite residences: Titus Annius Milo, a political figure of the first half of the first century BC, and Pompeia Celerina, mother-in-law of Pliny the Younger, both had villas in the area. In AD 69 it was involved in the struggle between the supporters of Vitellius and Vespasian, and it eventually became part of *Tuscia et Umbria* under Diocletian. Having being destroyed at the time of the Lombard invasion, for various reasons — including floods caused by the Tiber — it was abandoned in the course of the seventh century AD.

Trade with Rome was intense, thanks to the Porto dell'Olio, which remained active during the Imperial period, and the Via Flaminia; indeed, in the twentieth century, the Tiber was still used as a primary transport-route for minerals, wood, foodstuffs and building materials. In this respect it is worth mentioning the recovery of a *lignarius* weight (associated with official checks on wood cargoes), the famous Popilius's cups and brick kilns, stamps from which are well-known and commonly have been found in Rome.

Important monumental remains of the Roman town are still visible between the hill and the Tiber: the amphitheatre, the theatre, the 'Grandi' and 'Piccole Sostruzioni', the forum area and other public buildings such as the basilica, the baths and the nymphaeum. Monumental features are concentrated mainly near the San Vittore stream, a tributary of the Tiber, which flows down from Otricoli and which followed a different course in antiquity. This stream was channelled through a 300 m long subterranean conduit, cutting across the area occupied by the baths and the 'Grandi Sostruzioni', exiting below the theatre, and thus flowing into the Tiber beside the church of San Vittore.

The town, not surrounded with a wall, was traversed by the ancient Via Flaminia, whose path has been partly identified and which was lined with funerary monuments in its approach to the urban area. There are indeed many preserved funerary monuments along the Via Flaminia, and they constitute the first visible remains for those arriving from Rome. Much like a series of tall trees, they are aligned beside a long straight tract of the road, thus making it possible to reconstruct its original route. Not much is preserved of these tombs beyond their concrete cores, but a varied typology is attested: tower-like, with niches, square, drum-like, with facings in travertine and marble blocks that have been reused in the modern town or that are now part of museum and private collections. Largely dating to the later Republican and early Imperial periods, they are aligned with the road, on both sides of it, either interspersed at various distances or clustered (for example, as at località Pianacci); in total fourteen are easily recognizable by their scale and character.

The ruins of Ocriculum, visible to those who travelled along the Via Flaminia, are mentioned in texts from the sixteenth to eighteenth centuries that deal with Umbrian and Sabine antiquities. The first official excavations were carried out during the pontificate of Pius VI (second half of the eighteenth century) and were directed by the architect Giuseppe Pannini, who also had drawn the plan of the town and surveyed some monuments. Results from the 1775–1783 fieldwork campaigns were published by Giuseppe Guattani. Several monumental buildings were explored (such as the basilica and the baths) and the works of art that were found there were sent to the Vatican Museums, where they are still kept. Other material ended up in Italian and foreign museums (the Louvre in Paris; the Hermitage in St Petersburg). Important groups of finds are still to be found in Otricoli, partly reused in the modern town, partly in public and private collections.

Following various interventions in the course of the nineteenth century, the exploration of the area was revived through a series of activities carried out in the 1950–70s by the Ispettorato Archeologico per l'Umbria and then, following its institution, by the Soprintendenza alle Antichità: the amphitheatre, the baths, the theatre and part of the 'Grandi Sostruzioni' were thus investigated. In the last few decades, the Soprintendenza Archeologica per l'Umbria has, through a series of excavations, improved our knowledge of the layout of the ancient town. Most recently, this research has explored the sector immediately outside the urban area, bringing to light a tract of the Via Flaminia and a round funerary monument, whose original ownership I have identified recently (Cencaioli 2012b: 25–6).

The monument is adjacent to the Via Flaminia and only its upper perimeter was known previously. It is of the drum type, on a square base, or tumulus-type. Built in concrete, it was covered with tuff blocks and had an ashlar facing made of local limestone blocks (well coursed both vertically and horizontally), some of which show signs of *anathyrosis*. The square base is 19×19 m, 2 m in height, with four rows of block on each side (one protruding). On top of this is a drum (16 m in diameter; 6 m in height) with a moulded base. Only a few facing blocks have been preserved, and these have been put back into place; the rest of them have been removed or lost over the centuries. The drum was made up of blocks decorated with a floral frieze (one block has been reused in via Rosella and two have been recovered during the excavation of the crypt of the collegiate church) and moulded frames (recovered during excavation and currently under study).

The inside of the drum has no chamber for the deposition of the dead, whose ashes were instead placed in a marble cinerary urn, placed on top of the *bustum*, from which fragments of the bone funerary bed have been recovered. The monument, accessible through an architraved entrance, was surrounded by an enclosure (partly shared with nearby monuments) and had two cells for funerary deposits (in the front), together with a limestone seat (supported by nine lion paws) for funerary banquets. The front was closed by a gate, as suggested by the presence of a series of regularly-spaced holes along the outer edge of the limestone flooring slabs, whilst a circular hole might signal the presence of an altar for sacrifices.

Dated to the early Augustan period, it is a tumulus-style Roman funerary monument, a type that is attested in Umbria and more generally across Italy. The moulded frame can be compared with that from the mausoleum of Ennius Marsus at Saepinum. Due to the scattering and dispersal of the facing blocks, previously it had not been possible to identify the person to whom this monument belonged. However, a new analysis of inscriptions reused in other buildings has provided fresh evidence. Three fragmentary inscriptions, carved on blocks that are comparable in material and size, present similar features in the size, style and position of the letters and punctuation marks. These blocks, two of which feature *anathyrosis* on their right and lower parts, have been reused at San Vittore. The three inscriptions, already known but not linked with each other, are: *CIL* XI 4099, reading]I.C.F.ARN[, located on the wall of the church near to the right doorpost and made visible when, in 2008, restoration works removed the mortar that was covering it; *CIL* XI 4093a, reading]TUSCI.RE[, reused as a step of the ruined monastery; *CIL* XI 4093b, reading]OMIN[, reused in a door surround at the monastery (Cenciaioli 2012b: 32, figs 16–18).

Once put together, the three inscriptions read [L.C]OMINI.C.F.ARN.TUSCI.RE[, that is *Luci Comini Cai filius Arnensis Tusci* ('[belonging to] Lucius Cominius Tuscus, son of Caius, of the Arnensis tribe' — Cenciaioli 2012b: 24–6). The inscription (in genitive case) refers to a certain L. Cominius, whose name is known from two other inscriptions found in Ocriculum: one carved on a large block found near Palombara and showing the letters L. COM; the other, kept at the Villa Basili Floridi, which bears the name of the freedman L. Cominius Hilarus Tonsor (barber), perhaps a freedman of the above-mentioned Cominius. Tuscus is attested in Volsinii and Terni (*CIL* XI 7297, 4293).

The presence of the *anathyrosis* on the inscribed blocks and the funerary monument could be taken to suggest that they belonged together and that the inscription might have been located on the front, possibly on the base in *opus quadratum* beneath the seat. The large block with the inscription L.COM might have been part of the drum, placed in front of the mausoleum, and the pine cone-shaped stone, now in the Antiquarium of Casale San Fulgenzio, might have been placed on top of the funerary monument itself.

Important work has been carried out at the baths, the only ancient monument attested by epigraphic sources, which mention both their construction and restoration. Following the earthquake of 27 September 1997, restoration work took place in the octagonal chamber, and this made it possible to observe the layers beneath the coloured mosaic, which is now in the Sala Rotonda of the Vatican Museums and which was first brought to light by Pannini in 1780 (Cenciaioli 2012a). The layer beneath the floor is made up of mortar, a compacted *pozzolana*, with tile and tufa fragments; the walls are covered with a thick layer of plaster and marble slabs. The threshold, in *opus caementicium* with tiles and marble slabs, has been identified near to the opening of the eastern chamber. A black and white mosaic floor in a room adjacent to the octagonal chamber has been identified too, and its border, decorated with black and white bands, has been brought to light.

Also, a circular brick stamp has been identified among the *bipedales* of the northeastern niche of the rear wall. It mentions the *figlinae* of Lucilla Veri and dates to AD 145–50 (*CIL* XV 1078): *o(pus)(doliare) ex pr(aedis) Lucillae Veri (fecit) Merc(urius) Cl(audii) Quint(quatralis)*. This stamp, together with the other inscriptions, provides a definite chronology for the baths. Furthermore, important restoration work has taken place on the Roman theatre and the 'Grandi Sostruzioni' (the latter carried out in 2011).

Another important event has been the establishment of a national Antiquarium at Casale San Fulgenzio, in front of the church of the Madonna del Buon Consiglio. It holds materials from both recent and less recent excavations, together with finds from other museums. The opening, on 21 May 2006, coincided with the publication of a catalogue that presents the settlement history of the area from the pre-Roman to the Roman periods.

Besides field research, other studies have progressed too. Following the work of Carlo Pietrangeli, there have been guides and catalogues edited by the Soprintendenza and articles by various scholars, all attesting to the remarkable interest of Ocriculum. Among the most recent contributions one cannot fail to mention the relevant volume of the *Bollettino per i Beni Culturali dell'Umbria* (edited by Marilena Rossi Caponeri and Elisabetta David; published in 2012) devoted to the river Tiber, itself the catalogue of the 2011 exhibition *Il Tevere a Otricoli. Vita e fede sulle rive del fiume* (organized by Luana Cenciaioli and Elisabetta David). The great central Italian river is its subject, and it is approached from the perspective of Otricoli, ranging from geology to archaeology, from religious, artistic, economic and social life to the archival and bibliographic sources. The volume *Rilievi archeologici in Umbria* by Roberto de Rubertis published in 2012 also deals with Ocriculum and presents the archaeological survey of the monuments that was commissioned from the Soprintendenza Archeologica dell'Umbria. Last but not least, there is my own contribution to the dating of the baths (Cenciaioli 2012a).

The academic studies devoted to this most important town are many, and the volume that is presented here represents a further contribution to our understanding of the ancient town. Here are published the results of the urban survey that had been presented preliminarily at the conference *Mercator Placidissimus. The Tiber Valley in Antiquity* (Hay *et al.* 2008). The urban survey, carried out with the full support of the Soprintendenza per i Beni Archeologici dell'Umbria, began in 1997 as part of the Roman Towns in the Middle Tiber Valley Project of the British

School at Rome; re-commenced in 2002, and was completed in 2005. This survey was coupled with a geophysical survey that has identified new features, thus contributing to our understanding of the layout of the ancient town, known also thanks to the eighteenth-century maps of Pannini and the recent work of de Rubertis, who worked on behalf of the Soprintendenza per i Beni Archeologici dell'Umbria in the final decades of the last century.

The results from this research are especially relevant in terms of the preservation and promotion of the ancient town, as prescribed by law (D.M.7.12.1983). The archaeological area is today open to the public and benefits from the extensive work that is made possible by the professional and economic resources of the Soprintendenza and that, thanks also to a fruitful relationship with the Comune di Otricoli, is promoting further developments.

The results that are presented here, from the work of Sophie Hay, Simon Keay, Martin Millett and their collaborators, will bring this town to the attention of the academic world.

Luana Cenciaioli
(Soprintendenza per i Beni Archeologici dell'Umbria)

NOTES

1. Translated from the Italian by Dr Alessandro Launaro.
2. J.W. von Goethe *Italian Journey 1786–88* (translated by W.H. Auden and E. Mayer) (Harmondsworth, 1970), 126–7.
3. http://ricerca.repubblica.it/repubblica/archivio/repubblica/1985/10/05/chi-salvera-quei-tesori.html [last consulted 17.02.2013].

FOREWORD

I have been asked by Simon Keay and Martin Millett to write a short preface to this new book on the archaeological area of Otricoli. I am not an academic but have agreed with great pleasure to write a few lines with a view to explaining my connection to this very special place, showing how this is explained by the presence of my family there for several centuries.

My recollections extend back to the early 1960s, when my family and I returned home to Italy after a period of living overseas. It was then customary in the summer months to spend some of the holidays at Otricoli, at the house of my grandmother, with its broader agricultural estate, within which lay the archaeological area of the ancient city. Share-cropping was still practised then, and the houses on her land were occupied by farm-workers who were bound to us through their hard work and in terms of deep affection. Every day we would go out into the countryside with the farm-manager to inspect the estate, and as we moved from one farmhouse to the next, we routinely passed through the Roman ruins. The larger monuments were easily recognized, while others were completely covered by vegetation. An air of mystery pervaded the whole place, and the farm-workers often talked of hidden treasures, containers filled with gold coins, and a secret tunnel that ran through the countryside for a long distance. While the latter actually existed and can today be identified as a Roman conduit, the buried treasures remain the stuff of dreams!

There was considerable sensibility to ancient art in my family, and in the garden of the country house were many archaeological finds, some of which have been stolen in more recent years. In the company of my grandmother, we strolled in the Forum at Rome and through Ostia Antica many times, and she had an excellent relationship with Professor Carlo Pietrangeli, who had published his first book on Otricoli in 1943, and followed it up in 1978 with another publication (which is now very rare). When it was decided to found the Associazione Amici di Zeus in order to promote an understanding of the territory of Otricoli through cultural activities, I was very pleased that Professor Pietrangeli became a founding member, since we had established a degree of friendship despite our differences in age.

In the 1960s, the Soprintendenza Archeologica per l'Umbria began the large-scale restoration of ancient Ocriculum. Drainage of the land was undertaken over several years on a substantial scale, and a range of unexpected finds gradually began to appear, as if by magic. Every stroll through the archaeological area of the ancient site revealed something new.

At the British Embassy at the beginning of 1996 I had the opportunity to meet Andrew Wallace-Hadrill, who had only just arrived in Rome as Director of the British School at Rome. I invited him to take a stroll through Otricoli, and from that day onwards there developed an interesting rapport with the Anglo-Saxon world. The Duke of Gloucester and his family, followed by Princess Alexandra, wanted to visit the ruins. Several artists from the BSR came to the site to find inspiration, while students from the universities of Cambridge and Southampton, led by Professors Millett and Keay, undertook an important geophysical survey of the area. Today several new initiatives are underway that aim to improve visitor enjoyment of the site, such as an entrance with a model of the archaeological zone, a rest area with refreshment facilities, and, last but not least, a series of leaflets and publications with a detailed description of the archaeological area. I also hope to be able to make a contribution to Otricoli in terms of ideas and initiatives that should facilitate the experience of visitors, and that are inspired by the way that sites of historical interest are presented in Great Britain.

Enrico Floridi
Otricoli, October 2012

FOREWORD

The study of the site of Ocriculum is one of a number of such studies undertaken in recent years under the aegis of the British School at Rome. From the mid-'90s onwards, there were two closely overlapping initiatives: the Tiber Valley Project, led by Helen Patterson, and the Roman Towns in the Middle Tiber Valley Project, led by Simon Keay and Martin Millett. Much of the Roman Towns Project was a subset of the first, looking at the varieties of Roman urbanism within the area of the lower and middle Tiber valley, though it came to extend beyond this area as the opportunities for geophysical survey across central Italy grew. Ocriculum has a key role to play in both projects.

Modern Otricoli stands on the boundary where three regions meet: the southernmost point of Umbria, with Lazio and the Sabina to its south, and to its west that portion of modern Lazio that in antiquity was part of Etruria, and hence comes under the Soprintendenza dell'Etruria Meridionale. It is a meeting-point and a crossing-point. As the Tiber snakes between the volcanic hills to its west, and the mixture of volcanic hills and limestone mountains to its east, the modern A1, the principal north/south thoroughfare of Italy, having made its way out of the Tiber valley immediately north of Rome and cut across the hills, comes down again to rejoin the river valley just south of Otricoli. And this is what in antiquity, by a slightly different route, the Via Flaminia did, making Ocriculum the first significant city on the route north of Rome. It features on all the itineraries. It also features in Ammianus Marcellinus's account of the triumphal progress in AD 357 of the Emperor Constantius II to Rome, since he stopped off here to display his military glory (16.10). If you are marching on Rome, Ocriculum is the last crossing of the Tiber at which you stop off before the final stretch.

Otricoli is also, it should be said, a place of magical beauty. The great loops of the Tiber around the natural amphitheatre of its hills, the gentle folds of its undulating ridge, wooded on its slopes, the valley bottom with a rare surviving example of the old fashion of growing vines 'wedded' to a row of coppiced trees, all this forms a suggestive backdrop to Roman remains that fulfil every romantic ideal: masses of crumbling, brick-faced concrete forming arches and vaults that disappear into the undergrowth. My own first visit to the site, in September 1995, made a deep impression; and when, shortly after, I met a member of the Floridi family, which for centuries has been the principal landowner in the area, Conte Enrico Floridi, I needed little encouraging in the suggestion that the British School at Rome should take an interest in the site. A firm friendship grew up, which soon came to involve not only archaeologists but artists, who could scarcely resist the festival of San Vittore on 13 May, when the wooden image of the saint is carried up the Tiber by torchlight, to be greeted on the banks of the river by a re-enactment of his protracted martyrdom. Enrico Floridi provided hospitality both for the successive waves of archaeologists who over the years walked the land in detail, but also for an artist, Geoff Uglow, who lived there for two years, and some of whose works illustrate this volume (see the front cover and frontispiece).

Otricoli is hard to resist; but it is also surprisingly difficult to study. The magnetometry survey, which had delivered such spectacular results at Falerii Novi, only 20 km to the southwest, consistently refused to divulge a street grid, or even a definitive trace of the Via Flaminia, which in the section excavated is paved as solidly as any Roman road. In the lower portions of the site, the alluviation is too deep, while on the upper slopes, too much has been robbed out. It is a tribute to the tenacity of Simon Keay and Martin Millett and their team, led by Sophie Hay, that it has been possible to tease out what must count as a radical rethinking of the ancient site. Ocriculum was no Falerii. Though it has been possible to make out traces of a grid layout on the ridge above the theatre, it is evident that this was at best one element of a much more complex urban settlement.

It is precisely because it is not a Falerii that makes Ocriculum so interesting. The formula of the Roman town as grid has been studied to excess, dominating our picture of Roman life. But the grid is a feature of the settlements of the plains, and especially of those laid out in colonial circumstances of treating the territory as a blank canvas. Ocriculum tells a different story. It starts as a little Umbrian hilltop settlement, probably going back to the Archaic period, but equipped with well-cut stone walls around 300 BC, which had, it now emerges, a secondary settlement on the lower tongue of land where the church of San Vittore overlooks the Tiber. Shattered, as so many other towns in central Italy, by Roman reprisals after the Social War in the early first century BC, it now starts a transformation, as its place on the Via Flaminia gives it growing importance. Striking above all is the degree of monumentalization: theatre, amphitheatre, baths and the vast vaulted substructures of what was presumably a temple complex made the town truly impressive to any traveller on the Via Flaminia. Yet our best guess at the number of inhabitants, around 2,000, scarcely raises it above the level of a village. In this it might be compared to Herculaneum, a small Oscan town transformed after the Social War into a major monumental centre.

The comparison with Herculaneum extends to its statuary. What first attracted attention to Otricoli in the late eighteenth century, triggered by the example of Bourbon excavations at Herculaneum, was its potential as a quarry for statuary. The fine group of portraits of the early imperial family, including a Livia in the praying position described as 'Orans', are close in selection and style, if not material (being marble not bronze), to the group found in Herculaneum. It is a new archaeological fashion to ascribe these to a building type now labelled 'Augusteum', though a remarkably similar group from Veleia in north Italy, also the product of late eighteenth-century exploration, certainly came from a basilica. But the important point is not the name of the building type. It is that in what by our standards were tiny settlements, Ocriculum, Veleia and Herculaneum, the first century AD saw a boom of monumentalization, driven by patterns of local benefaction that radiated from Rome, and with a heavy emphasis on the cult of the imperial family.

The peak of glory of Ocriculum was in the first and early second centuries AD, something confirmed by the distribution of pottery that this study shows to conform to the general pattern of the Tiber valley. But even in late antiquity, it retained some importance, shown by the construction of new city walls, and also, by implication, by the visit of Constantius II. And though it may have shrunk in late antiquity, there is evidently, as elsewhere in the Tiber valley, at small sites like Forum Novum/Vescovio, a continuity into the Early Middle Ages, when the churches of San Vittore and San Fulgenzio were founded.

The project at Ocriculum is thus a methodological experiment, in which the limits of magnetometry may have been shown, but also the strengths of combining it with close contour topographical survey to achieve an understanding of the transformations of an urban landscape. It is also a case-study of another, non-orthogonal, type of Roman town in which the high degree of monumentalization seems not to correlate with the scale of the urban population.

It would be wrong not to finish with thanks: not only to Enrico Floridi, but to the Soprintendenza dell'Umbria, and especially to the archaeologist responsible for the site, Luana Cenciaioli, who generously allowed the British School at Rome to experiment with new technologies at the site it has always regarded as the jewel in its crown.

Andrew Wallace-Hadrill
October 2012

ACKNOWLEDGEMENTS

The fieldwork that has led to the production of this book was undertaken over a long period and has involved a variety of people whose help we gratefully acknowledge. Our work was made possible by the Soprintendenza per i Beni Archeologici dell'Umbria. We acknowledge the support of the successive Superintendents, Anna Eugenia Feruglio, Mariarosaria Salvatore and, especially, Luana Cenciaioli, who has been responsible for the site throughout our project. Work on the site would not have been possible at all without the kind help and support of Enrico Floridi and his family. The team was welcomed and provided with help and support by the Comune di Otricoli.

The project was undertaken under the aegis of the British School at Rome and benefited throughout from the enthusiastic support of the then Director and Assistant Director, Professor Andrew Wallace-Hadrill and Dr Helen Patterson. In the final phases of the publication work the current Director, Professor Christopher Smith, has been generous in his support.

The exploratory fieldwork in 1997 was made possible by a grant from the University of Durham. The subsequent fieldwork in 2002–5 was undertaken as part of the Roman Towns in the Middle Tiber Valley Project, funded by the then AHRB. The final two seasons of fieldwork were supported by funds from the University of Southampton, the University of Cambridge Faculty of Classics, the McDonald Institute for Archaeological Research and the Society for the Promotion of Roman Studies. The University of Cambridge Faculty of Classics also provided funding for the preparation of the illustrations in this volume.

The work in the field was undertaken by a variety of people, including students from the Universities of Cambridge, Durham and Southampton. In addition to those who have contributed to this volume, Paul Johnson, Jeremy Taylor and Helen Woodhouse all helped with the supervision of the work at different times.

In the preparation of this report we have benefited much from the comments provided on draft text by Dr John Patterson, Dr Lacey Wallace, Professor Andrew Wallace-Hadrill and Bryan Ward-Perkins, as well as the two anonymous referees.

Finally, we are most grateful to Geoff Uglow for allowing us to use his pictures for the frontispiece and cover of this volume. They admirably exemplify the links between artists and archaeologists long fostered by the BSR.

INTRODUCTION

Martin Millett

This volume presents the results of an archaeological survey of the Roman town of Ocriculum (Otricoli, Province of Terni), the fieldwork for which was initiated in 1997 and completed in 2005. The work was undertaken as part of our project investigating Roman towns in the Tiber valley (Keay *et al.* 2004), itself part of the British School at Rome's broader Tiber Valley Project (Patterson and Millett 1998; Patterson *et al.* 2000; Patterson 2004). Our work on urban sites investigated within that project deployed a range of surface survey techniques to produce comparative information about urban centres ranging from small roadside settlements to the urban port complex of Portus. Work was completed at the following sites in addition to Ocriculum: Falerii Novi (Keay *et al.* 2000; Hay *et al.* 2010), the lesser urban sites of Baccanae, Castellum Amerinum and Forum Cassii (Johnson, Keay and Millett 2004), Portus (Keay *et al.* 2005), Capena (Keay, Millett and Strutt 2006) and Falerii Veteres, Vignale (Carlucci *et al.* 2007). A previous paper has discussed some of the preliminary results of the survey at Ocriculum (Hay *et al.* 2008). Another paper (Keay and Millett in press) places some of the results in a broader context.

The challenges presented by survey at Ocriculum were very different to those of the other sites investigated in the project, since it is characterized by geological deposits and buried structures that do not respond very well to magnetometry, while the complex physical topography of the site is difficult to understand on the ground, as a result of extensive tree cover and marked local variations in elevation. In addition, fragmentary standing remains of a series of Roman buildings survive, most of which have not previously been planned accurately. For these reasons, the production of a detailed topographical survey was fundamental to an understanding of the site. The problems of undertaking such a detailed survey in a difficult landscape, and appreciating the relationship of the standing structures to the different forms of evidence from geophysical survey, thus determined the nature of our work. Furthermore, our results needed to be reconciled with the important evidence from eighteenth-century plans of the site published by Giuseppe Guattani in 1784 (see below, pp. 13–20).

Ocriculum lies at the very southern tip of Umbria, on the eastern bank of the Tiber, close to the point where it is crossed by the Via Flaminia (Fig. 1.1). The medieval and modern village of Otricoli occupies a hilltop overlooking a former meander in the river Tiber (Fig. 1.2). The medieval core of the modern village occupies a spur at *c.* 200 m above sea level (henceforth asl), its walls reusing those of a pre-Roman Umbrian centre (see below). The Roman settlement was located on lower ground and occupied a ridge that descends towards the Tiber to the southwest of the village (Fig. 1.3). The northern flank of this ridge formed a cliff standing directly beside the river-bank on a large meander in the Tiber until the river changed its course in 1846 (Pietrangeli 1978: 342). The ridge slopes down from an elevation of *c.* 100 m asl at the east, to a plateau just above 80 m asl at its west. It is defined to the south by the valley of the San Vittore stream, a minor tributary of the Tiber that originates at a spring on the hillside just south of the modern village (Fig. 1.2).

At the western end of the ridge the small eighteenth-century chapel of San Vittore now overlooks the Tiber, whilst towards the top of the slope to the east stands the church of San Fulgenzio. Both buildings generally are considered to be of early Christian origin (see below, p. 11). A farm track runs along the spine of the ridge connecting the two and continues eastwards to form a junction with the modern via Flamina (SS 3). Midway between the two churches, a north–south track crosses the ridge, continuing northwards down a steep slope to fields in the area of the former river port known as the Porto dell'Olio, which lay on the eastern bank of the now-silted meander of the Tiber (Fig. 1.2). To the south, this track curves down into the valley of the San Vittore stream, which it then follows for a distance before ascending its southern slope to join the modern via Flaminia. Both these farm tracks now occupy deep cuttings where their routes have eroded the

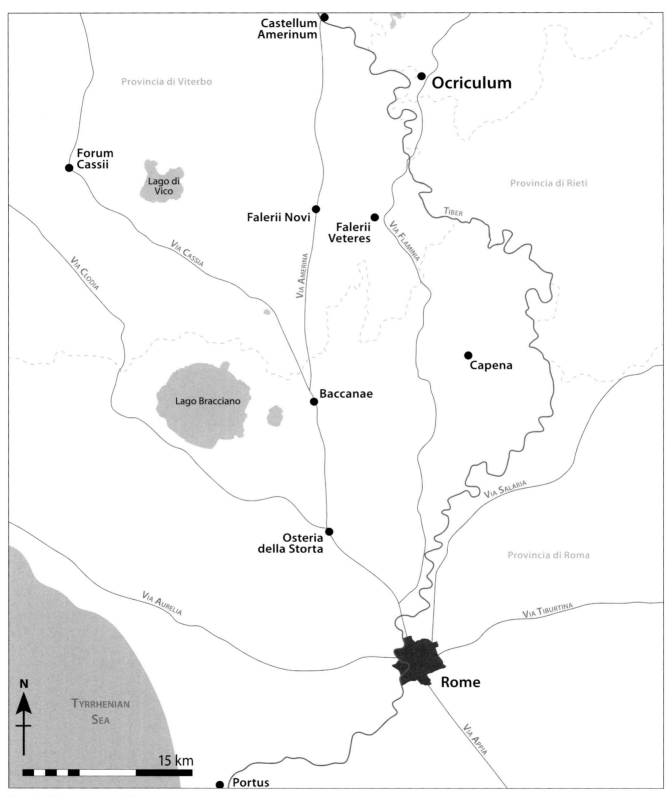

Fɪɢ. 1.1. The location of Ocriculum.

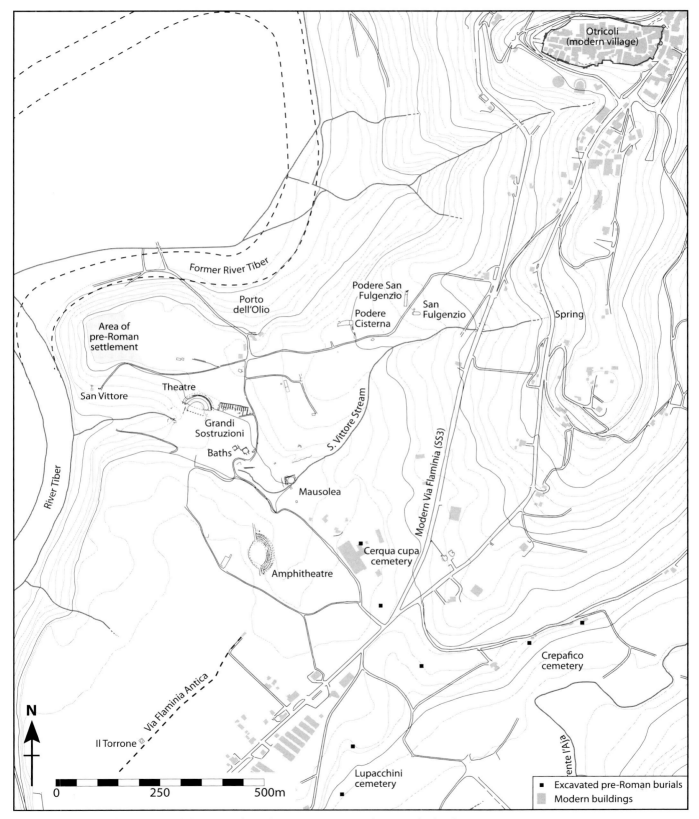

Fɪɢ. 1.2. The site of Ocriculum and the principal standing monuments in relation to the local area.

FIG. 1.3. General view of the site of Ocriculum from the modern village of Otricoli looking southwest. *(Photo: Martin Millett.)*

soft bedrock, implying a long period of use. In some places these sunken trackways have cut through a series of Roman buildings whose foundations are now exposed along the sides. Elsewhere on the site there are extensive standing remains of Roman buildings, including the amphitheatre, theatre, baths and concrete vaults ('Grandi Sostruzioni'), as well as fragments of buildings that are less visible because they are either incorporated within standing buildings or hidden beneath dense vegetation around the margins of fields. When considered together, these architectural remains represent a very significant set of Roman structures whose urban context hitherto has remained undefined.

The absence of an accurate contour map of the site has contributed to the problem of understanding the relationships between the various structures. The plans reproduced in most previous publications (Pietrangeli 1978: carta 1; Cenciaioli 2000: 9; Cenciaioli 2006: 36) are derived from that drawn by O. Visca in 1941 for a publication by Carlo Pietrangeli (1943: fig. 2), which lacks contours (Fig. 1.4). The most

recently published plans do include contours, but only of the southern part of the site in the vicinity of the theatre, amphitheatre and baths (de Rubertis 2012: 105–7, figs 1–2). Understanding the topographic context of all the monuments was thus a key objective of our survey, which was designed to complement the important programme of work being undertaken on the site by the Soprintendenza per i Beni Archeologici dell'Umbria (Cenciaioli 2008).

GEOLOGICAL BACKGROUND

Ocriculum lies at the very eastern edge of a series of lava flows derived from the Middle Pleistocene volcanoes of South Etruria to the west (Bertacchini 2006). Volcanic tuff deposited during these eruptions now forms a plateau at between 80 and 90 m asl on the eastern side of the Tiber valley, dissected by the river and its tributary streams. This erosion has created the ridge on which the principal Roman structures were built (Fig. 1.5). The amphitheatre, theatre and the

'Grandi Sostruzioni' were constructed against the edges of the tuff plateau, which was quarried and sculpted to form parts of their structures.

The tuff, overlain in places by a superficial deposit of weathered clayey sand, forms only a relatively thin stratum that overlies a sequence of Lower Pleistocene conglomerates, sands, clays and silts (Bertacchini 2006: fig. 2; Bertacchini and Cenciaioli 2008: 841–3). These deposits outcrop on the lower slopes of the valley of the San Vittore stream on the south side of the ridge and on the cliffs that define the northern and western ends of the ridge, although in some places obscured by landslip deposits. On the ridge top, the eastern margin of the tuff is reached on the eastern side of the Roman town, just downslope of the church of San Fulgenzio, so the Pleistocene sedimentary sequence that is sealed beneath the tuff elsewhere also outcrops at the surface here. This geological boundary coincides with the increased angle of slope rising towards the village of Otricoli. The valley of the San Vittore stream to the south of the site was modified significantly by major engineering works during the Roman period and will be discussed below (pp. 149–51).

ARCHAEOLOGICAL AND HISTORICAL BACKGROUND

There is considerable archaeological evidence for the presence of a pre-Roman Umbrian centre at Otricoli. This has been summarized by Gabriele Cifani (2003: 126–31) and Luana Cenciaioli (2006: 18–20; 2008: 813–15). Settlement evidence comes from both the hilltop occupied by the modern village and from the western part of the ridge overlooking the Tiber in the vicinity of San Vittore. The evidence from the ridge indicates the existence of a settlement dating from the eighth century BC and covering c. 4 ha. An important fragment of an early sixth-century BC architectural terracotta decorated with images of warriors was found at the Podere Cisterna (Dareggi 1978; Pietrangeli 1978: 24, fig. 6; Cenciaioli 2006: 20), c. 0.5 km further up the ridge to the east. This may imply the presence of a temple, although Pietrangeli (1978: 22) raised the possibility that it indicates the production of terracottas here. However, our survey perhaps suggests the presence of a later temenos in the vicinity (see below, pp. 147–9).

Evidence for the seventh–sixth centuries BC also comes from three excavated cemeteries at Fondo Lupacchini, Cerqua Cupa and Crepafico (Stefani 1909; 1929). They are all located on the west side of the valley of the Torrente l'Aja to the south of Otricoli, about a kilometre to the east of the settlement at San Vittore. Rock-cut chamber-tombs and *fossa* burials are attested, together with important ceramic assemblages (Cenciaioli 2006: 21–34). The styles of tomb architecture and ceramics have been taken to indicate close linkages with the Faliscans on the opposite bank of the Tiber. At the most recently excavated site, Crepafico, there is also evidence for continued use down to the Roman Imperial period.

The walled *enceinte* on the hilltop at the core of the present-day village of Otricoli presents problems in dating and interpretation (Figs 1.6 and 1.7). The *opus quadratum* wall has been dated variously to the late fifth–fourth centuries BC on the basis of parallels with Etruscan and Faliscan city walls (Fontaine 1990: 60–5), or to the late fourth–early third centuries BC, based on an hypothesized association of its construction with the alliance between Rome and the Umbrians from 308 BC (Cipollone and Lippolis 1979: 58–64; see below). In reality, there is little difference of opinion about the dating, since Paul Fontaine prefers a date towards the end of his suggested range, in the context of the conflict between Rome and the Faliscans before their treaty of 343 BC (Fontaine 1990: 65; Livy 7.22.4–5, 7.38.1). A date in the second half of the fourth century BC thus seems probable. Recent archaeological work has not clarified the date of the origins of the wall, but has demonstrated that there was a phase of late antique refortification (Cenciaioli 2008: 812). Whatever its date of origin, it also remains uncertain whether the hilltop enclosure was occupied contemporaneously with the settlement beside the Tiber and, if so, how these centres functioned in relation to one another. There is a widespread assumption that the valley-bottom settlement replaced that on the hilltop in the late Republic, but this is no more than an hypothesis.

There is extensive textual evidence concerning the history of Ocriculum. Its people (the Ocriculani) came into alliance (a *foedus aequum*) with Rome in 308 BC, following her victory in the battle of Mevania (Livy 9.41.20; Oakley 2005: 273–4, 532). A physical connection with the City of Rome seems to have been provided at first by the Via Tiberina and was certainly in existence by 299 BC, when a Colonia Latina was founded at Narni (ancient Narnia: Livy 10.9–10; Ashby and Fell 1921: 126). The subsequent construction of the Via Flaminia in c. 220 BC provided an improved and more direct link, presumably

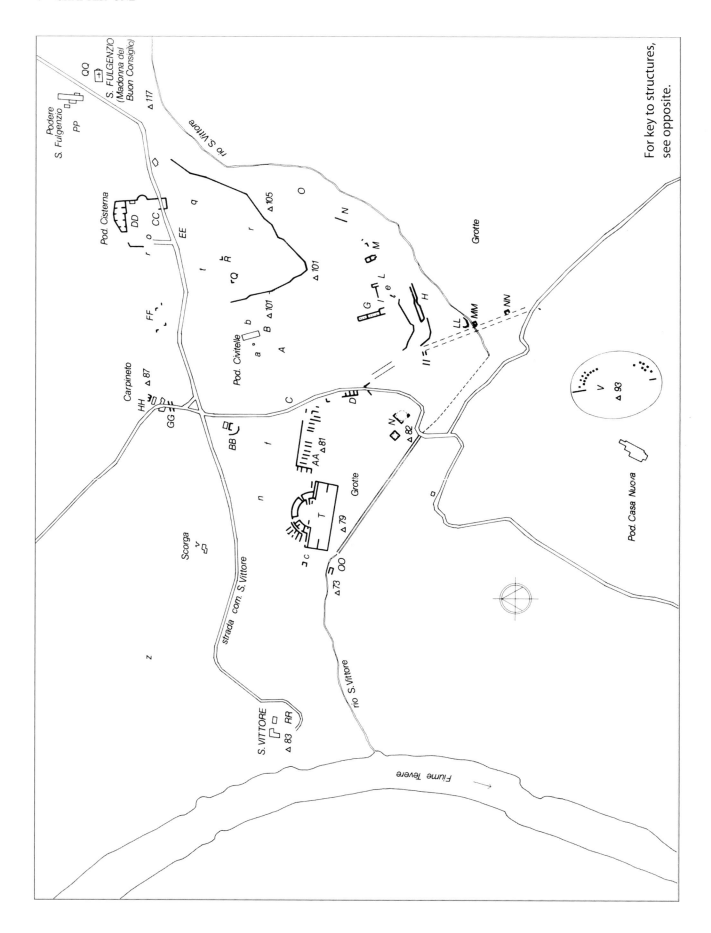

For key to structures,
see opposite.

FIG. I.4. Plan of Ocriculum. (After Pietrangeli 1978.)

Key: VISIBLE OR CERTAIN RUINS — A. foundations by the Podere Civitelle; B. vaults beneath the Podere Civitelle; C. brick ruins beside the track; D. substructures (= Pannini no. 7); E. vaults beneath the track; F. remains of the Via Flaminia; G. double cistern; H. wall with architectural decoration; I. late antique structures; L. foundations; M. cistern; N. concrete wall foundations; O. opus reticulatum wall; P. Foundations beneath the Podere Civitelle including an opus listatum stairway; Q. concrete wall foundations; R. corner of a travertine block wall; S. concrete wall foundations; T. theatre (= Pannini no. 10); U. probable theatre foundations; V. amphitheatre (= Pannini no. 3); Z. 'Terme' (= Pannini no. 5); AA. 'Grandi Sostruzioni' (= Pannini no. 9); BB. foundations (= Pannini no. 11); CC. foundations in opus listatum (= Pannini no. 22); DD. cistern at the Podere Cisterna (= Pannini no. 23); EE. remains of a road; FF. brick foundations at the Podere Cisterna; GG. cistern excavated beneath the track; HH. building in opus reticulatum; II. pier of a city gate; LL. circular funerary monument; MM. tower tomb above a columbarium; NN. tomb with a niche; OO. exit of an underground conduit; PP. cistern under the Podere San Fulgenzio; QQ. church of San Fulgenzio; RR. San Vittore and abbey ruins.

REMAINS THAT ARE NOT VISIBLE: a. mosaic under the Podere Civitelle; b. probable site of the basilica (= Pannini no. 15); c. findspot of a palaeochristian cross; d. Podere Civitelle — site of a probable forum; e. site of a palaeochristian building; f. ancient walls; g. ancient walls; h. 'Terme invernali' (= Pannini no. 6); i. 'Terme'; l. 'Magnifico Palazzo' (= Pannini no. 8); m. 'Conserua d'Acqua' (= Pannini no. 4); n. scaena of the theatre; o. 'Stadio' (= Pannini no. 12); p. excavated remains at the Podere Cisterna; q. excavated marble stairs; r. 'Foro' (= Pannini no. 17); s. 'Tempio' (= Pannini no. 14); t. 'Pozzi' (= Pannini no. 16); u. 'Colleggio' (= Pannini no. 13); v. 'Nobile Abitazione' (= Pannini no. 19); z. 'Palazzo Pubblico' (= Pannini no. 18). NOTES: Letters in italics appear in Pietrangeli's key but are not shown on his plan. Letters omitted are evidently misplaced. Letters underlined are not listed by Pietrangeli.

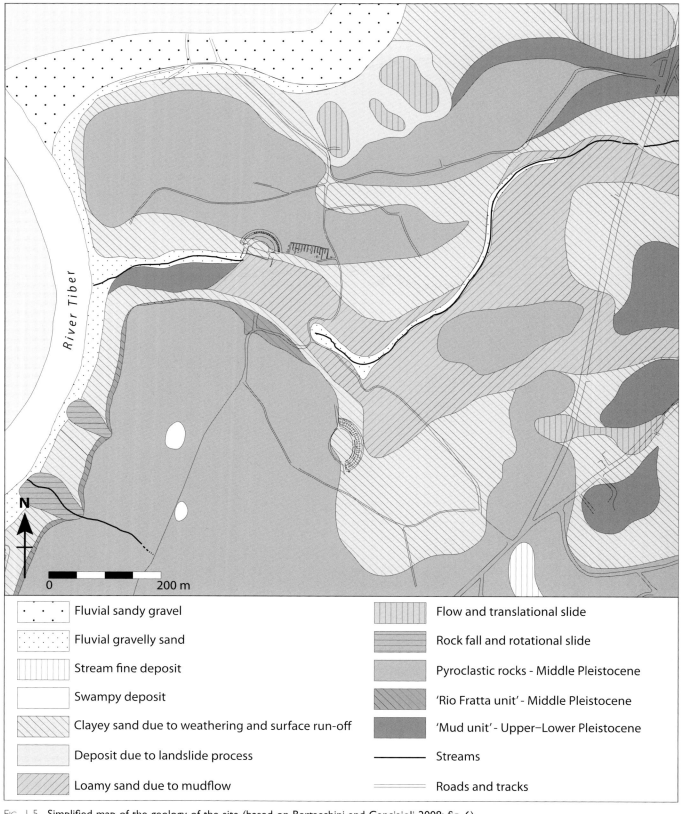

Fluvial sandy gravel

Fluvial gravelly sand

Stream fine deposit

Swampy deposit

Clayey sand due to weathering and surface run-off

Deposit due to landslide process

Loamy sand due to mudflow

Flow and translational slide

Rock fall and rotational slide

Pyroclastic rocks - Middle Pleistocene

'Rio Fratta unit' - Middle Pleistocene

'Mud unit' - Upper–Lower Pleistocene

Streams

Roads and tracks

Fɪɢ. 1.5. Simplified map of the geology of the site (based on Bertacchini and Cenciaioli 2008: fig. 6).

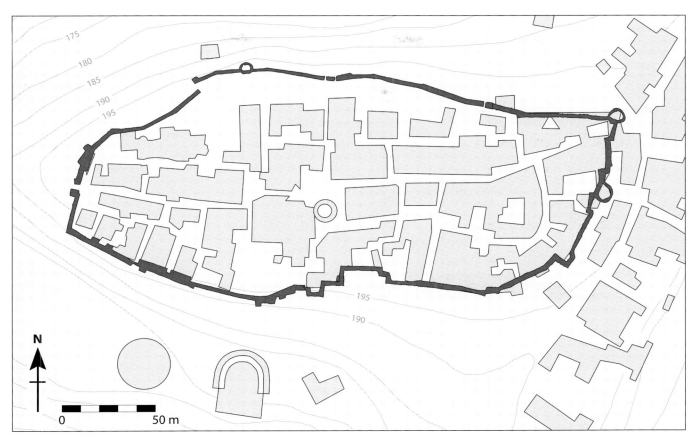

FIG. 1.6. Plan of the walled enclosure of presumed Umbrian origin at the modern village of Otricoli (based on Pietrangeli 1978: pull-out III).

FIG. 1.7. View of the western wall of presumed Umbrian origin at the modern village of Otricoli. *(Photo: Martin Millett.)*

FIG. 1.8. Inscription on the base of a statue to L. Iulius Iulianus (*CIL* XI 4087), probably dating to the first century AD, now in the wall of the Casa Squarti in Otricoli. *(Photo: Martin Millett.)*

stimulating its prosperity. It generally has been assumed that this consular road was first routed to the hilltop *enceinte* on the understanding that this was then the nucleus of settlement of Ocriculum (Ashby and Fell 1921: 165). However, the exact route of the road remains uncertain (see below, pp. 136–41) and Thomas Ashby's assumption that the hilltop was the main location of settlement at this date is questionable, given the subsequent discovery of evidence for the existence of a substantial settlement on the ridge overlooking the Tiber. Whatever its precise course, the construction of the Via Flaminia reinforced the advantageous geographical location of Ocriculum since it developed as a key point for the transfer of goods and people between road and river. A quay at the site now generally known as the Porto dell'Olio (Fig. 1.2) became a key port on the Tiber. Its importance in the communications network can be demonstrated during the second Punic War when, following the Battle of Lake Trasimene, Q. Fabius Maximus,

newly-appointed dictator in 217 BC, relieved the consul Cn. Servilius Geminus of his command beside the Tiber near Ocriculum (Polybius 3.88.8; Livy 22.9.5).

During the Social War, Ocriculum opposed Rome and, when defeated, is reported to have been destroyed completely (Florus 2.6). As it is not clear which part of the settlement was being occupied at this date, there is not yet any archaeological evidence of this supposed destruction. Subsequently, Ocriculum was enrolled into the *tribus Arnensis* as a municipium in 90 BC (Pietrangeli 1943: 29, note 10) and *quattuorviri* are attested on several inscriptions, the earliest perhaps dating from the mid-first century BC (**Fig. 1.8**: *CIL* XI 4087 and 7804; Pietrangeli 1943: nos. 30–3; Bispham 2007: Q61, Q92 and Q93). The Ocriculani appear in Pliny's list of region VI (*Historia Naturalis* 3.14.114) while Strabo also lists the town (5.2.9–10).

The region around Ocriculum was the location of a series of élite villas in the late Republican and early Imperial periods (Marzano 2007: 710–11, map 23). One belonging to Titus Annius Milo was mentioned by Cicero (*Pro Milone* 24.64), while Pliny the Younger's mother-in-law, Pompeia Celerina, had large estates here in the late first century AD (Pliny, *Epistulae* 1.4.1). The evidence of brick stamps confirms that important brick manufacturing estates in the surrounding area used the Tiber to transport their products to Rome (Steinby 1981: 238–9; Champlin 1983: 259). Similarly, evidence for the timber trade at Ocriculum is attested by the recent discovery of an inscribed stone weight dated to the end of the fourth century AD. This was used for the weighing of timber and attests to the role of the town in the control of this important trade (Cenciaioli 2006: 110–11; Diosono 2008: 262–3).

It is notable how perceptions of Ocriculum are reflected in the surviving texts. Polybius's account (3.88.8) of events in 217 BC, written in the second century BC, uses the *colonia* of Narnia as its geographical point of reference. By contrast, writing of the same episode in the reign of Augustus, Livy (22.11.5) locates them near to Ocriculum, with emphasis on the passage of both armies along the Via Flaminia. This reflects its enhanced significance and familiarity as a place frequently passed through when travelling to and from Rome along the Via Flaminia, or indeed on the Tiber. Reference to it as a place where historical events were located is seen also in later sources. In AD 69, after leaving Narnia, Vespasian's forces paused to celebrate the Saturnalia at Ocriculum,

FIG. 1.9. **View of the church of San Fulgenzio from the south. For the location, see Fig. 1.2.** (*Photo: Martin Millett.*)

before travelling on down the Via Flaminia to confront Vitellius's army just north of Rome (Tacitus, *Histories* 3.78). Late antique sources also confirm this continued importance as a place on the road system: Ammianus Marcellinus records that Constantius II passed through it en route to Rome in AD 357 (16.10.4). Similarly, Hymetius was brought to the town for his trial in front of Ampelius, *praefectus* of the City of Rome, in AD 368 (Ammianus Marcellinus 28.1.22). Finally, when Heraclianus, *comes Africae*, unsuccessfully attempted to invade Italy in AD 413, the battle that left 50,000 dead (Hydatius 24) is located as being in the region of Ocriculum. The Via Flaminia also played an important role in the Gothic Wars, leading Pietrangeli (1943: 33) to surmise that Ocriculum may have been destroyed in this period, although there is no direct evidence for this.

The late antique period also provides the context for the establishment of the churches of San Vittore and San Fulgenzio. The present building at San Vittore is a small eighteenth-century structure on the site of a Benedictine monastery, although the building itself has late Roman origins. It housed the relics of Saint Victor before they were translated to the collegiate church of Santa Maria Assunta in the village of Otricoli in the fourteenth century. A sixth-century inscription, now in the church in Otricoli, records the construction of an altar over the tomb of Saint Victor, who is believed to have been martyred in Syria in AD 168 (Pietrangeli 1978: 94–100). The other church on the

site is dedicated to the sixth-century bishop, Saint Fulgentius, who dedicated this altar. The origins of the church are uncertain, although structural remains within its standing walls (Fig. 1.9) have been taken to suggest an early Christian origin (Pietrangeli 1978: figs 99–100). Its location would be consistent with the building having originated within a cemetery of the Roman town (Pietrangeli 1978: 100–5). A sixth-century metrical inscription found near the Podere Civitelle in 1938 records the dedication of a baptistery (Pietrangeli 1978: 94–5, pl. 93), whilst a palaeo-christian monogram was also found in the same area in 1926 (Pietrangeli 1978: 94, pl. 92). These were taken by Pietrangeli as evidence for further early Christian buildings in the centre of the town, although their context remains unclear.

The date and circumstances of the abandonment of Ocriculum and a possible shift to the site of the modern village of Otricoli are subject to debate. Pietrangeli (1978: 42) concluded that the Roman city was abandoned in the seventh century as a result of flooding and the unhealthy environment. Others prefer to date its abandonment to the eighth or ninth century, relating it to the occupation of the area by the Lombard King Desiderius in 772 (*Liber Pontificalis, Vita Hadriani* 18). As this text refers to the *castrum*, it is most likely to refer to the hilltop centre rather than the site of the Roman town. It is also notable that the collegiate church in the village has its origins in the seventh century.

PREVIOUS ARCHAEOLOGICAL WORK[1]

Martin Millett

EIGHTEENTH-CENTURY EXPLORATION

Ocriculum was the subject of a major series of excavations in the eighteenth century under the patronage of Pope Pius VI. These were integral to his development of the Vatican Museums and provided him with important objects for display there. The excavations were under the direct control of the papacy and there are references to the finds in contemporary correspondence (Bignamini and Hornsby 2010: 114). The centrepiece of the Sala Rotonda in the Museo Pio Clementino is a mosaic taken from the baths at Ocriculum at this date, while many of the sculptures in the same part of the museum also derive from the excavations there (Werner 1998: 147–71, inventory nos. 45751–61). Other sculptures from the site have been dispersed to various museums including the Louvre and the Hermitage, as well as various private collections.

The principal excavations were undertaken between 1775 and 1783 under the supervision of the architect Giuseppe Pannini, who produced a series of plans and reconstruction drawings of the structures explored (Figs 2.1–2.7). These were published by Giuseppe Guattani in his volume *Monumenti antichi inediti* of 1784. This work provided an overall plan with a key listing the various buildings identified (Fig. 2.1), as well as plans and elevations of the theatre (Fig. 2.2), the amphitheatre (Fig. 2.3), the plan of a building referred to as a basilica (Fig. 2.4), an elevation of the concrete vaults — the 'Grandi Sostruzioni' (Fig. 2.5), and a view of the baths (Fig. 2.6). A fuller account of these excavations was to have been published by Giovanni Battista Visconti, but this never appeared (Ashby and Fell 1921: 163). A general view of the 'Grandi Sostruzioni' (Fig. 2.7) was published by Guattani in his *Monumenti sabini* (1827–32: II, 180).

The overall plan (Fig. 2.1) shows a series of ancient structures within the context of an apparently wooded topography. The various buildings shown on the plan are not orientated correctly in relation to one another, but sufficient of them can be related to the modern topography to understand the general layout (cf. Chapter 6). In the description that follows, the numbers shown on this plan and labelled in its key are referred to using the terminology given there with the reference numbers shown in brackets. The eighteenth-century roads, 'strade moderne' (24), mainly correspond to the farm tracks still in use, except that the approach from the south is not the principal one used today (which passes to the north of the amphitheatre). Instead, the route shown follows the present track, which passes to the south of the amphitheatre before curving down the slope to go in front of the theatre, passing between the baths and the 'Grandi Sostruzioni', a route now only followed by a small path. The Tiber is shown to the west (21), and the route of the 'Via Flaminia' (1) is shown running north–south across the site with two 'Sepolcri' (2) on its western flank (and another further away to the east). The relationship of these to the present standing remains is uncertain, although they may represent respectively the mausoleum known as Il Torrone on the stretch of the Via Flamina to the south of the town (Fig. 1.2) and one of those in the field to the northeast of the amphitheatre (Fig. 1.4, MM and NN). The 'Anfiteatro' (3) and 'Terme' (5) are identified readily, and are also shown in more detailed illustrations (Figs 2.2 and 2.6). The 'Conserua d'Acqua' (4) shown between the two is probably to be identified with the substantial below-ground cistern in the valley floor (see below, p. 60), although the shape shown is not easily related to the surviving structure. The 'Terme Hiemali' (6) and 'Magnifico Palazzo' (8) are not now extant, and their relationship with the standing remains of the baths is uncertain. If 'Gran Muro' (7) is to be identified with the extant retaining wall, now referred to as the 'Piccole Sostruzioni' (see below, p. 60), as seems certain, then the representation of the orientation of these buildings (5, 6 and 8) on the published plan must be

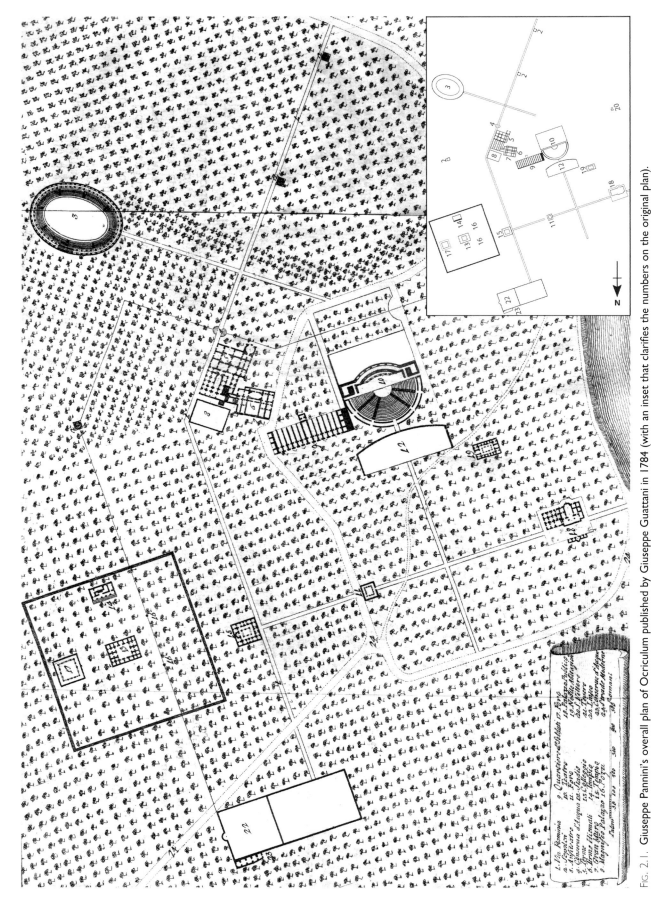

FIG. 2.1. Giuseppe Pannini's overall plan of Ocriculum published by Giuseppe Guattani in 1784 (with an inset that clarifies the numbers on the original plan).
The key reads: 1. Via Flaminia; 2. Sepolcri; 3. Anfiteatro; 4. Conserua d'Acqua; 5. Terme; 6. Terme Hiemali; 7. Gran Muro; 8. Magnifico Palazzo; 9. Quartiere d' Soldati; 10. Teatro; 11. Foro; 12. Stadio; 13. Colleggio; 14. Tempio; 15. Tempio; 16. Pozzi; 17. Foro; 18. Palazzo Publico; 19. Nobile Abitazione; 20. S. Vittore; 21. Tevere; 22. Ninfeo; 23. Conserua d'Acqua; 24. Strade Moderne.

T·I

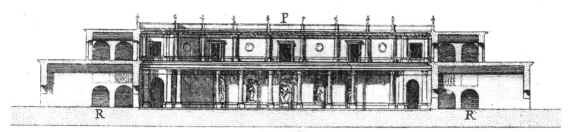

Fig.III.

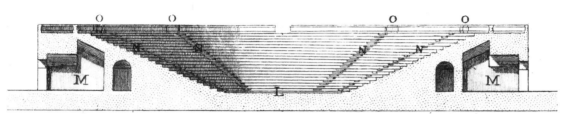

Fig.II.

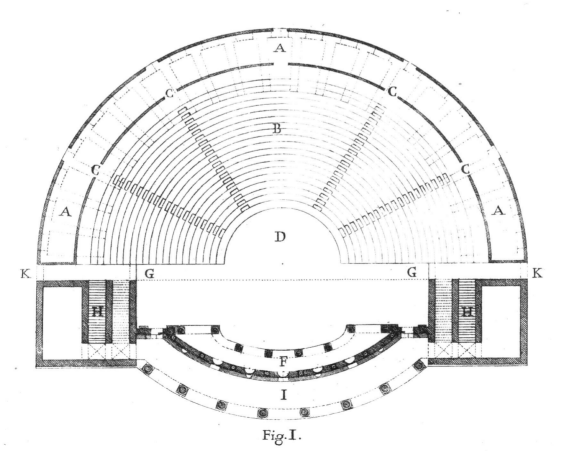

Fig.I.

FIG. 2.2. Pannini's plan and elevations of the theatre published by Guattani in 1784.

T.I.

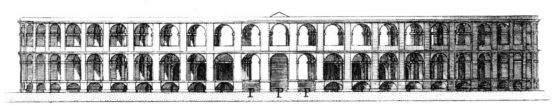

Fig.III.

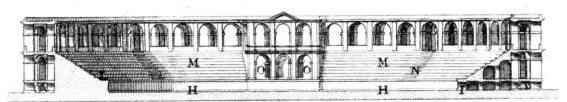

Fig.II.

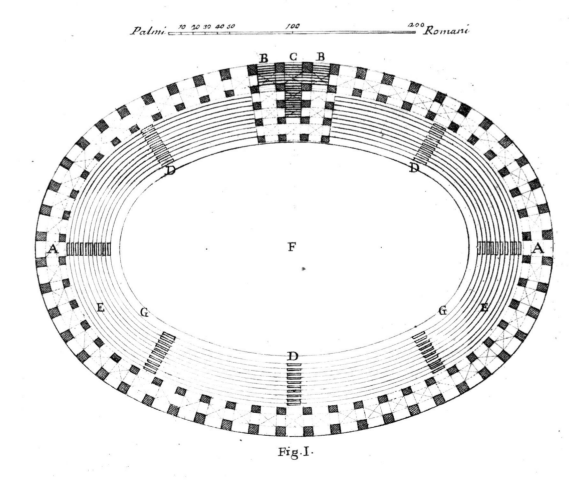

Fig.I.

FIG. 2.3. Pannini's plan and elevations of the amphitheatre published by Guattani in 1784.

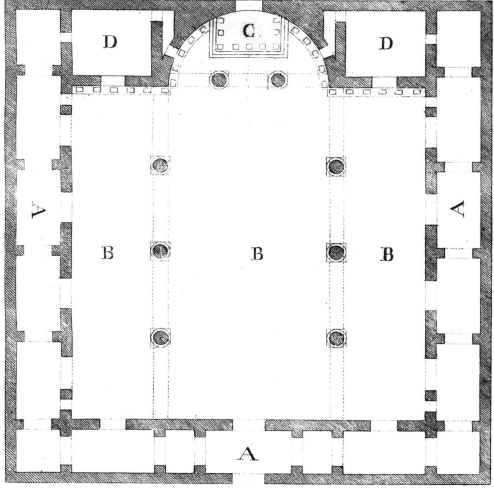

FIG. 2.4. Pannini's plan and elevation of the *tempio*, the so-called 'basilica', published by Guattani in 1784.

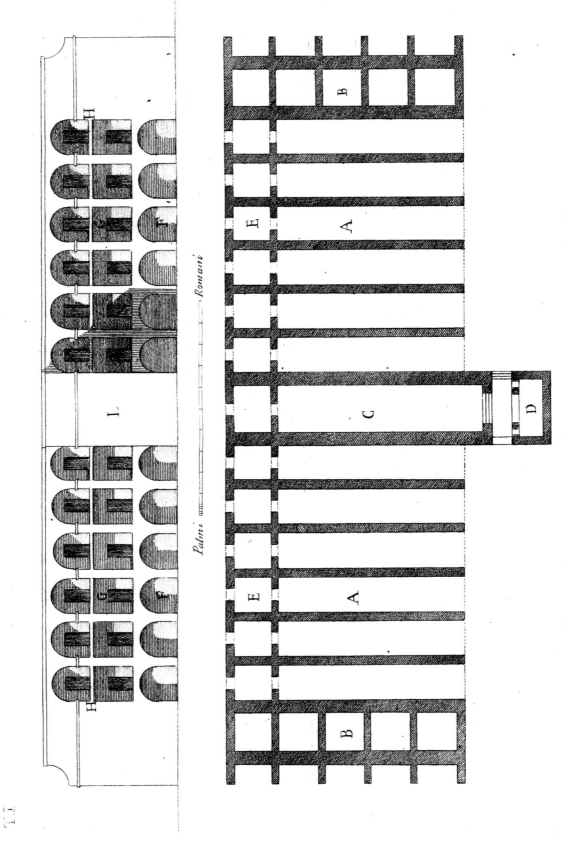

FIG. 2.5. Pannini's plan and elevation of the 'Quartiere d' Soldati', now known as the 'Grandi Sostruzioni', published by Guattani in 1784.

T.I.

FIG. 2.6. Pannini's view of the 'Terme' published by Guattani in 1784.

mistaken. This conclusion is supported by the relative positions of the two domed rooms shown to the west on the plan of the 'Terme' (5), which imply that this building was rotated through 35° anticlockwise (see below, p. 133).

The 'Quartiere d^e Soldati' (9) is clearly to be identified with the so-called 'Grandi Sostruzioni', which are shown in their correct topographical relationship to the 'Teatro' (10), and both buildings are also shown in other drawings (**Figs 2.2** and **2.5**). The identification of the 'Foro' (11) is unclear, but previous scholars have placed it in our Field 19 (see **Fig. 3.2**). The 'Stadio' (12) shown behind the *cavea* of the theatre is not now extant, although its straight northern boundary may be related to features revealed by the surveys in Fields 3 and 19 (see below, pp. 48, 135). To the west a 'Nobile Abitazione' (19) is shown with the plan of an atrium house. The location indicates that it is to be identified with the present farm building at the Podere Scorga, which incorporates *opus reticulatum* walls within its cellars although the extent of these remains

is unclear (see below, p. 48). This is shown in the correct topographical relationship to the theatre and track, as is 'S. Vittore' (20). The large structure labelled 'Palazzo Publico' (18) generally has been related to the now heavily-overgrown foundations on the edge of the river cliff in the northern part of Field 3, although it is impossible to evaluate the accuracy of the plan of this building. The orthogonal system of streets shown on the plan linking this building with the 'Foro' and 'Stadio' are inconsistent with the actual relationship between these buildings on the ground; to create this pattern the 'Foro' (which, if correctly located in Field 19, is actually roughly aligned with the 'Stadio' and 'Nobile Abitazione') has been displaced to the north.

The same hypothesized street connects the 'Foro' with a 'Tempio' (15), an apsidal aisled hall that is also shown in another illustration (**Fig. 2.4**). The location of this structure, often referred to as the 'basilica', generally has been identified with the present Podere Civitelle (see below, p. 54). To the north of this, the plan shows a square enclosure within which are several buildings. The enclosure probably can be identified with the standing late Roman wall in the boundaries of Fields 16 and 17 (see below, p. 64) with the plan rationalized into a square (see below, p. 133). Within this, three buildings are shown, a 'Colleggio' (13) in the centre, a 'Tempio' (14) to the south, and another 'Foro' to the east (17), in addition to two 'Pozzi' (16) to the west. This group cannot be related to any standing remains in Fields 16 or 17, although the overgrown remains of a concrete foundation in the middle of Field 16 (below, Fig. 3.36, [T]) perhaps may be identified with the 'Colleggio' (13) (see below, p. 72).

Finally, a pair of rectangular enclosures with an apsidal niche at the eastern end is labelled as a 'Ninfeo' (22), with a 'Conserua d'Acqua' (23) flanking its northern side. The latter is identifiable with the standing remains of cisterns now built into the Podere Cisterna. The apse and adjacent walls survive in the boundary of the garden surrounding the house (see below, p. 72).

In common with other works of the era, Pannini's more detailed illustrations (Figs 2.2–2.6) combine exact observation of the structures with knowledge of the ideals of classical architecture to produce reconstructed plans and elevations that are difficult for us to evaluate (see Chapter 6). The extant remains of the standing buildings enable us partially to evaluate the drawing of individual structures shown in his illustrations, something that will be attempted in Chapters 3 and 6. Interpretation of the general plan is more problematic, as some aspects of the layout shown appear entirely fanciful and bear no obvious relationship to the topography of the site. Understanding this plan is, nevertheless, vital to the interpretation of Ocriculum as a whole, and will be considered further in relation to the survey results and topography in Chapter 6.

In addition to Guattani's publication, Vatican archives relating to the eighteenth-century excavations enabled Carlo Pietrangeli to produce a key synthesis that draws together the large collection of sculpture and epigraphy from the site now housed in diverse museums, and relates certain of them to the buildings in which they were found (1943; 1978). The sculptures that can be related to particular structures are summarized in Table 2.1, and some are illustrated in Figures 2.8–2.13. Other significant sculptures from the site but without certain provenance include the famous head of Jupiter (Pietrangeli 1978: 116–17, no. 4), a statue of Venus Victrix (Pietrangeli 1978: 121, no. 8), three togate figures (Pietrangeli 1978: 132,

nos. 14–16), a cuirassed figure (Pietrangeli 1978: 134–5, no. 17), and busts of Septimius Severus, Julia Mammea, Plautilla, Octillia Severa and Antoninus Pius (Pietrangeli 1978: 1,136–42, nos. 19–23).

More recently, the so-called basilica has been reinterpreted as an Augusteum. This argument is based on parallels between the plan of the building, which certainly cannot be a basilica, and other examples of Augustea; it is supported by the identification of the statues from therein as a coherent cycle of imperial portrait sculptures (Dareggi 1982).

RECENT WORK

There was comparatively little further exploration of the site during the nineteenth and twentieth centuries, although a considerable effort was made to reinterpret earlier work. Occasional finds and further exploration is documented, including examination of heated rooms within a building at the Podere Cisterna (Pietrangeli 1978: 77–90, figs 87–9) and clearance of a sector of the Via Flaminia at Civitelle (Pietrangeli 1978: 45–6). There was also significant work in the amphitheatre and theatre in the 1950s and '60s (Cenciaioli 2000: 16–17, 34–5; 2006: 53–4), but none of this work has benefited from extensive publication. New work was begun in 2011 to investigate the theatre, with a resumption of excavations at the *scaenae frons*.

The latter forms part of a broader programme of work, including both excavation and conservation, initiated by the Soprintendenza per i Beni Archeologici dell'Umbria (Cenciaioli 2008). As part of this campaign, Roberto de Rubertis drew a series of architectural plans and elevations of individual standing monuments on the site. These drawings were published in a volume with limited commentary (de Rubertis 2012) only as the present volume was going to press. We have thus revised our text and illustrations to take his material into account.

The Soprintendenza's work also has included important research on the pre-Roman cemeteries just south of the town and significant new excavations that have explored a mausoleum and an adjacent stretch of the Via Flaminia in Field 8 (see above, pp. xii–xiii; Cenciaioli 2000: 22–7; Cenciaioli 2006: 45–52; Cenciaioli 2012b: 24–6; de Rubertis 2012: 124–7, 156, figs 16–19; and see below, Fig. 3.32). The mausoleum is probably datable to the late first century BC or the early first century AD, and comprises a square podium, 19 × 19 m, with a circular drum 16 m

TABLE 2.1. Details of sculpture from Ocriculum with known contexts.

Building (excavation dates)	Sculpture	References
Baths (1778–9)	Standing female figure Vatican Museums, Galleria delle Statue 268 (inv. no. 745)	Visconti and Visconti 1782–1807: II (1785), tav. XX; Pietrangeli 1978: 114, no. 2
Basilica (November 1778–June 1779)	Venus Vatican Museums, Gabinetto delle Maschere 429 (inv. no. 816) Fig. 2.9	Visconti and Visconti 1782–1807: III (1790), 41, tav. VIII; Pietrangeli 1978: 115, no. 3
Basilica (November 1778–June 1779)	Nude figure of Augustus Vatican Museums, Sala a Croce Greca 565 (inv. no. 181) Fig. 2.8	Visconti and Visconti 1782–1807: III (1790), 3, tav. III; Pietrangeli 1978: 122, no. 9; Dareggi 1982: 12–14
Basilica (November 1778–June 1779)	Orans figure of Livia Vatican Museums, Sala Busti 352 (inv. no. 637) Fig. 2.10	Visconti and Visconti 1782–1807: II (1785), 94, tav. XLVII; Pietrangeli 1978: 124, no. 10; Dareggi 1982: 18–21
Basilica (?) (November 1780–June 1781)	Togate figure of a Julio-Claudian prince Vatican Museums, Sala a Croce Greca 597 (inv. no. 199) Fig. 2.11	Visconti and Visconti 1782–1807: II (1785), 93, tav. XLVI; Pietrangeli 1978: 126, no. 11; Dareggi 1982: 14–16
Basilica (November 1780–June 1781)	Standing figure of a young Julio-Claudian prince Vatican Museums, Galleria dei Candelabri IV, 93 (inv. no. 2622) Fig. 2.12	Visconti and Visconti 1782–1807: III (1790), 32, tav. XXIV; Pietrangeli 1978: 128, no. 12; Dareggi 1982: 16–18
Basilica (November 1778–June 1779)	Head of Claudius Vatican Museums, Sala Rotonda 551 (inv. no. 242) Fig. 2.13	Visconti and Visconti 1782–1807: VI (1797), 57, tav. XLI; Pietrangeli 1978: 130, no. 13; Dareggi 1982: 23–4
Theatre (1782)	Seated female figure (Muse) Vatican Museums, Sala a Croce Greca 587	Visconti and Visconti 1782–1807: II (1785), tav. XXV; Pietrangeli 1978: 119, no. 5
Theatre (1782)	Seated female figure (Muse) Vatican Museums, Sala a Croce Greca 569	Visconti and Visconti 1782–1807: II (1785), tav. XXIV; Pietrangeli 1978: 119, no. 6

in diameter and perhaps 6 m high set upon it. The concrete core is faced in very finely cut travertine ashlar. The funerary deposits from a nearby *ustrinum* included some extremely fine fragments of carved bone decoration from a bed, as well as marble urns. The public fountain immediately to the northwest was built of *opus reticulatum* and was fed by the underground water system (see below, p. 62).

Finally, excavation of part of the aqueduct and the recording of the major cistern complex at the Podere San Fulgenzio preceded the opening of the building as a museum (Cenciaioli 2006: 8–9). Information from the results of all previous work will be drawn upon where relevant in the description of the different areas presented in the survey results below.

FIG. 2.7. View of the 'Grandi Sostruzioni' published by Guattani in 1827–30 (vol. 2, page 180).

FIG. 2.8. Nude figure of Augustus, Vatican Museums, Sala a Croce Greca 565 (inv. no. 181). *(Photo: Vatican Museums. Reproduced courtesy of the Vatican Museums.)*

FIG. 2.9. Venus, Vatican Museums, Gabinetto delle Maschere 429 (inv. no. 816). *(Photo: Vatican Museums. Reproduced courtesy of the Vatican Museums.)*

FIG. 2.10. Orans figure of Livia, Vatican Museums, Sala Busti 352 (inv. no. 637). *(Photo: Vatican Museums. Reproduced courtesy of the Vatican Museums.)*

FIG. 2.12. Standing figure of a young Julio-Claudian prince, Vatican Museums, Galleria dei Candelabri IV, 93 (inv. no. 2622). *(Photo: Vatican Museums. Reproduced courtesy of the Vatican Museums.)*

FIG. 2.11. Togate figure of a Julio-Claudian prince, Vatican Museums, Sala a Croce Greca 597 (inv. no. 199). *(Photo: Vatican Museums. Reproduced courtesy of the Vatican Museums.)*

FIG. 2.13. Head of Claudius, Vatican Museums, Sala Rotonda 551 (inv. no. 242). *(Photo: Vatican Museums. Reproduced courtesy of the Vatican Museums.)*

NOTE

1. Note that throughout the text we refer to field numbers for ease of reference in discussing locations. The field numbers used are shown in Figure 3.2.

Survey methods and results

Sophie Hay, Simon Keay, Martin Millett and Tim Sly, with a contribution by Salvatore Piro

SURVEY METHODS

Our field methodology at Ocriculum followed the same principles as employed at other sites surveyed in the Roman Towns in the Middle Tiber Valley Project (Keay *et al*. 2004), integrating a range of topographical and geophysical surveys with some limited surface collection in order to maximize information from the site. A network of 30×30 m grids was established over the site using a Leica TC 805 total station, with the topographic data processed using LisCAD 6.2 software (Fig. 3.1). This provided the framework for the geophysics and field-walking, as well as a local grid coordinate system for our topographical survey. The latter was conducted both to record the basic plans of the standing remains and to provide an accurate contour map of the whole archaeological site. Microtopographic detail was therefore recorded, with measurements taken at 4–5 m intervals plus additional points on the breaks of slope and to plan the standing structures; the survey also incorporated the modern features recorded on the published 1:10,000 maps, so that our detailed topographical survey could be related to them.

Since much of the site was covered with dense vegetation and woodland, the survey work was time-consuming, and some areas, such as the floor of the San Vittore stream valley, could not be recorded fully. Nevertheless, by combining the results of our detailed survey with digitized topographical data from the published maps, we have been able to create a new and more precise overall plan of the whole site using ArcGIS. This facilitated the creation of a digital elevation model of the site and its immediate surroundings, which provides a crucial tool for understanding its complex topography (cf. Figs 6.8 and 6.9). Our new survey also provides a framework for interpreting the results of the other prospection techniques, allowing variations in the topography to be related to features identified by the geophysical survey.

The standing remains of the Roman structures on the site and the fragments of structures cut through by the farm trackways (see above, pp. 1–4) were also mapped using the total station during the topographic survey. Although the production of full plans and elevations of the standing remains lay outside the remit of our project, we endeavoured to record their plans in sufficient detail so that we could relate their remains to the results of the geophysical survey. In the case of the principal buildings (the theatre and amphitheatre, for example), available published information has been used in conjunction with our survey data to generate the plans included here. For the more fragmentary structures, notes and photographs taken during the project have been used to provide information and illustrations as required.

The geophysical survey at Ocriculum used magnetometry as the principal method. Despite the relatively poor response of the site to this technique, its rapidity meant that the whole area available for survey was covered relatively quickly, producing some useful results. The magnetometer survey was carried out using Geoscan Research FM36 and FM256 fluxgate gradiometers, where possible using a ST1 encoder trigger to record measurements automatically. Measurements were taken with reference to the site grid, with readings taken at 0.5 m intervals on 1 m traverses. Grid numbers were recorded in notebooks to allow the magnetometer survey results to be integrated correctly and to provide a numerical framework for the collection and recording of finds made during the survey. Readings stored in the internal data-logger of each instrument were downloaded onto a laptop computer in Geoplot 3.0 software. Modern boundaries divide the site into multiple small fields (Fig. 3.2), each of which was processed separately as a single composite. The data from each composite were processed in Geoplot to remove variations produced in the course of the survey.

FIG. 3.1. General view of the site showing the topographic survey in progress. *(Photo: Martin Millett.)*

These were then manipulated in turn to remove any iron 'spikes', before a zero mean traverse function was applied to remove the effect of drift caused by changes in the Earth's magnetic field and a low-pass filter was used to eliminate any high-frequency anomalies. The data were subsequently interpolated along the north–south axis of each composite, providing a 0.5 nm resolution to complement that along the axis of the traverses. Finally, the data were exported as a series of greyscale bitmaps. The results are presented below by area (**Fig. 3.3**), with an overall plan of the results shown in **Figure 3.4**.

In the light of the uneven results from the magnetometry it was decided to attempt other techniques of geophysical survey (electrical resistance and ground-penetrating radar) in areas of the site where this was possible. Because of the dry soil conditions during our regular September season, electrical resistance work could be undertaken only in the winter. This

was carried out in two areas, in the west and near the centre of the site (Fields 2, 3 and 16), using a Geoscan Research RM15 resistance meter with a standard twin parallel array and probes spaced 0.5 m apart. Readings were taken at 1 m intervals on 1 m traverses within the site grid. Readings were stored in the internal data-logger of the instrument and downloaded into Geoplot 3.0 for processing. The data were processed to remove any distorting 'spikes' caused by localized high-resistance readings, whilst variation in the range of readings between adjacent grids was removed using the edge-match function. High-pass and low-pass filters were used to eliminate any low- and high-frequency anomalies. The data were then interpolated along the north–south and east–west axes of each composite, providing a 0.5 × 0.5 m resolution, before being exported as a series of greyscale bitmaps. Ground-penetrating radar survey (GPR) was also undertaken, in September 2003 and September 2004 (**Fig. 3.5**), by Salvatore Piro of ITABC-CNR, in two areas in Fields 8 and 18 near the centre of the site, where our evidence suggested that deposits were comparatively deep (see below, pp. 77–90).

During the topographical and geophysical surveys of the site, members of the team also collected significant finds that were seen on the surface, including sculpture, inscriptions and architectural terracottas. The location of each find was recorded in relation to the site grid, and the information has been used to provide additional information about buildings in different parts of the site. Since only a few areas of the site were under arable cultivation at the time of our work, more extensive surface collection was generally not possible. However, in 2003, intensive field-walking was undertaken to address specific questions in two areas of the site, Fields 7 and 9. These finds are reported upon in Chapters 4 and 5.

Ground conditions near the centre of the site, in Field 9, were suitable for surface collection across a substantial area, providing us with a good sample of pottery with which to evaluate the full chronological span of settlement in this central part of the town. Despite some vegetation regrowth limiting surface visibility, the main part of the field was systematically grid-walked within a 10 × 10 m grid, with the aim of achieving total surface collection (see p. 91; cf. **Figs 4.2–4.8**). Larger, but more irregular, collection units were used on the slopes towards the San Vittore stream on the southeastern side of this field, where the topography was more uneven and there was limited surface visibility.

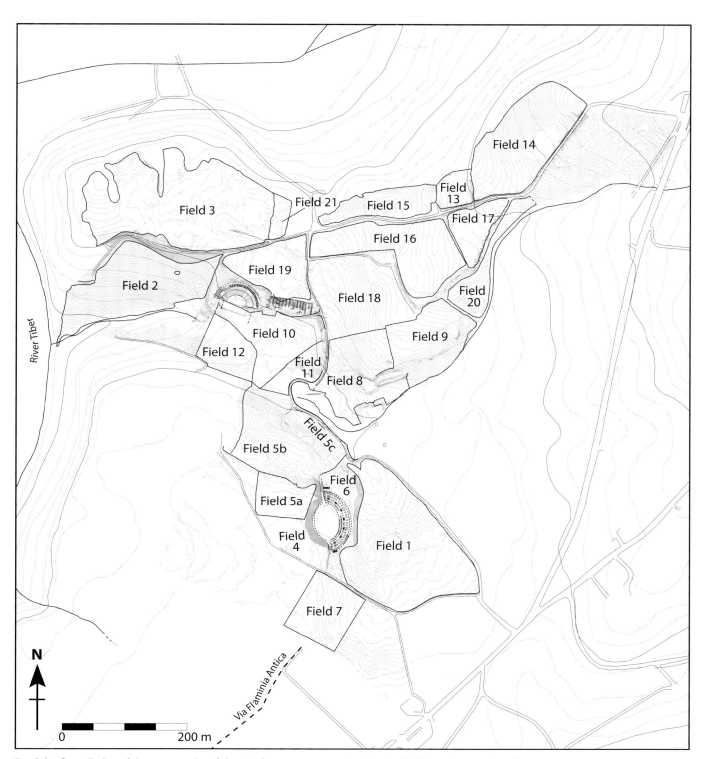

FIG. 3.2. Overall plan of the topography of the site from our survey showing the Field numbers used in the text.

An area near the southern edge of the survey, in Field 7, which had been ploughed and weathered, was also selected for field-walking in the same season. It lay astride the Via Flaminia, to the south of the amphitheatre, and the objective here was to evaluate the chronology of settlement on either side of the road as it approached the Roman town. Thus, five transects 30 m apart, perpendicular to the Roman road, were walked, with the lines

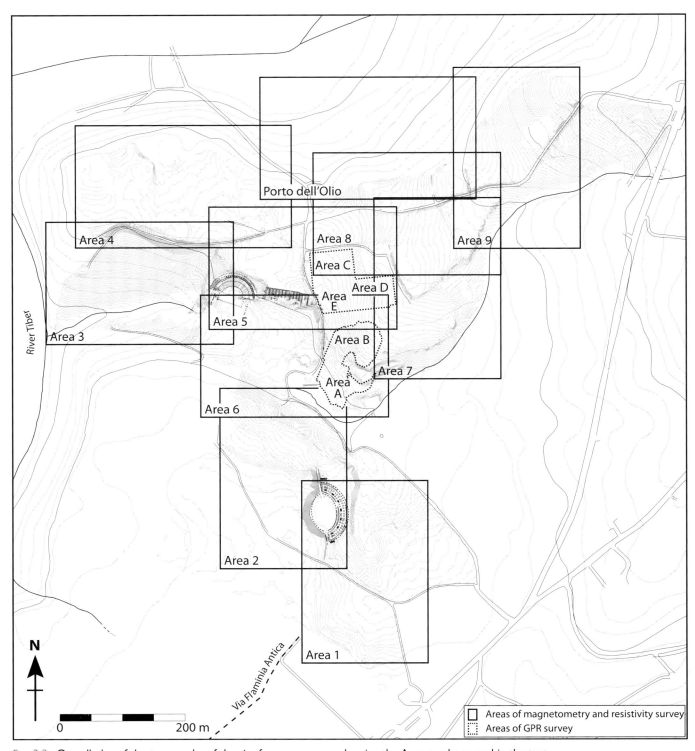

Fig. 3.3. **Overall plan of the topography of the site from our survey showing the Area numbers used in the text.**

divided into 30 m collecting stints (cf. **Fig. 4.1**). The field-walkers collected all visible material on the surface within view of their line, thus providing a sample of about 7% of the area. The material from both these

fields was washed and bagged by collection unit and the finds analysed by specialists after the survey.

The results of these different surveys were integrated using a variety of computer software packages. The

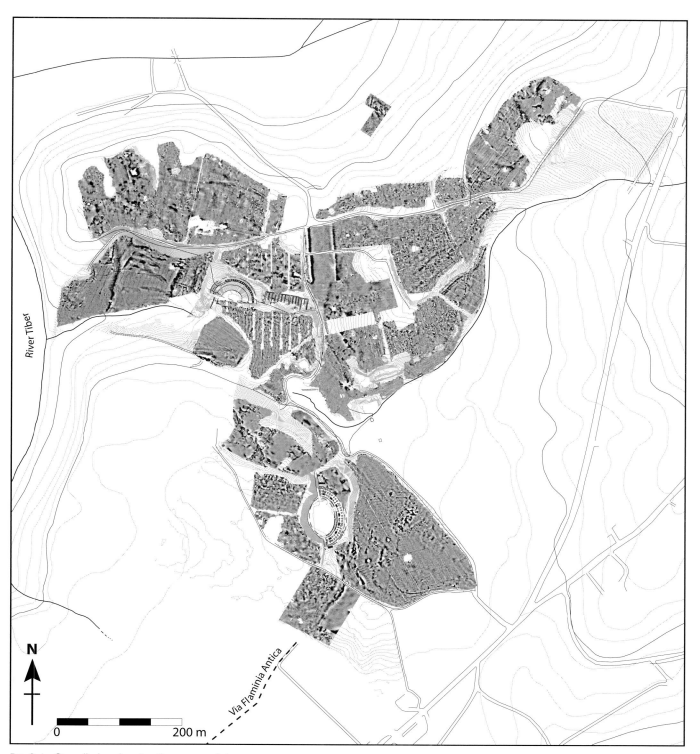

River Tiber

Via Flaminia Antica

N

0   200 m

FIG. 3.4. **Overall plan showing the extent of the magnetometry survey.**

geophysical survey and topographic data were compiled in AutoCAD, together with the available published map data. These were then exported into Adobe Illustrator (CS5) to provide the basis of the published maps and illustrations. The grid network for the site was imported into ArcMap and the ceramic data for the site were attached, in database format, to the grid system. The results of the field-walking for each material type were then exported and integrated with the other survey data in Adobe Illustrator.

FIG. 3.5. Georadar survey in progress in Field 8. *(Photo: Martin Millett.)*

SURVEY RESULTS: TOPOGRAPHY, STANDING REMAINS, MAGNETOMETRY AND ELECTRICAL RESISTANCE

The survey work at Ocriculum was undertaken within the confines of the separate fields into which the site is now divided. During the survey these fields were referred to using the numbers shown on Figure 3.2. These numbers are used also for locating the finds discussed below (Chapters 4 and 5). For the presentation and discussion of the survey results, the site has been divided into Areas 1–9 (Fig. 3.3), with the results from each presented in plans reproduced at a scale of 1 : 1,500. For each of these areas, the evidence from the magnetometer survey (and, where appropriate, also the electrical resistance survey) is presented together with an interpretative plan, which also shows the topography and the standing remains, together with the location of any finds that were collected. For ease of reference, each of the features discussed is referred to using a unique number or letter. Figure 3.3 provides a key to the area numbers, and an index to the figures used in this section is provided in Table 3.1. To facilitate comparison, the results of the geophysical surveys from each separate field (as in Fig. 3.2) have been presented, with the values shown as deviations from the mean for that field. The absolute values for the range in each field are shown in Table 3.2 for reference. The results from the GPR survey are presented separately at the end of this chapter, and

those from the systematic field-walking of Fields 7 and 9 are presented in Chapter 4.

AREA 1 (Figs 3.6 and 3.7)

Area 1 lies in the southern part of the site and covers parts of Fields 1, 4, 6 and 7. It lies on the edge of the plateau, with the land falling away to a valley to the

TABLE 3.1. Key to the Area and Field numbers used in the descriptions of the magnetometry and resistivity surveys. For the locations, see Fig. 3.3.

Area	Fields	Figure numbers for survey plans
1	1, 7, and parts of 4 and 6	3.6–3.7
2	4, 5, and part of 6	3.9–3.10
3	2, and parts of 3, 10 and 12	3.11–3.13
4	3 and 21	3.15–3.17
5	10, 19, and parts of 12, 16 and 18	3.18–3.19
6	8, 10, 11, 12, and part of 18	3.26–3.27
7	9, 20, and parts of 16 and 17	3.34–3.36
8	13, 15, 17, and parts of 14, 16 and 18	3.39–3.40
9	14, and parts of 13 and 17 plus part of the Porto dell'Olio	3.43–3.45

TABLE 3.2. Absolute values used in the scales of the geophysical survey plans for each field.

Magnetometer (gradiometer) survey		
Measurement values [nT]		
Field	Maximum	Minimum
1	19.65	−18.37
2	20.89	−20.35
3	25.11	−24.39
4	35.32	−35.13
5a	79.66	−79.59
5b	136.53	−129.54
5c	50.33	−28.91
6	104.11	−104.10
7	65.65	−65.26
8	37.46	−36.93
9	25.85	−25.62
10	11.51	−11.50
11a	16.54	−16.63
11b	7.99	−8.39
12	15.72	−15.74
13	25.39	−24.38
14	17.22	−16.80
15	25.61	−25.10
16	18.80	−18.85
17	20.99	−20.42
18	31.99	−31.60
19	60.47	−57.64
20	15.36	−14.84
21	75.90	−73.92
Porto dell'Olio	15.74	−15.67

Resistivity (electrical resistance) survey		
Measurement values [Ohms]		
Field	Maximum	Minimum
3	15.89	−15.67
16	14.32	−14.26

north. Here the ground slopes irregularly down towards the San Vittore stream, with tuff outcrops close to the surface. To the southeast the ground rises again to a plateau that continues eastwards towards the modern via Flaminia. There obviously has been some quarrying within the valley where it approaches the farm track that separates Field 1 from Field 7, and it is evident that there has been recent infilling of the valley floor. However, it is equally clear that the hollow here is natural in origin. The amphitheatre (**Fig. 3.8**) occupies the western edge of this valley and is cut into the edge of the tuff plateau. The *agger* of the Via Flaminia is visible running across the fields immediately to the south (**Fig. 1.2**) and the road enters the survey area at the southwestern edge of Field 7. Magnetometry covered the whole of Field 1 as well as a central strip flanking the route of the Via Flaminia in Field 7. Dense vegetation around the eastern and southern sides of the amphitheatre restricted survey in these areas. Along its eastern side the topography has been modified by the construction of a platform flanking the amphitheatre. Although some of this material may derive from excavations that have taken place since the eighteenth century, most of it is probably contemporaneous with the construction of the building, since access was required from this side in antiquity.

The remains of the amphitheatre as excavated in 1958 are now open to visitors (Pietrangeli 1943: 64–6; 1978: 60–3; Figs 2.3 and 3.8). Plans, axonometric views, elevations and a reconstruction drawing of it have been published recently by Roberto de Rubertis (2012: 116–23, 155–6, figs 10–15). These provide a valuable record of the structure and especially of the rock-cut features that are now heavily overgrown. Our survey shows that the maximum dimensions of the outer perimeter of the building are approximately 100×78 m, while for the *arena* (as defined by its inner wall), they are *c*. 63×40 m. (The external dimensions recorded are significantly smaller than the 120×98 m quoted by Pietrangeli (1943: 66) and repeated in all later accounts.) The *arena*, the western side of the *cavea* and the passages for both its northern and southern entrances, have all been cut through the natural tuff bedrock. Stone-cut steps provided access up the slope outside the perimeter at both the north and south (see also **Fig. 3.10** for Area 2). By contrast, the seating on the eastern side was constructed on a series of concrete vaults, supported on concrete piers, the internal faces of which use *opus reticulatum*. The extant structure here comprises:

- an inner wall of *opus reticulatum* defining the perimeter of the *arena* and set at the level of its floor;

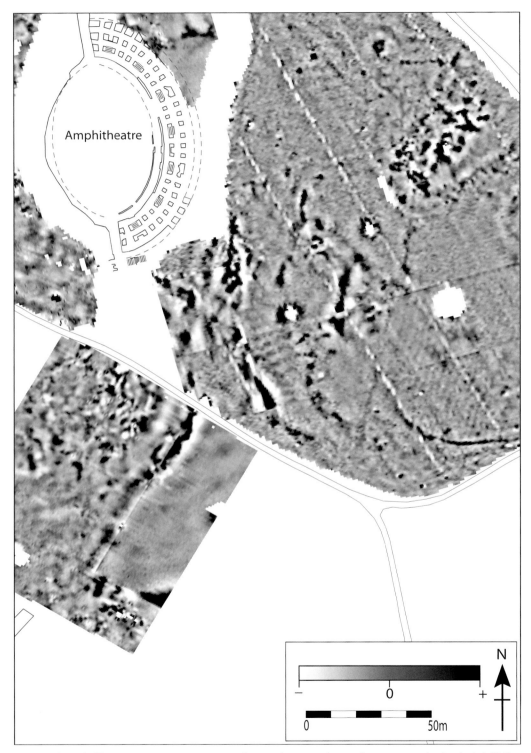

FIG. 3.6. Area 1. The magnetometry survey results in relation to the modern topography (scale 1:1,500). For the location, see Fig. 3.3; and for the geophysics scales, see Table 3.2.

- a wall of *opus reticulatum*, founded on the bedrock and set at a higher level than the inner wall and defining the inner edge of the seating banks;
- an inner row of piers, faced with *opus reticulatum*,

supporting the vaults of the seating banks. Stairways providing access up to the seats are set between every fourth pair of piers;
- a middle row of piers to support the seating, most

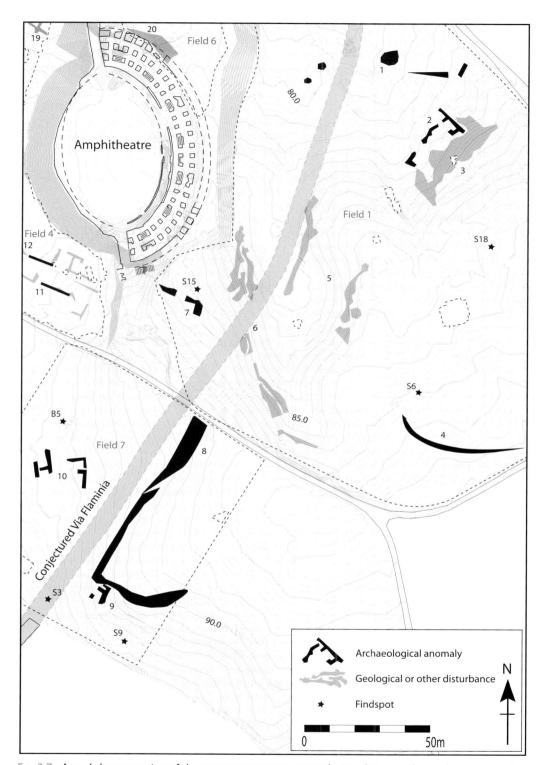

FIG. 3.7. **Area I.** Interpretation of the magnetometry survey results in relation to the modern topography and standing monuments (scale 1:1,500). For the location, see Fig. 3.2.

being built on stone-cut bases with *opus quadratum* above, although some having been replaced in *opus reticulatum*. Blockings between four pairs of these piers match alternate stairways in the inner row of

piers and must have supported stairways up to the seating from a passage at an upper level;

- an outermost row of piers with rock-cut bases and kerbs, constructed in rusticated ashlar blocks.

FIG. 3.8. **View of the eastern side of the amphitheatre from the southeast.** *(Photo: Martin Millett.)*

The external façade on the exterior to the east was faced with rusticated *opus quadratum* blocks and semi-engaged columns, although there is no clear evidence for which order was used (cf. Pietrangeli 1978: figs 61–3). There is evidence in the standing remains for a barrel-vaulted passage running immediately behind the façade. This is separated from an inner ambulatory by the two rows of piers that support the seating above on another barrel vault. There are the remains of seven sets of steps that provided access to the upper seating banks, and the geometry of the structure implies that the amphitheatre rose to three storeys in height. Its complexity, and a series of irregularities in the surviving structure, suggest that it had a varied constructional history, perhaps involving an increase in its height in a secondary phase. It clearly would benefit from a full and detailed analytical architectural study.

Outside the rock-cut passages that provided access to the arena at the north and south, our contour survey indicates that the rock was cut away to create entrance approaches. The entrance lying to the south (**Fig. 3.7**) is *c.* 15 m wide and extends for more than 30 m to the south, towards the Via Flaminia. At the north (below, **Fig. 3.10**) the narrow rock-cut passage extends for *c.* 22 m before opening onto the natural slope through a constricted space.

The use of *opus reticulatum* generally has been taken as evidence for an Augustan date for the building. This relies on an assumption that the original structure had not been altered significantly after its initial construction; it seems clear from the surviving remains, however, that there were later alterations, and this casts doubt on the accepted chronology. We may note that the similarly-sized and fully rock-cut amphitheatre at Sutrium was 'probably first-century BC' (Welch 2007: 248). Equally, Katherine Welch has identified a series of changes in the design of amphitheatres in Italy prior to the construction of the Colosseum that would suggest that the Ocriculum building probably should be dated to somewhere in the first half of the first century AD. This is consistent with the Julio-Claudian date indicated by Jean-Claude Golvin (1988: 166).

The magnetometer survey identified a series of anomalies in the vicinity of the amphitheatre, although the heavy ploughing of Fields 1 and 7 meant that conditions for survey were not ideal. In Field 1 features mostly flank the sides of the valley (**Fig. 3.7**). At the north a positive anomaly ([1]), *c.* 7 m across, perhaps represents the foundations of a mausoleum. A linear positive anomaly running eastward from this may be a wall. To the south is a series of linear positive anomalies ([2]), just below the brow of the slope and aligned with it, which may also represent funerary structures. Although they alternatively may indicate areas where the tuff bedrock has been exposed by the plough, their linear form is more consistent with an interpretation as archaeological features. In contrast, the more diffuse anomaly upslope to the southeast

([3]) seems to result from the accumulation of deposits behind [2]. To the south, a clearly defined curving positive anomaly ([4]) may indicate the presence of a former boundary. Along the sides of the valley, substantial positive anomalies [5] and [6] seem to indicate outcrops of tuff near the surface along the slopes. A large L-shaped positive anomaly ([7]) cuts across the slope a short distance to the west and seems most likely to represent an archaeological feature, perhaps a foundation running along one side of the Via Flaminia adjacent to the entrance of the amphitheatre. It is notable that three finds from Field 1 (S6, S15 and S18), two fragments of inscriptions and a head from a sculpture in travertine (see below, pp. 118–21), are all likely to derive from funerary contexts.

To the south of the farm track in Field 7, the magnetometer survey results provide evidence for fewer features. At the southeast, a major positive linear anomaly ([8]) appears to represent the edge of a quarry, *c*. 80 × 30+ m, cut into the tuff with the greater depth of soil in the quarried area showing as a zone of quiet readings to its east. The northeastern edge coincides with the farm track, so it is most likely that this is a comparatively modern feature. At its southwest a series of positive anomalies in rectilinear form ([9]) may represent a structure, perhaps a truncated mausoleum. Up the slope to the northwest, another group of positive anomalies forming a rectilinear pattern ([10]) may represent a similar structure, but their alignment with the slope makes it more likely that they result from an outcrop of the natural tuff. A fragment of a sarcophagus (S3) and a cornice moulding (S9) from the field are compatible with the predominantly funerary landscape suggested by many of the archaeological features detected in the field (see below, pp. 91–2) (**Fig. 3.7**). A brick stamp (B5) was also found in the fieldwalking survey (see below, p. 130).

In that part of Field 4 that lies within this area, a series of weak positive anomalies ([11]–[12]) lie on the plateau above the amphitheatre and continue into Area 2 (below, **Fig. 3.10**). Whilst these possibly may represent the foundations of buildings related to the Podere Casa Nuova, to the west, they appear more likely to reflect variations in the surface of the natural tuff caused by patterns of cooling cracks in the rock, as seen elsewhere on the site (see pp. 37–8).

The main puzzle with the results from Area 1 concerns the line of the ancient Via Flaminia, which is far less clearly visible than might have been expected. Its route is evident with adjacent standing funerary monuments as it approaches Field 7 from the southwest, and its *agger* is now followed by a series of field boundaries (see **Fig. 6.2**). It is not clear whether, in this part of its route, its surface was made of basalt blocks, as seems most likely and as known in the city centre (cf. **Fig. 3.32**), or of gravel and, if of basalt, whether the blocks have been robbed out. A gravel surface or the robbing of blocks would make the road more difficult to identify in the geophysical survey and could account for its lack of visibility in the results here. However, it is not clearly visible elsewhere in the survey (see below, pp. 46–64, Areas 5 and 6), probably as a result of masking by soil cover and the lack of difference from the background geology.

In this area, the known alignment would suggest that the road passed along the northwestern flank of the recent quarry edge ([8]). A faint negative anomaly at the north, close to the modern farm track, may represent the road itself. Beyond the farm track to the north its course is less certain, and there are two alternative routes that it may have taken. The first lies up the slope passing close beside the amphitheatre. Here, it may be visible flanked to the west by a possible foundation ([7]) and crossing an outcrop of the bedrock ([6]). From here it would have followed a course very close to the foot of the bank below the terrace around the amphitheatre and may now lie buried by soil that has eroded down this slope. Alternatively, and more probably, it took a route a little further to the east, cutting down the slope and then following the floor of the valley, where it is now obscured by colluvium. In either case, the route that it took would have been dominated along this stretch by a series of funerary monuments constructed on the valley sides. Further north in this area, the Via Flaminia is not visible and must lie buried beneath colluvial deposits (cf. **Fig. 3.32**). However, its general route here is indicated both by the presence of a surviving pair of funerary monuments (**Figs 1.2** and **1.4** = Pietrangeli 1978: carta 1, MM 'Tomba a torre' and NN 'Tomba a nicchia'), which presumably lie immediately to its east, in the stretch leading up to the excavated section in Field 8 (see p. 62).

AREA 2 (**Figs 3.9** and **3.10**)

This area lies to the northwest of Area 1 and overlaps the area around the amphitheatre, the features of which have been discussed above (pp. 31–4). It occupies part of the plateau to the south and the slope

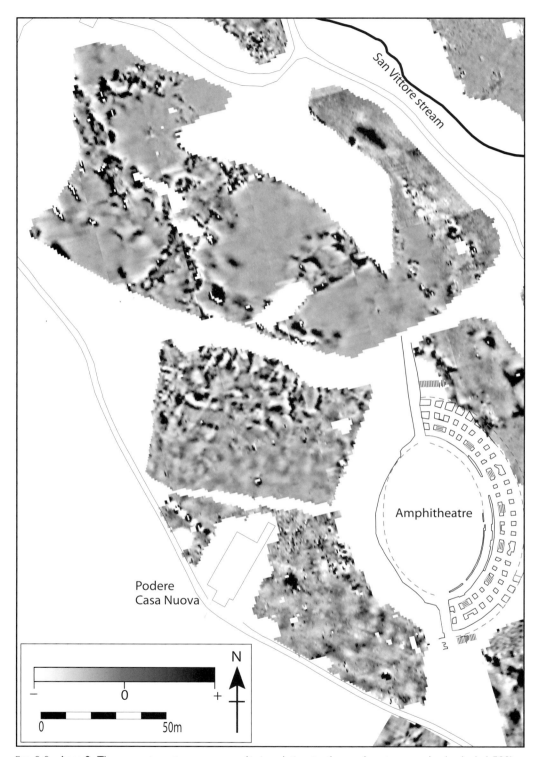

FIG. 3.9. **Area 2.** The magnetometry survey results in relation to the modern topography (scale 1 : 1,500). For the location, see Fig. 3.3; and for the geophysics scales, see Table 3.2.

northwards down to the San Vittore stream, incorporating the whole of Field 5 and parts of Fields 4 and 6. In this stretch, the stream now flows in the bottom of a deep gorge that has cut through the deposits that accumulated as part of an artificial infilling of the valley in the Roman period (see p. 149).

Survey of the plateau top revealed a series of faint rectilinear positive anomalies ([11]–[13], [15]–[19]). As

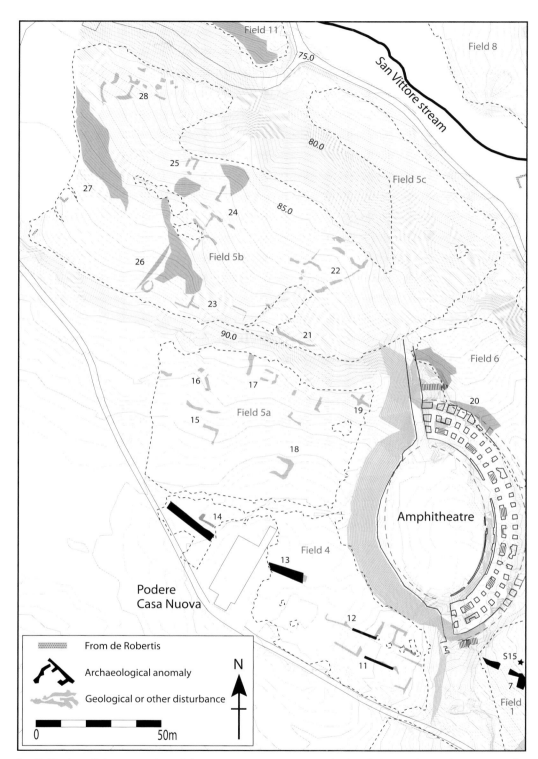

FIG. 3.10. **Area 2. Interpretation of the magnetometry survey results in relation to the modern topography and standing monuments (scale 1 : 1,500). For the location, see Fig. 3.3.**

noted above, although these align with the modern Podere Casa Nuova, they most likely resulted from fracturing during the natural cooling of the tuff bedrock. A dipolar anomaly ([14]) is most probably a modern pipe

leading to the house. On the valley slope below, the topography is characterized by a series of slight hollows skirted by sets of positive anomalies ([21]–[28]) that indicate tuff outcropping near the surface and are indicative of a distinctive pattern of geological features across the slope. There was no evidence on the surface of this area for any archaeologically significant features except those associated with the amphitheatre already discussed (above, p. 34).

AREA 3 (Figs 3.11–3.13)

This area lies to the north of the San Vittore stream in the western part of the survey area. It encompassed the western part of the valley, with Field 2 on its northern side being the main area surveyed. At its western edge lies the church of San Vittore (see p. 11). The track that marks the northern edge of Field 2 runs along just below the edge of the tuff plateau, with Field 3 on the plateau above and to its north. The theatre is discussed within Area 5 (pp. 55, 58), while parts of Fields 10 and 12 to the east are discussed under Area 6 (pp. 58–64) and Field 3 at the north is included in Area 4 (pp. 42–8). The southern side of the valley was not included within the geophysical survey, although part of it was included within our topographic survey. Unfortunately the floor of the valley itself was largely inaccessible and could not be included within the topographic coverage.

Field 2 lies entirely on steeply sloping Lower Pleistocene conglomerates, clays and silts, but there was a scatter of surface finds all along its northern side. Finds included a fragment of a marble statue (S7), a marble table top (S13) and a terracotta antefix (T14) (**Fig. 3.13**; see below, pp. 119–20, 122, 124). Furthermore, in the overgrown areas in the middle of the northern part of the field and along the boundary to the north, there was evidence for surviving structures, including pieces of *opus signinum* flooring *in situ* ([A]). The whole of Field 2 was surveyed using a magnetometer (**Fig. 3.11**), whilst the eastern part was examined also by means of electrical resistance survey (**Fig. 3.12**).

To the west, positive magnetometry anomalies [29] and [30] suggest the existence of foundations belonging to substantial buildings near the top of the field. Similar features ([31]), but more plough-damaged, lie adjacent to the exposed fragment of Roman floor make-up ([A]). These all suggest that there was a series of structures extending down the slope from the north — a pattern repeated along the edge of the ridge in Area 7 to the east. Further down the slope from these structures, a series of other anomalies seems to represent the vestiges of terracing. To the east, and sharing the same alignment as the other buildings, is a coherent series of rectilinear magnetic and resistance anomalies ([32]–[36]) that flank the western side of the theatre, with several of their walls sharing the same axis as its southern façade. These cover an area *c.* 30 m wide along the eastern edge of Field 2 and represent a series of substantial buildings running down the slope. It is notable that a substantial upstanding masonry pier ([B]), in the heavily overgrown area to the south of these anomalies, shares the same general alignment and is probably part of the same complex.

The area in the floor of the valley of the San Vittore stream to the southwest of the theatre is heavily overgrown, but is of crucial importance for understanding the site. From this point westwards, the stream flows along the floor of its natural valley, but to the east the valley has been infilled behind a revetment wall that rises to a maximum of *c.* 10 m (**Fig. 3.13**; see below, pp. 149–50). This is now largely obscured by soil slippage and vegetation, but in the valley floor we were able to survey the brick-faced concrete walls that defined the canalized stream channel as it disgorged from the conduit running beneath the infilled valley to the east. There seems little doubt that while the structures found here ([C]) have been reused in more recent times, they actually incorporate elements of an important Roman structure (**Fig. 3.14**). This revetment wall is aligned parallel with and slightly to the west of a partly exposed wall ([D]), which is clearly linked to the *scaenae frons* of the theatre (see pp. 55, 58).

The plans published by de Rubertis (2012: 105–7, figs 1–2) show a series of three apses aligned parallel with the revetment wall and about 30 m to its west. These lay in an area that was too heavily overgrown for us to investigate, and they are not discussed by de Rubertis. However, it is notable that his plan associates them with the pier ([B]) we recorded further to the north (but which was certainly not apsidal). They align with the features noted above ([32]–[36]), which seem to have formed the western flank of the theatre, perhaps suggesting that this monumental façade extended across the valley to the south.

AREA 4 (Figs 3.15–3.17)

This area comprised Fields 3 and 21, and it occupies the western end of the ridge top to the north of Areas 3 and 5, and it adjoins Area 6 to the east. It is bounded to the north and west by the wooded and heavily overgrown slopes and cliffs overlooking the old course of the Tiber. To the south, in Area 3, the edge of the ridge is formed by a low cliff above the modern trackway,

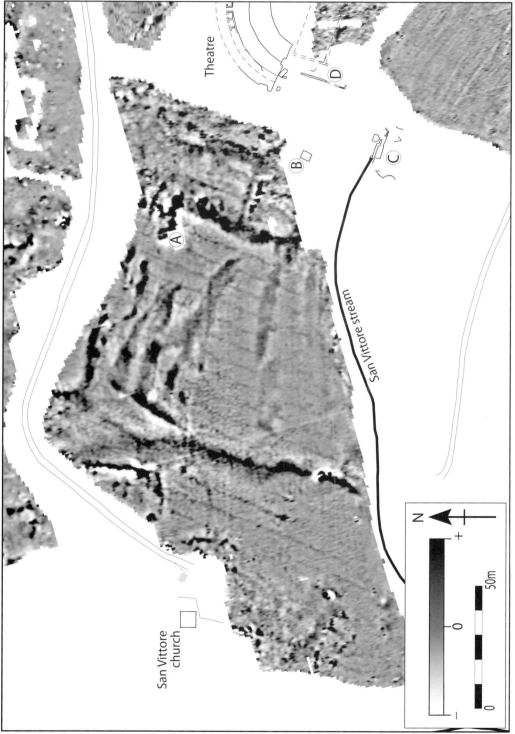

FIG. 3.11. Area 3. The magnetometry survey results in relation to the modern topography (scale 1:1,500). For the location, see Fig. 3.3; and for the geophysics scales, see Table 3.2.

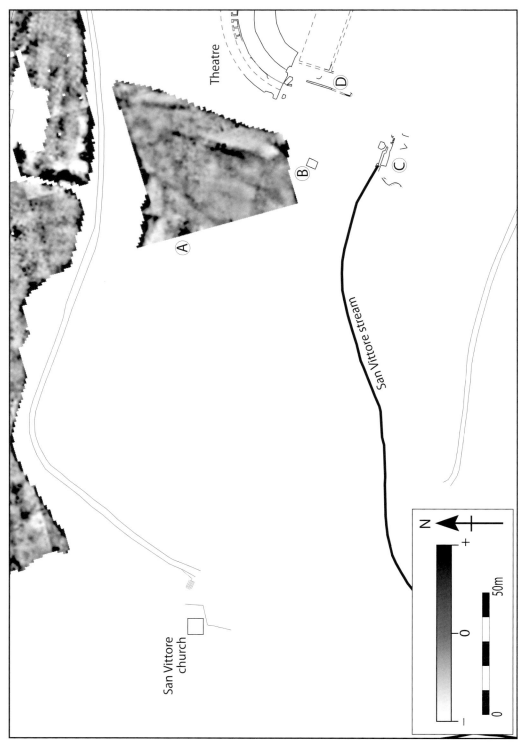

FIG. 3.12. Area 3. The electrical resistance survey results in relation to the modern topography (scale 1:1,500). For the location, see Fig. 3.3; and for the geophysics scales, see Table 3.2.

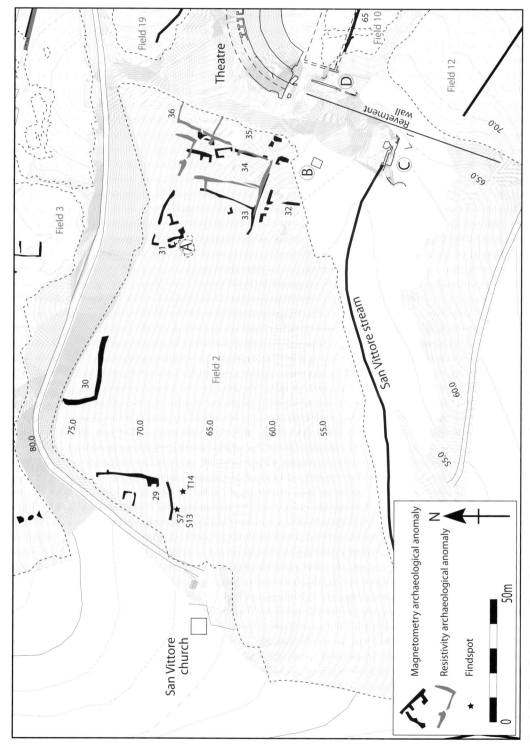

FIG. 3.13. Area 3. Interpretation of the magnetometry survey results in relation to the modern topography and standing monuments (scale 1:1,500). For the location, see Fig. 3.3.

FIG. 3.14. View of the structures in the floor of the San Vittore valley (C on Fig. 3.13) including the exit of the culvert, viewed from the northwest. *(Photo: Martin Millett.)*

below which is the slope of the San Vittore stream valley. The ridge top is at its broadest in this area, and is entirely covered by agricultural land that is relatively flat, although it is cut by three narrow wooded and steep-sided valleys that cut back into the plateau and drain it to the north.

This part of the site has been identified as the location of a settlement dated to the eighth century BC (Cifani 2003: 126–31; Cenciaioli 2006: 18–20; Cenciaioli 2008: 813–15) (Fig. 1.2). The 'Palazzo Publico' shown on Pannini's plan (Fig. 2.1) has been presumed to be located in the most easterly of the valleys on the northern side of the area, which contains some very overgrown structures. The Soprintendenza plan (Cenciaioli 2000: 9) shows a large structure here, as well as a small building in the most westerly of the three valleys. These were not surveyed and it is difficult to relate anything now visible to the elaborate structure drawn by Pannini. The 'Nobile Abitazione'

also shown in this area on Pannini's plan must lie in the vicinity of the present farmhouse of Scorga, where *opus reticulatum* walling is built into the cellar walls. The 'Stadio' shown on his plan, just behind the theatre, also lies within this area (see p. 135).

There was a large collection of surface finds from this field, mostly comprising terracottas that were found in a zone across the middle of Field 3 (Fig. 3.17; Chapter 5: T1–2, T6–11, T15–21, T25–6 and T28–9). Many were from a rock heap derived from local field clearance. These finds suggest the presence of major buildings in this part of the site, although one fragment (T29) may derive from a mould, which could instead indicate that production took place here. There were also three brick stamps from the field (Chapter 5: B1, B2 and B3).

The whole area was surveyed using magnetometry (Fig. 3.15), with extensive electrical resistance survey in Field 3 only (Fig. 3.16). The combined interpretation is shown on Figure 3.17. The electrical resistance results are heavily influenced by rows of trees in the field, the planting of which has led to the creation of lines of dry ground that show up as strips of high resistance. The magnetometer survey results show generally subdued responses, as well as some evidence for variations in geology, surface rubble and the tree rows.

Towards the northwest of the field, the electrical resistance results show a series of features that could possibly be a product of earlier tree planting but coincide with evidence for surface rubble in the magnetometry. Within these can be discerned a probable rectangular structure ([37]). This measures *c.* 35 × 30 m, is aligned west/southwest–east/northeast and comprises a series of fairly regular rooms. The scale and regularity of these features suggest that there was a major building here, perhaps to be identified with the 'Palazzo Publico' shown on Pannini's plan (Fig. 2.1, no. 18), given its general resemblance. A series of three other rectilinear resistance anomalies on different alignments may indicate other structures of different phases. To the south, a series of positive magnetometry anomalies probably reflects the underlying geology. However, rectilinear anomalies detected in the electrical resistance ([38]) and magnetometry ([39]) surveys seem to indicate other structures on the same alignment and perpendicular to the slope that may perhaps form part of the same building. Other anomalies in the southwestern corner of the field may relate to structures that have been destroyed but that may be connected with the foundations ([29]) located further down the slope in Area 3 (see above, p. 38).

FIG. 3.15. Area 4. The magnetometry survey results in relation to the modern topography (scale 1:1,500). For the location, see Fig. 3.3; and for the geophysics scales, see Table 3.2.

FIG. 3.16. Area 4. The electrical resistance survey results in relation to the modern topography (scale 1:1,500). For the location, see Fig. 3.3; and for the geophysics scales, see Table 3.2.

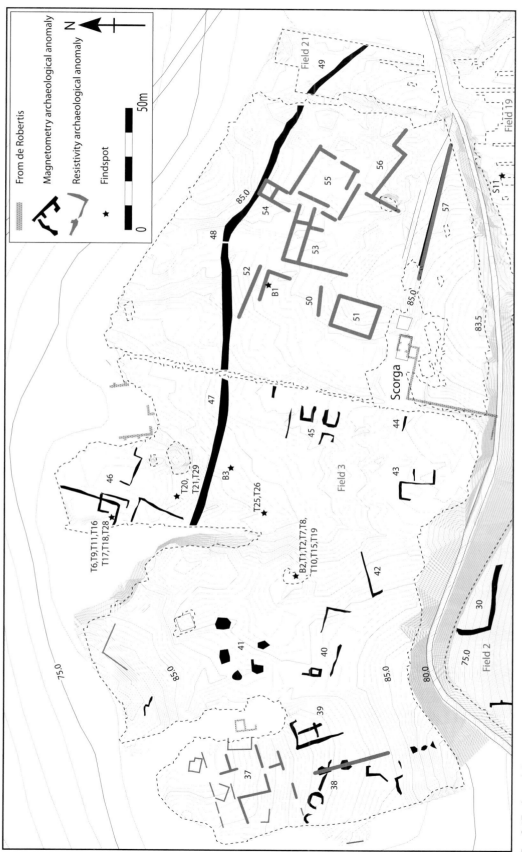

Fig. 3.17. Area 4. Interpretation of the magnetometry survey results in relation to the modern topography and standing monuments (scale 1:1,500). For the location, see Fig. 3.3.

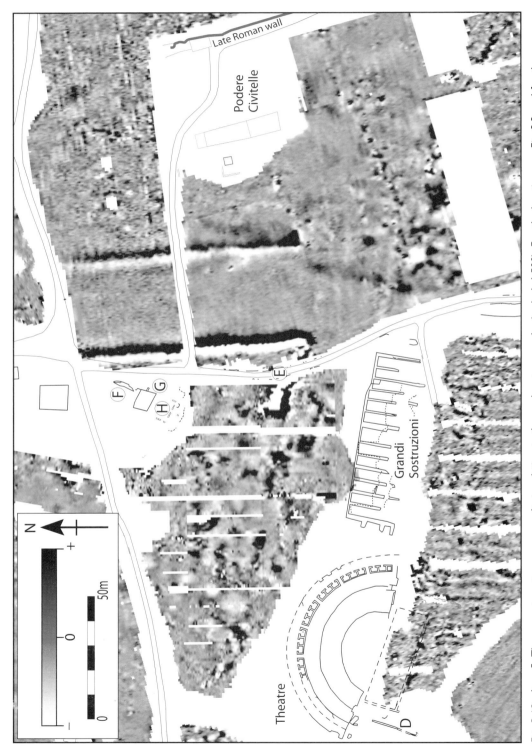

Fig. 3.18. Area 5. The magnetometry survey results in relation to the modern topography (scale 1:1,500). For the location, see Fig. 3.3; and for the geophysics scales, see Table 3.2.

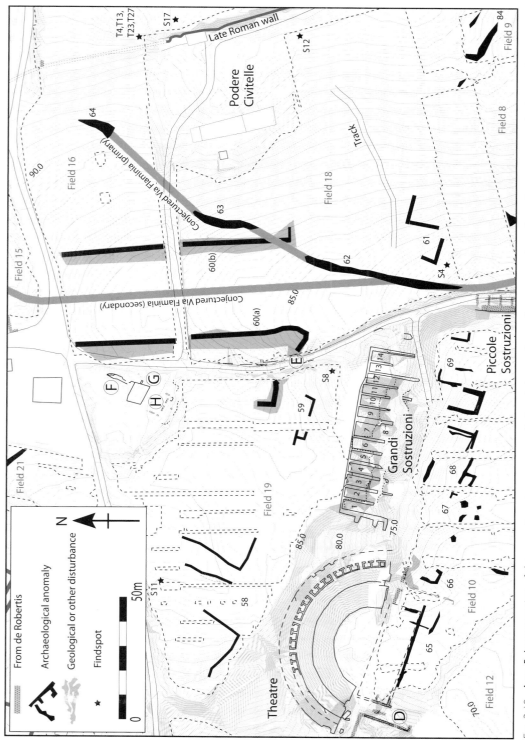

Fig. 3.19. Area 5. Interpretation of the magnetometry survey results in relation to the modern topography and standing monuments (scale 1:1,500). For the location, see Fig. 3.3.

Further to the east the magnetometer survey shows traces of another building ([40]), *c*. 30 m long by 10 m wide, that lies on a significantly different alignment from the structures to the west. To the north of this is a series of positive magnetic anomalies ([41]) that may represent the truncated remains of foundations. Although these may result from geological features, the proximity of a dump of terracottas could support their interpretation as structures. A further positive magnetic anomaly ([42]) a little to the east certainly appears to represent a major wall. It shares the alignment of features [37]–[39] to the west, but is at an angle to [40] nearby and [30] to the south in Area 3; it lies perpendicular to the slope.

To the east of this, towards the middle of Field 3, the magnetic anomalies form a more coherent pattern aligned west/northwest–east/southeast like structures [30]–[36] in Area 3 and also the remains incorporated into the farmhouse of Scorga to the east. These features show up best in the magnetometer survey, as the results of the electrical resistance survey are largely masked by the planting lines for trees that share the same alignment. To the south, there are rectilinear anomalies ([43]) that are indicative of parts of a building measuring *c*. 15 × 15 m. A series of parallel walls and rooms, [44] and [45], stretching for *c*. 50 m north–south along the modern boundary, may belong to a single building, further evidence for which is provided by surface rubble to the west. It is possible that this complex is to be identified with the 'Nobile Abitazione' also shown in this area on Pannini's plan (**Fig. 2.1**, no. 19). This complex is bounded to the north by a major curvilinear feature that shows up as both a strong positive magnetic anomaly and as a line of high resistance ([47]) continuing to the east to the edge of Field 3 ([48]) and onwards into Field 21 ([49]). This major feature could possibly be a road, although since its course follows the brow of the hill, it is more likely to represent an earthwork bank. If this is the case, then this is very likely to be an enclosure relating to the pre-Roman settlement noted above (p. 5). As such it potentially provides very important new evidence for the character of the site in this period.

To its north is a rectilinear series of positive magnetic anomalies ([46]) that suggest that a further substantial building ran northwards down the hill slope for more than *c*. 50 m and extended for a similar distance from east to west. These structures are associated with a substantial group of architectural terracottas that are indicative of a significant building. These walls could possibly relate to the 'Palazzo Publico' shown by

Pannini (**Fig. 2.1**, no. 18) although [37] seems a more likely candidate.

In the eastern part of the field both the electrical resistance and magnetometer survey results show evidence for a series of substantial but damaged structures ([50]–[56]), some sharing the alignment of the buildings to the west, others apparently respecting the line of the earthwork ([48]) to their north. Although they are large, the evidence for these buildings is insufficiently clear to allow a precise interpretation to be offered. This complex of structures is bounded to the south by a major linear feature ([57]), which shows up as both a positive magnetic anomaly and a line of high resistance. It runs for more than 60 m on the approximate alignment of the buildings to the north and lies a little to the south of the modern track that approaches the farm of Scorga; it also coincides with a marked change in the level of the ground surface. The remains of a revetment wall are visible at the edges of the track where this cuts it to the east. The *opus reticulatum* walling that survives in the cellar wall of the Scorga farmhouse may form part of this structure. Its continuation to the east in Area 5 is discussed below (p. 51). It is notable that this wall and the buildings aligned with it to the north are all parallel with the front of the theatre (see p. 55), indicating that this represents a major orthogonal axis in the planning of the urban nucleus on the ridge top (see the discussion below, pp. 55, 58).

The location of this wall suggests that it must be identified with the straight back wall of the 'Stadio' shown by Pannini (**Fig. 2.1**, no. 12). If this is so, then the change in level, which coincides with the modern field boundary to the southwest of Scorga, presumably represents the western end of the structure that he mapped. Resistance anomalies along this boundary appear to result from drying of the soil along the bank, and the area available for magnetometer survey was limited also, so our survey provides no certain evidence for a retaining wall here. However, the plan published by de Rubertis (2012: 105, fig. 1) does record a wall in exactly this location, which supports this identification. The southeastern part of Field 3 lies beneath a vineyard, with the tree-planting lines unfortunately obscuring the results of the electrical resistance survey.

AREA 5 (Figs 3.18 and 3.19)

This area lies to the southeast of Area 4 and to the east of Area 3, and encompasses two of the principal standing monuments visible on the site, namely the theatre and the 'Grandi Sostruzioni'. It comprises Fields 18 and 19, and parts of Fields 10, 12 and 16. Fields 3 and 21 to the northwest have been discussed already above (Area 4). The remainder of Fields 10 and Field 12 are discussed under Area 6 (pp. 58–64), whilst the eastern part of Field 16 is within Area 7 (pp. 64–72).

The western part of the area covers the ridge top with the theatre and 'Grandi Sostruzioni' constructed along its southern flank. To the south Fields 10 and 12 lie on the floor of the infilled valley of the San Vittore stream. To the east, the ridge rises gently and broadens out to the south. The modern rock-cut track climbs this at the point where it broadens out, with the ground falling away steeply close to its western side, where the cliff is revetted by the 'Piccole Sostruzoni' (see below, pp. 60–2). At the eastern boundary of Field 18 are the substantial remains of a late Roman enclosure wall (see below, pp. 64–6). The available areas were surveyed with magnetometry, whilst part of Field 18 was included within the GPR survey reported on separately below (pp. 77–90). Several pieces of marble sculpture and architectural ornament (Chapter 5: S4, S8, S11 and S12) suggest that there were important structures in this part of the site (Fig. 3.19).

In Field 19 the magnetometer survey was made difficult on account of the presence of north–south rows of vines, while the northeastern corner of the field had to be excluded because it was in use as a chicken run; nevertheless, visible structures within this compound were planned (see below, pp. 51–4). Since the field was relatively flat and the soil depth was minimal, with the exception of the northeastern corner, the magnetometer results largely provided evidence for the underlying geology. Two sets of positive magnetic anomalies seem to represent archaeological features. Behind the theatre are two sets of rectilinear features ([58]), probably walls belonging to a large structure. To the east of these is a series of features ([59]) that follows the overall alignment of the walls of the 'Grandi Sostruzioni' and seems to represent a major L-shaped wall c. 10×5 m, with a further pair of parallel walls c. 12 m to the south. A surviving fragment of a masonry wall in the side of the trackway ([E]) lies parallel with this and perhaps represents the east side of the L-shaped structure that thus would be c. 18 m wide. It is notable that there is a complex series of standing structures and substantial fragments of collapsed masonry along this stretch of trackway that would repay clearance and more detailed study. These may include remains identifiable with the fragment of vault shown above and to the right of the 'Grandi Sostruzioni' in Giuseppe Guattani's view of the site (Fig. 2.7). These features need to be considered in the context of the 'Grandi Sostruzioni' themselves.

The 'Grandi Sostruzioni' (Pietrangeli 1943: 72–4; 1978: 76–86) were constructed in such a way as to extend the ridge top southwards by building in front of the tuff cliff (Figs 2.5, 2.7 and 3.20). Plans, elevations

FIG. 3.20. General view of the 'Grandi Sostruzioni' from the south. (*Photo: Martin Millett.*)

and an axonometric drawing have been published by de Rubertis (2012: 112–13, 155, figs 7–9). The structure as a whole runs for *c*. 70 m and is *c*. 20 m wide. It comprises two superimposed tiers of concrete vaulting, the lower one of which is now largely obscured; and the surviving overall height of the complex is *c*. 18 m. It is built of *opus reticulatum*, suggesting a date in the first century BC or the beginning of the first century AD, although there is no other evidence to corroborate this.

The back wall, built against the cliff to the north, runs straight from the northwestern corner for *c*. 50 m, before kinking slightly to the south. This feature might suggest that the easternmost pair of vaults is a later addition to the complex. Alternatively, however, the symmetry of the overall plan would indicate that this irregularity in the back wall was a result of other factors, and may have been conditioned by the line of the natural cliff behind. At the western end of the complex, Pannini's plan shows the end wall as having four lesser vaults built perpendicularly against it and facing the eastern side of the theatre (de Rubertis 2012: 112–13, figs 7–8). The three surviving masonry projections here, however, suggest that these formed buttresses with intervening recesses rather than vaults. Straight joints between them and the end wall of the 'Grandi Sostruzioni' suggest that these are secondary, rather than being part of the original structure. Pannini's plan shows a similar set of four vaults against the eastern end wall, but these no longer exist and it has been impossible to establish whether his plan was accurate in this respect. However, the eastern end

wall as it now survives does comprise a pair of walls built directly against one another, suggesting an addition to the original complex like that lying to the west (de Rubertis 2012: 114–15, fig. 90). The southern façade of the building is no longer visible, but its position is indicated by the intact western wall, which makes it clear that its plan formed a rectangle. It lies at a slight angle to the predominant west/northwest–east/southeast alignment of the other structures in this part of the site. However, it should be noted that it aligns with the southern wall of the eastern side of the *cavea* of the theatre to its west.

The uppermost row of vaults that opens to the south consists of thirteen full vaults and one partial one (**Fig. 3.20**; cf. de Rubertis 2012: 114–15, fig. 90). From the west, the pattern is as follows (measurements given are their internal widths):

- projecting end wall (this has a straight joint with the main set of vaults to the east and is clearly secondary);
- Vault 1, 3.75 m (collapsed);
- Vault 2, 3.79 m (with a lower vault visible below);
- Vault 3, 4.03 m (with a lower vault visible below);
- Vault 4, 3.76 m (with a lower vault visible below);
- Vault 5, 3.74 m;
- Vault 6, 4.34 m (collapsed);
- projecting wall between vaults;
- Vault 7, 5.68 m;
- Vault 8 — a partial vault resting against a major projecting wall to the east (**Fig. 3.21**), the structure of which includes large blocks of travertine (cf. the

FIG. 3.21. **Detail of Vault 8 in the 'Grandi Sostruzioni' and an earlier wall from the southwest.** *(Photo: Martin Millett.)*

'Piccole Sostruzioni' below and Fig. 3.31). This projecting wall must pre-date Vault 8, but is apparently contemporaneous with Vault 9;

- Vault 9, 4.08 m;
- Vault 10, 4.18 m (with a lower vault visible below);
- Vault 11, 3.51 m (with a lower vault visible below);
- Vault 12, 4.07 m (with a lower vault visible below);
- projecting wall between vaults;
- Vault 13, 3.56 m;
- Vault 14, 3.97 m;
- projecting end wall — with evidence for a secondary wall built against it to the east.

The complete vaults range between *c*. 3.5 m and *c*. 4.3 m in width, except for the central one (Vault 7), which has a width of *c*. 5.7 m. This also has more substantial walls that incorporate a stone string-course of travertine near the top. Pannini's plan (Fig. 2.5) reconstructs a central square structure in front of this middle vault, but there is no sign of this today and it is not shown on the nineteenth-century view (Fig. 2.7). Carlo Pietrangeli (1978: 76–7) suggested that the vaults were of different dates, as those lying to the west have different wall widths from those to the east. A close inspection of the standing remains suggests an alternative conclusion, with the structure representing at least three phases. The first comprises a central structure the walls of which survive in the support for Vaults 7/8; in the second phase the flanking sets of six vaults were added; and, in the third, the sets of transverse supporting structures were added to the west and east. The structures revealed in Field 10 to the south of the 'Grandi Sostruzioni' are considered below (p. 58).

The substructures evidently were constructed to provide a building platform that extended the surface of the natural ridge further to the south and provided the town with a monumental façade prior to the infilling of the valley. This platform is reminiscent of later Republican temple platforms, and this indeed would seem to be the obvious interpretation for it (Cenciaioli 2000: 32–3). Given the plan, the broader central vault may have supported the temple itself, which could have faced northwards across the ridge and have been visible to traffic travelling down the Tiber. According to this interpretation, Field 19 to the north of the 'Grandi Sostruzioni' lay within the temenos, and building [59] may have been set within this complex. Alternatively, if the wider central vault is irrelevant, the temple may have faced southwards and the features shown in the magnetometer survey might themselves form part of a temple.

In the northeastern corner of Field 19, bounded to the north and east by the modern trackways, a fenced-off area around a derelict agricultural building was being used as a chicken coop at the time of the survey. The presence of rubbish and disused agricultural equipment meant that it was impossible to do any magnetometry here, but it was clear from the topographic survey that a podium *c*. 1 m high occupied this area (Fig. 3.22). It extended for *c*. 40 m north–south from the corner of the field by the crossroads, with the step down on its southern side aligned west/northwest–east/southeast and clearly forming a continuation of the alignment of the revetment ([57]) described in Area 4 (above, p. 48).

On the surface of this platform two principal sets of surviving structures were recorded. First, to the northeast, close to the side of the track flanking the east of the compound, is part of an apse ([F]), with an estimated internal radius based on the limited element surviving of *c*. 2.3 m (Figs 3.22 and 3.23). It is faced internally with *opus reticulatum* and now stands exposed above the ground surface. The wall of the apse was *c*. 0.6 m thick and had an original opening through it at the east, presumably marking the central axis of the building and suggesting that it shared the west/northwest–east/southeast alignment of the platform. The interior, to the west had some surviving evidence for a concrete floor preparation. This clearly represents a substantial building and appears to be that which Pietrangeli recorded as having a surviving mosaic (1978: carta I, BB = Fig. 1.4). He attributed this to the structure labelled as 'Foro' by Pannini (Fig. 2.1, no. 11). However, it may be noted that this structure is not shown by Pannini as having had an apse, whilst the building he calls the 'Tempio', also referred to as the 'basilica' (Figs 2.1, no. 15, and 2.4) and located by Pietrangeli under the Podere Civitelle to the east (see p. 54), is shown with an apse that has three openings through it, including one on the axis of the building like that recorded here. Gianna Dareggi (1982: 3) estimated the size of the 'basilica' as 16.30 m wide by 19.43 m long on the basis of Pannini's plan. The apse was shown by Pannini as occupying one third of the width, which would suggest a radius of *c*. 2.7 m, marginally larger than the surviving structure recorded here. Overlaying Pannini's plan on that of the apse and adjusting the scale to fit the surviving fragment provides a good fit, but would suggest that the building was somewhat smaller than Dareggi suggested at 14 × 14.6 m (Fig. 3.22). It should be noted also that Pannini showed the apse set within

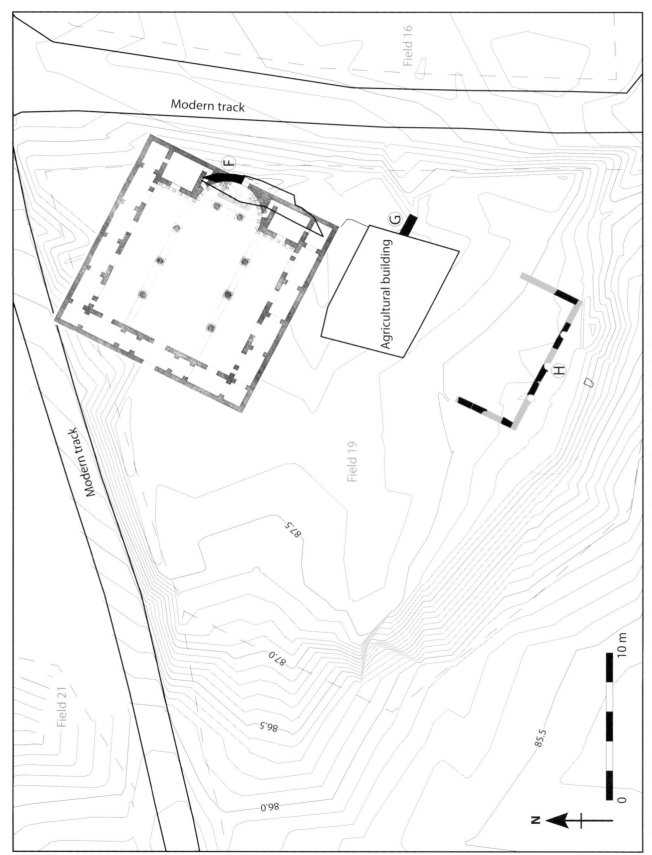

FIG. 3.22. Detailed plan of the structures in the northeastern corner of Field 19 with Pannini's plan of the basilica (Fig. 2.4) superimposed.

and forming three sides of a structure *c.* 10 m long, aligned parallel with the Augusteum to the north and with the edge of the platform to the south (**Figs 3.22** and **3.24**). The blocks appear to be *in situ*, with those on the exterior on the southwestern side having a series of equally spaced niches, *c.* 0.45 m across, cut into them. Three surviving niches are spaced almost equidistantly at 1.94 m and 1.98 m apart, and one had an apparent integral pilaster defining its western margin. The location of the niches, and the survival of some concrete sub-flooring to their southwest, indicates that they may have formed the back wall of a portico opening onto the suggested temenos. These niches cannot be related easily to any of the structures drawn by Pannini, although they clearly belong to a major Roman public building. It is perhaps possible that the building can be identified with the 'Foro' shown on Pannini's plan (**Fig. 2.1**, no. 11), but this

Fig. 3.23. Detail of *opus reticulatum* apse [F] viewed from the south above (cf. Fig. 3.22). Scale bar = 0.3 m. *(Photo: Martin Millett.)*

the rectangle of the building's outer perimeter and not with a curved outer wall as in the surviving fragment. However, it is also evident that following our scaling of the building, its western end and northeastern corners would coincide with surviving topographic features. There therefore seem to be very strong grounds for arguing that this building is to be identified with the 'basilica', which is generally interpreted as an Augusteum and from which much of the sculpture found in the eighteenth-century excavations was derived (see above, pp. 20–1). It is notable both how the building recorded by Pannini fits within this area and that it lies parallel with the other structures and the podium wall to the south.

Immediately to the south, the present stone building that is used to house animals overlies another wall ([G]) that extends a short distance to the east (**Fig. 3.22**). Further to the south of this, there were sections of white marble foundation ([H]) visible on the surface

Fig. 3.24. Marble foundation [H], showing the niches at the east and centre. Note the pilaster on the far niche (cf. Fig. 3.22). *(Photo: Martin Millett.)*

would require the relationship between the 'Foro' (no. 11) and the 'Tempio' (no. 15) to be shown incorrectly on his plan. This seems unlikely, and it is more probable that their locations have been transposed (see below, p. 136). Although it was not possible to make a thorough study of them in our survey, they clearly deserve further investigation.

To the east Fields 16 and 18 occupy a col in the ridge, with the ground rising gently to the east. The magnetometer survey reveals a parallel pair of major positive anomalies, [60a] and [60b], $c.\,38$ m apart, which can be traced for $c.\,90$ m up to the track at the north. They terminate here, with no evidence for continuation further north in Field 15 (see Area 8 below, pp. 72–3). Curiously these major features were not found in the results of the GPR survey (p. 80). Their character and positions in relation to the topography suggest that they formed a pair of revetment walls defining the sides of an open area cut through the ridge that is visible in the contour survey. The function of this feature is discussed further below. The southern end of the westerly feature ([60a]) turns to the west towards structure [59] in Field 19. Similarly, the southern end of [60b] also has a right-angle turn to the east. These two features would be consistent with the idea that the anomalies represent revetment walls. It should be noted also that westerly feature [60a] is on the same general alignment as the 'Piccole Sostruzioni' to the south (see below, p. 60).

Further to the south, a series of positive anomalies seems to indicate damaged structures. One set of walls ([61]) is discernible, defining a building $c.\,15 \times 25$ m on the west/northwest–east/southeast alignment of the features to the west. It continues the line of the 'Grandi Sostruzioni' to the west and may link with [84] in Area 7 (below, p. 69), although the intervening area was not available for survey because it was in use as a vineyard. To the north of these anomalies a feature running up the hillside is interpreted as a recent trackway that continues the line of the present path that passes in front of the 'Grandi Sostruzioni'.

Two further positive linear anomalies, [62] and [63], are aligned with one another, running for a total of $c.\,110$ m on a north/northeast–south/southwest axis that is perpendicular to structure [61] and others in the central part of the site. This is almost certainly the line of the Via Flaminia, also located in the results of the GPR survey (see p. 80). Its location is consistent with the evidence for the excavated section of road illustrated by Pietrangeli (1978: 46, fig. 42, carta 1;

Fig. 1.4). His photograph shows a section of road paved in basalt blocks that had been cleared during agricultural work, but this is not located precisely on his plan. It certainly lies in the southern part of Field 18, and it appears from his photograph that it was probably at the very western end of the vineyard. This being the case, magnetic anomalies [62] and [63] show the continuation of the route followed by the paved road further up the slope. The results of the magnetometry in Field 16, to the north, are dominated by the effects of surface rubble and deep ploughing. A positive anomaly ([64]) suggests the presence of a major foundation, possibly a continuation of the line of the Via Flaminia. Features to the east in this field are discussed under Area 7 (below, pp. 64–72). The line of the road appears to be cut by eastern revetment wall [60b]. We would thus suggest that the Via Flaminia, represented by these magnetic anomalies, originally passed up the slope from the south and conformed to a major axis in the orthogonal grid of this part of the town. Subsequently it was decided to create an open space in the town centre by making a cutting across the ridge top, thereby reducing the gradient of the road. This open space, revetted by major walls [60a] and [60b] to the west and east, was cut on a north–south axis at a slight angle to the earlier grid plan. The Via Flaminia, which is visible in the results of the GPR (below, Figs 3.53 and 3.54, no. 1), now passed through this space, which also may have been designed to form a piazza flanked to the west by a series of existing public buildings.

The magnetometry did not reveal any further features in the remainder of Field 18. This is notable since the Podere Civitelle, located on the slope in the eastern part of the field, usually is identified with the location of the 'basilica' (see above, p. 51). The platform on which the present farmhouse is built was not suitable for geophysical survey. Pietrangeli (1978: 48–9, carta 1, A, B and a; Fig. 1.4) recorded the presence of Roman structures within and around the present farmhouse, including a mosaic to the west of it. The GPR results also confirm the presence of buried structures just downslope from the present house, in the area where the mosaic is recorded (Figs 3.54–3.56, nos. 5–6). This certainly confirms the presence of important buildings, but there seems no reason beyond the evidence of Pannini's plan to identify these remains with the 'basilica'. Indeed, the remains here are much more extensive than the size of the 'basilica', $c.\,16 \times 19$ m, as estimated by Darregi (1982: 3). If, as suggested above, Pannini transposed

Fɪɢ. 3.25. **View of the theatre from the east.** *(Photo: Martin Millett.)*

the location of the 'Tempio' and 'Foro' on his plan (**Fig. 2.**1), the latter might be sought here, although this too appears comparatively small.

Field 10, in the south of this area, occupies the artificial floor above the infilled valley of the San Vittore stream. The southern part of this field is discussed under Area 6 (below, p. 58). The northern side of the field lies below the 'Grandi Sostruzioni' at the east and the theatre at the west. The ground rises towards them, partly at least as a result of the spread of rubble from them, and this somewhat obscures the results of the magnetometry.

The theatre has been known since the eighteenth-century excavations (**Fig. 3.25**; Pietrangeli 1943: 61–4; 1978: 52–9). Following excavation in 1964 (Cenciaioli 2000: 34–7), it is now the subject of further study and renewed excavation; it has been considered also by Frank Sear (2006: 161–2). Plans, a section, axonometric views and a reconstruction drawing have been published recently by de Rubertis (2012: 108–11, 155, figs 3–6). The theatre faces south and comprises a *cavea*, with a diameter of *c.* 79 m, which is cut into

the tuff cliff in such a way that the lower seating tiers were built into the bedrock. The upper tiers are supported by radial vaults with *opus reticulatum* facing, while the barrel vault of the *ambulacrum* is supported on rusticated piers of *opus quadratum*. The southern ends of the seating are supported by massive retaining walls of *opus quadratum*. The *scaenae frons* does not survive above ground, although exposed remains from past excavations are still visible at a considerable depth in front of the *orchestra*. New excavations are investigating its southwestern corner and have revealed a probable portico along its southern side. A wall perpendicular to the end of the *cavea* ([D]), to the west, extends for *c.* 25 m before turning eastwards; this is mirrored by another excavated wall *c.* 58 m to the east. Between these, the foundations of the eastern and northern sides of the *scaenae frons* are also exposed (see below, p. 57).

Sear (2006: 161–2) has suggested an Augustan date for the construction of the theatre. An early first-century AD inscription records games donated by the *quattuorvir* Passenius Ataedius, son of Lucius, to celebrate

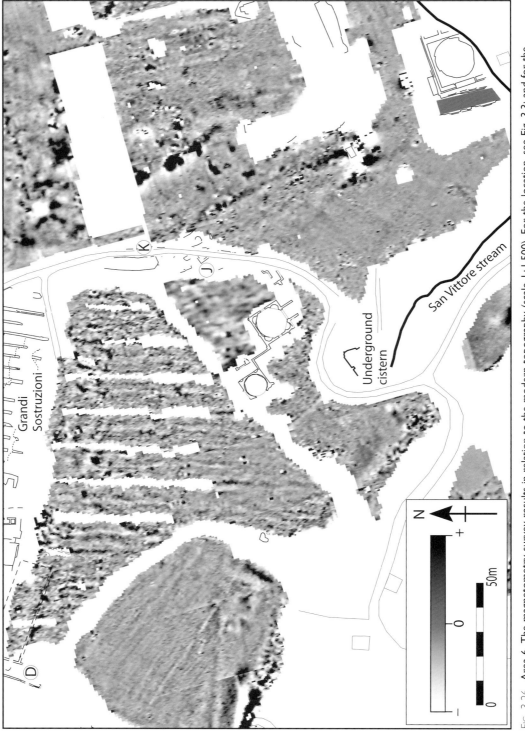

FIG. 3.26. Area 6. The magnetometry survey results in relation to the modern topography (scale 1 : 1,500). For the location, see Fig. 3.3; and for the geophysics scales, see Table 3.2.

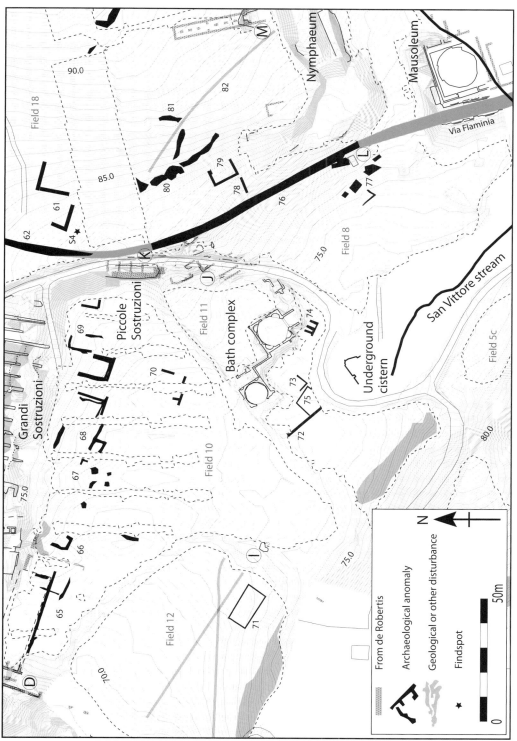

FIG. 3.27. Area 6. Interpretation of the magnetometry survey results in relation to the modern topography and standing monuments (scale 1 : 1,500). For the location, see Fig. 3.3.

the dedication of the *scaenae* (*CIL* XI 7806 = Pietrangeli 1943: no. 23). There is also a monumental inscription in the Vatican (*CIL* XI 7807–8) recording a dedication by the same person, which Pietrangeli suggested probably derived from the *scaenae frons* (1978: 52, fig. 18). A pair of statues of seated muses of Antonine date is believed to come from the *scaenae frons* (Pietrangeli 1978: 119, figs 118–19; Musei Vaticani, Sala a Croce Greca, nos. 569 and 587).

The magnetometer survey shows further walls of the *scaenae frons* ([65]) as positive anomalies. When these are considered with the excavated walls, they indicate that it measured *c.* 42 × 12 m and was positioned symmetrically in front of the *cavea*, separated by a passage *c.* 3 m wide. At the eastern end, there is also evidence for further walls, one to the south lying parallel with the *scaenae frons* and the other crossing it. Further east there is evidence for a sequence of buildings ([66]–[69]) that shares the alignment of the theatre and other buildings further to the north; the axis, however, diverges slightly from that of the frontage of the 'Grandi Sostruzioni' (see above). These buildings are very substantial, comprising individual units *c.* 10 m wide and covering a strip *c.* 18 m deep that continues the alignment of the back of the *scaenae frons*. The evidence is too fragmentary for a secure interpretation, but they resemble the *tabernae* that surround some *fora*. Given the open area of the infilled valley lying immediately to their south, it could be argued that they fulfilled a similar function here, although this seems doubtful given the likely position of the *pomerium* (see below, p. 151).

AREA 6 (Figs 3.26 and 3.27)

This area lies to the south of Area 5 and covers the floor above the infilled valley of the San Vittore stream in Fields 10, 11 and 12, as well as the slope up to the ridge to the east in Fields 8 and 18. The standing remains of the baths dominate the area, while the recently excavated mausoleum and stretch of the Via Flaminia are located at its southeastern corner. In addition, there is a huge underground cistern (its standing wall being at least *c.* 5 m high) concealed beneath the artificial fill of the valley just to the south of the baths. To the southeast of this feature, the San Vittore stream now runs along the bottom of a ravine that cuts through the valley fill, whilst to the northwest it still runs though a conduit beneath this fill (see below, pp. 149–54). The modern trackway, which climbs northwards up the side of the ridge, is cut deeply into

the slope to the northeast of the baths and thus has sliced through a series of ancient structures.

The features in the northern part of Field 10 have been described under Area 5 (p. 55 and this page). In the centre of the field, despite the presence of rows of vines and surface rubble, there is evidence for a further building ([70]), *c.* 10 × 10 m, which shares the same alignment as those to the north. The location of this suggests that it probably should be identified with the 'Terme Hiemali' shown on Pannini's plan (**Fig. 2.1**, no. 6). In the overgrown boundary between Fields 10 and 12 are the standing remains of a concrete arch ([I]) (**Fig. 3.28**). This is evidently the base of a tomb monument with an arched niche at its base that is very similar to the much better preserved example a little further to the south beside the Via Flaminia (Pietrangeli 1978: 90, fig. 91, tav. VI, carta 1, NN; **Fig. 1.4**). The magnetometer survey does not provide any further information for its context, but its presence does confirm that the ground level here remains at approximately the same height as in antiquity. It must imply also that this area, on the southern side of the valley, lay outside the *pomerium* of the town. The area to its north seems to have been left largely open, perhaps forming some sort of piazza in front of the theatre and baths.

Field 12 is generally devoid of magnetic anomalies. Two linear features are probably recent, that to the south an east–west trackway, the other associated with cultivation. A single rectangular anomaly ([71]) may be a building, *c.* 15 × 8 m. Its alignment parallel with a modern agricultural feature implies that it may be comparatively recent, although, given its proximity to standing funerary monument [I], a similar function is perhaps possible.

Field 11 contains the standing remains of the baths (**Figs 2.1** and **2.6**). The baths themselves (Pietrangeli 1943: 67–71; 1978: 64–75) are amongst the best-preserved monuments on the site (**Figs 2.6** and **3.29**). The visible remains comprise a domed octagon with a segmented vaulted roof to the southeast, from which came the famous mosaic now in the Vatican Museums (see above, p. 13). This was entered through an ante-room from the southeast. The octagon opened onto a square room to the northwest, which had a further square room to its southwest built in *opus latericium* roofed with a round dome. Pannini's overall plan (**Fig. 2.1**) shows the baths in the context of other structures that are now no longer visible. The standing remains are clearly identifiable as his '5 Terme', but he has rotated them so that their relationship with the

FIG. 3.28. The base of the funerary monument with a niche ([I]) in the boundary between Fields 10 and 12 viewed from the southeast. *(Photo: Sophie Hay.)*

'Grandi Sostruzioni' and the theatre is shown incorrectly. To one side he shows '8 Magnifico Palazzo' and the adjacent '7 Gran Muro', now generally referred to as the 'Piccole Sostruzioni' (see

below, p. 60). The epigraphically attested '6 Terme Hiemali' are shown between these and the 'Grandi Sostruzioni'.

The baths themselves are well dated by inscriptions. One, recording that their construction was funded by L. Iulius Iulianus, is on a statue base dedicated by his daughter, Iulia Lucilia, and is dated to the second century AD (*CIL* XI 4090 = Pietrangeli 1943: no. 24). Pietrangeli (1978: 69) noted a further inscription (*CIL* XIV 98) found in 1784, and previously erroneously attributed to Ostia, which dates the construction to AD 139. Finally, a brick stamp dated *c*. AD 145–50 was found *in situ* in the superstructure of the octagon during recent work (see p. xiii; Cenciaioli 2012a: 173). This evidence also provides a secure *terminus ante quem* for the infilling of the valley, perhaps in preparation for their construction.

A restoration of the winter baths (*thermae hiemalium*), by C. Cluvius Martinus and M. Caesolius Saturninus on *XVI kalendas decimbres* in AD 341, is recorded in another inscription (*CIL* XI 4095 and 4096 = Pietrangeli 1943:

FIG. 3.29. General view of the octagonal room in the baths from the south. *(Photo: Martin Millett.)*

nos. 25–6). There is also a record of a further restoration, by C. Volusius Victor on *III nonas nobembres* [*sic.*], sometime in the late fourth or early fifth century (*CIL* XI 4094 = Pietrangeli 1943: no. 28).

The standing remains have been published recently in a series of plans, elevations and axonometric drawings (de Rubertis 2012: 130–7, 156–7, figs 22–8). Our survey did not reveal much further evidence for structures in the immediate vicinity of the baths, largely because of the presence of surface rubble. To the south is a series of walls ([72]–[75]) that is not aligned with the standing buildings and thus may be later. To the northeast, walls [J] were visible beside the track at the southern end of the 'Piccole Sostruzioni'. These walls are aligned with the standing structures and probably can be identified with the complex shown by Pannini as lying between the 'Terme' and the 'Magnifico Palazzo'.

In Figure 3.30 we have superimposed the plan by Pannini on the extant remains, adjusting the scale of the eighteenth-century plan to make a best fit with the standing structures. There can be little doubt that Pannini's plan is an idealized representation, but this exercise does provide some further evidence for the character of the buildings, and it is clear that some elements of his plan are reliable. He shows the main range as symmetrical, with the octagon at the centre of a square surrounded by rooms of equal size. Behind this lies a further range of pairs of smaller rooms, with the domed room projecting from one side. On the opposite side is a further square block of smaller rooms, with a rectangular structure (the 'Magnifico Palazzo') beyond. The square block of smaller rooms is also shown connected on one side to the 'Terme Hiemali', which is shown as a square block around an axial courtyard with an apparently vaulted room at the west behind. The reconstructed plan of the extant remains published by de Rubertis (2012: 131, fig. 23) provides some useful detail but does not add further to the understanding of Pannini's plan.

The surviving remains are partly consistent with Pannini's plan, and it is notable that the boundary between Fields 10 and 11 basically coincides with the back of the main block of building that he showed. However, following his plan, the 'Magnifico Palazzo' would lie uphill on the far side of the Via Flaminia to the east. Although it is possible that it can be associated with the magnetic anomalies ([78]–[80]) in this area, this is perhaps doubtful. Equally, the plan of the 'Terme Hiemali' as shown by Pannini is inconsistent with the evidence from the survey. The 'Piccole Sostruzioni' ([K]) and magnetic anomalies [69]–[70]

are all on a completely different alignment. Whilst it is possible that these are the buildings shown by Pannini, there is nothing distinctive in their forms to support this identification.

By contrast, Pannini's plan of the 'Terme' is closely comparable with results of the survey. The domed structures and exposed walls ([J]) form a reasonable match, while the line of the Via Flaminia also appears consistent with his plan. On this evidence we may accept tentatively his general plan, which makes reasonable sense at least as far as the area around the octagon is concerned. The main entrance, on the southeastern façade, led via an anteroom, perhaps flanked by *apodyteria*, into the octagonal hall, which presumably formed a central *frigidarium*. There were exits from this on each of the main sides, making this hall the central circulation area. Beyond the octagon lay the suites of *tepidaria* and *caldaria*, with the flanking domed room presumably forming a *laconicum*, accessed from the northeast (not via the present opening, which appears comparatively recent). Although the layout has obvious generic links with major urban bath-houses of the early Imperial period, there are no close parallels for the plan, and its axial symmetry may have been exaggerated by Pannini. Further survey using GPR would be useful to clarify the plan.

It is notable also that the baths are aligned roughly parallel with the Via Flaminia to their northeast. Furthermore, their layout, with the entrance via the surviving octagonal room, shows that the baths faced to the southeast, with access from the Via Flaminia, and that they did not open onto the piazza below the theatre and the 'Grandi Sostruzioni' to the northwest. This is significant for understanding the layout of the town. The underground cistern to the south of the baths can be identified with the 'Conserua d'Acqua' illustrated by Pannini (Fig. 2.1, no. 4). There seems no doubt that this is a cistern, although it recently has been interpreted as a revetment wall associated with the infilling of the valley (Bertacchini and Cenciaioli 2008: 840–1). This issue is discussed further below (p. 150).

The 'Piccole Sostruzioni' comprise a standing wall that rises vertically to a height of *c.* 9 m at the eastern end of Field 10 (Fig. 3.31), extending for *c.* 20 m on a north–south alignment. They are built of concrete and incorporate large horizontal travertine blocks. These are very similar to those used in the wall between Vaults 8/9 of the 'Grandi Sostruzioni' (cf. Fig. 3.21). The modern track cuts through them to the east ([K]), revealing that the thickness of their southern wall is in excess of 1 m and exposing the tops of a series of three vaults running from east to west behind the

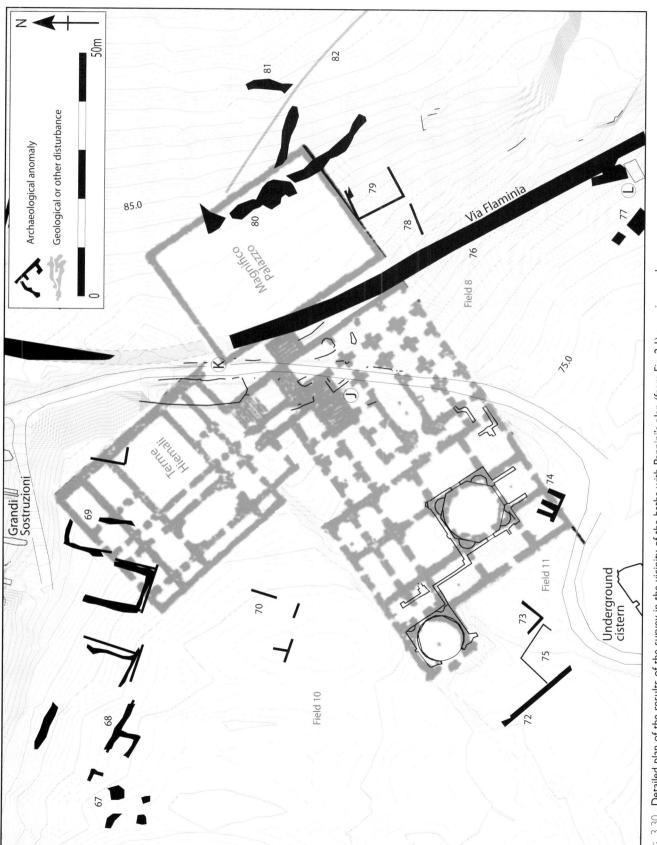

FIG. 3.30. Detailed plan of the results of the survey in the vicinity of the baths with Pannini's plan (from Fig. 2.1) superimposed.

FIG. 3.31. **View of the 'Piccole Sostruzioni' from the west.** *(Photo: Martin Millett.)*

western façade (which we were not able to plan but are recorded by de Rubertis — 2012: 131, fig. 23). The central vault is *c.* 2.7 m wide, with those on each side being *c.* 1 m wide. It seems clear that the structure was designed to extend the ridge outwards beyond the cliff-face in a manner similar to the 'Grandi Sostruzioni'. In this position, the 'Piccole Sostruzioni' seem most likely to have been built as a retaining wall for the western side of the Via Flaminia as it climbed up

the flank of the ridge. In this context, their alignment with major retaining wall [60a] to the north in Area 5 is thus significant.

In Field 8 to the east, the ground rises from the infilled valley of the San Vittore stream up onto the ridge. At the southern edge of the field lie the excavated remains of a mausoleum and a section of the Via Flaminia (see above, pp. xii–xiii). The road is deeply buried beneath *c.* 3 m of alluvium (**Fig. 3.32**),

FIG. 3.32. **View from the northwest of the excavated stretch of the Via Flaminia in Field 8, with the circular funerary monument (left) and *columbarium* (right) behind. Note the level of the modern ground surface to the left, which shows the depth of burial of the deposits in this part of the site.** *(Photo: Sophie Hay.)*

FIG. 3.33. View looking south along the line of the Via Flaminia in Field 8. The previously-supposed gate pier, reinterpreted here as a funerary monument ([L]), stands to the right of the Via Flaminia, with the circular funerary monument and *columbarium* in the background standing to its left. *(Photo: Martin Millett.)*

which may explain why it was not detected in the magnetometer survey to the south in Area 1 (above, p. 35). A further section of the road upslope to the north, discussed under Area 5 (p. 54), was buried less deeply, and its continuation was noted in the magnetometer survey ([62]–[63]). A linear positive anomaly ([76]) links these sections and must also represent the basalt blocks of the road surface. It is also visible in the results of the GPR survey (see below, Fig 3.49). Beside this, to the west near the foot of the slope, is a free-standing rectangular monument in *opus reticulatum* (Fig. 3.33), with brick quoins and string-courses, and with a niche on its northwestern face ([L]). This has been identified as a gate pier (Pietrangeli 1978: 48, fig. 43; Cenciaioli 2000: 22–3; de Rubertis 2012: 129, 156, fig. 21), although there is only limited evidence for a matching pier on the opposite side of the road to the northeast and no sign of the springing of an arch in the surviving structure. To its west there is a group of positive magnetic anomalies ([77]), which also show up as features in

the GPR survey (see below, Fig. 3.49). These might suggest that, if there were an arch here, it would have stood to one side of the road. A gate in this position would certainly make good sense if it marked the point where the road crossed the *pomerium* as it entered the town. However, given that it was a monument that stood to one side of the road, and that it was aligned also with the funerary monuments flanking the Via Flaminia to the south (Fig. 3.33), it is probably better understood as another such funerary monument.

To the east of this monument there is a large area that has been excavated behind the nymphaeum wall (see below, p. 64), with the spoil having been dumped on the slope and thus meaning that a large area was unavailable for survey. Structures in this area were shown by Pietrangeli (1978: 50, 94, carta 1, I, L and e; Fig. 1.4), including a probable palaeochristian building. The entrance to an underground cistern (Pietrangeli 1978: carta 1, G), on the northern edge of this area ([M]), was not accessible for survey, but its full extent northwards is clearly visible in the results of the GPR survey (see below, Figs 3.48–3.51). The evidence of the GPR shows that this formed part of a more extensive complex of buildings that continues to the west. These structures were not visible in the results of the magnetometry, probably because they are deeply buried and masked by rubble; the foundations only become clear at a depth of more than 1 m in the GPR survey.

The remaining parts of Field 8 lie on the west-facing slope that forms the side of the ridge. Near the crest of the slope, eroded building floors and foundations are visible. The magnetometer survey results provide some evidence for the form of these buildings. Rectilinear positive anomalies [78] and [79] indicate the existence of foundations of a building, c. 10 m wide and 15 m long, running perpendicular both to the slope and to the Via Flaminia. Above this, a major series of positive anomalies ([80]) along the line of the slope probably represents the foundations of a building parallel to the slope and to the road. This complex shows much more clearly in the results of the GPR (see below, Figs 3.48–3.52, no. 1). Further upslope, a series of more diffuse positive anomalies ([81]) may indicate another building obscured by surface rubble. Finally, a fainter linear anomaly ([82]) running for c. 75 m across the site probably is to be identified with a modern trackway that can be seen on recent maps.

AREA 7 (Figs 3.34–3.36)

This lies to the east of Areas 5 and 6, and it adjoins Area 8 to the north and Area 9 to the east. It covers the main part of the ridge, to the west of the San Vittore stream, in the zone where it rises steadily to the northeast. The description here includes Fields 9 and 20, as well as the eastern part of Field 16 (the western part having been discussed under Area 5, p. 54)). Field 17 is discussed under Area 8 (below, pp. 72–3). Field 9 was also field-walked intensively, with the results presented in Chapter 4. As a result, some pieces of sculpture (S5, S16), terracotta (T5) and bricks stamps (B4, B6, B8 and B9) were found there. Significant pieces of sculpture (S2, S14 and S17) and terracottas (T4, T13, T23 and T27) were recovered in the eastern part of Field 16, with further sculpture (S10) and terracottas (T12, T22, T24, T31, T32 and T33) being found near the southern boundary of Field 20. Fields 16 and 20 showed evidence for the recent disturbance of archaeological deposits by ploughing. In contrast, Field 9 evidently had been left unploughed for some years, although exposed foundations and flooring showed

that the archaeological deposits had been heavily eroded in the past.

Two major standing monuments are located in this area. At the south there is the façade of a revetment wall in brick-faced concrete, with alternating rectangular and apsidal niches faced with *opus reticulatum* (Fig. 3.37 — Pietrangeli 1978: carta 1, H; Fig. 1.4), which has been interpreted as a nymphaeum (Cenciaioli 2000: 28–9).

To the north, in the southeastern boundaries of Fields 16 and 17, and in the boundary separating Fields 16 and 18, heavy undergrowth masks the presence of a very substantial wall, which forms the edge of a terrace (Fig. 3.38). This is labelled as 'Late Roman wall' on our plans. It is marked on the plans published by Pietrangeli (1978: 50, carta I; Fig. 1.4) and Cenciaioli (2000: 9). The former suggested that it should be identified with the square enclosure on Pannini's plan. The core of the wall is built in layers of concrete poured over stone, and in some places it incorporates layers of very large squared blocks. It has lost most of its facing, but the remaining fragments suggest that it was probably *opus mixtum*, indicative of a late Roman date. It stands up to c. 3 m high, and can be traced from the track at the eastern apex of Field 17 southwestwards for about 130 m to the boundary between Fields 16 and 17. Here there is a kink in its path, at which point there are the remains of an internal structure ([N]), possibly a tower; this feature is marked on Pietrangeli's first plan (1943: fig. 2). Another wall, following the terrace edge in the boundary between Fields 16 and 17, probably joined it here, although the only trace of it comprises a short section towards the north ([O]). The main wall continues southwestwards for c. 110 m, on a slightly different alignment, in the boundary between Fields 9 and 16. It then turns very sharply northwards in the boundary between Fields 16 and 18, continuing as a visible structure for c. 100 m to the corner of Field 18. The remains of the wall are then lost as it crosses Field 16, although its course can be detected clearly in the results of the contour survey as it continues northwards across Field 16; it then runs across beneath the track and on into Field 15, where it appears in the magnetometer survey results (see below, p. 72, [104]). Here it presumably turned east to run along the edge of the ridge, but has now been lost through erosion. The magnetometer survey did not locate it in these fields, and the line of its northern side remains unknown.

This wall is evidently a key feature in the urban plan, and it would appear that the *enceinte* comprised two

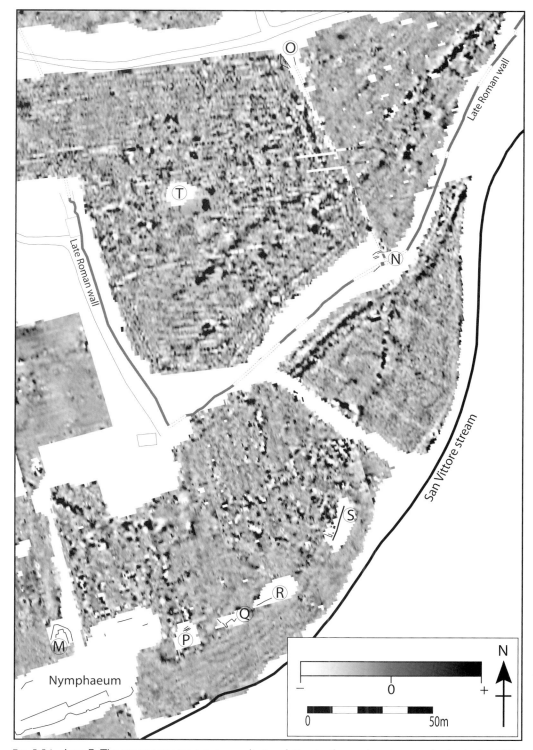

FIG. 3.34. **Area 7.** The magnetometry survey results in relation to the modern topography (scale 1:1,500). For the location, see Fig. 3.3; and for the geophysics scales, see Table 3.2.

attached enclosures. The first, to the west, occupies the upper part of Field 16 and the adjacent part of Field 15, is sub-rectangular and measures *c.*180 m north–south by 100 m east–west. The second lies

uphill to the east, sharing a boundary with the first enclosure along the line of the hedge that now separates Fields 16 and 17. It is triangular, occupying Field 17 and parts of Fields 13 and 14. Its southeastern wall

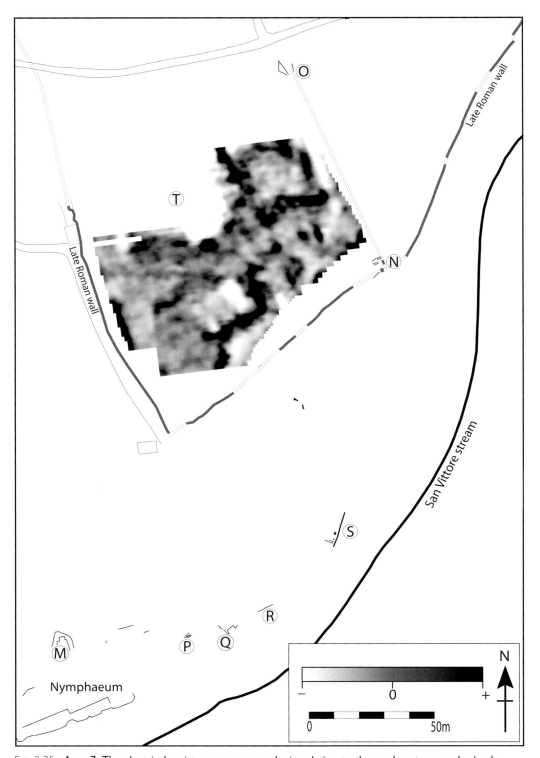

FIG. 3.35. Area 7. The electrical resistance survey results in relation to the modern topography (scale
1:1,500). For the location, see Fig. 3.3; and for the geophysics scales, see Table 3.2.

continues the line of that of the first enclosure for a
further *c.* 140 m. The enclosure to the west clearly
should be identified with the square enclosure on
Pannini's plan (**Fig. 2.1**), which is shown as containing

three major buildings, '13 Colleggio', '14 Tempio' and
'17 Foro'.

The available land in Fields 9, 16 and 20 was
surveyed by magnetometry, whilst an area in Field 16

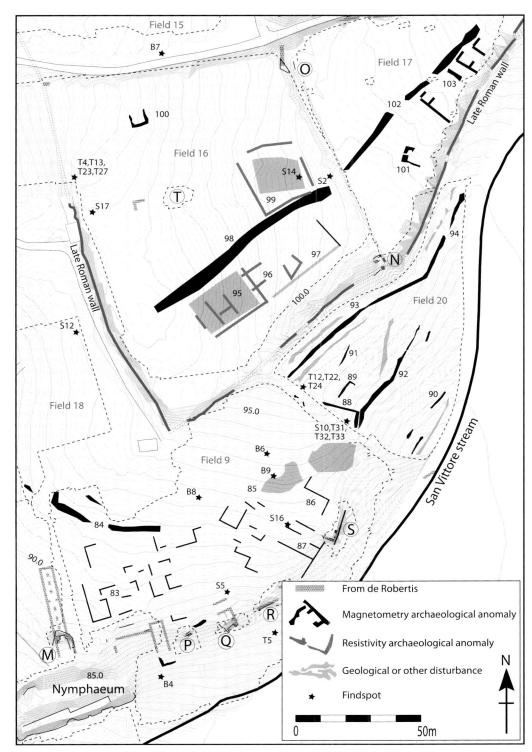

FIG. 3.36. **Area 7.** Interpretation of the magnetometry survey results in relation to the modern topography and standing monuments (scale 1:1,500). For the location, see Fig. 3.3.

was also surveyed with electrical resistance (although this work could not be completed because the landowner withdrew permission). Field 9 occupies the edge of the ridge and the steep slope down to the San Vittore stream along the southeastern side. Along its brow the eroded remains of a series of standing structures are exposed. These include a fragment of wall in *opus reticulatum* ([S]), pieces of *opus signinum*

FIG. 3.37. **View of the nymphaeum in Field 8 from the southwest.** *(Photo: Martin Millett.)*

flooring ([P] and [R]) and a vaulted cistern ([Q]) that was noted also by Pietrangeli (1978: 50, carta 1, M; **Fig. 1.4**). The most northerly structure ([S]) comprises a long stretch of retaining wall faced in *opus reticulatum* that was pierced by drains made from amphorae (Pietrangeli 1978: 50, carta 1, N; **Fig. 1.4**) and can be traced further north in the results of the magnetometer survey (see below Field 20, [92]).

On the ground beside the San Vittore stream the magnetometer survey did not reveal any features, probably because of soil accumulation. A positive anomaly on the slope between the nymphaeum and the standing remains of a fragment of wall ([P]) may represent a further part of its structure. On the flatter ground of the ridge top immediately to the north the results are masked by considerable interference from surface rubble. However, a complex of walls ([83]) is partially visible, revealing a building, *c.* 35 × 35 m, comprising a series of rooms, *c.* 5 m wide, aligned west/southwest–east/southeast, parallel with the slope. This alignment is shared with the nymphaeum and cistern [M], immediately to the west in Area 6 (see

FIG. 3.38. **View of a standing stretch of the late Roman enclosure wall in the boundary between Fields 16 and 18, viewed from the west.** *(Photo: Martin Millett.)*

above, p. 63). The form of the building is uncertain, but it may be either a peristyle house, or perhaps part of the palaeochristian complex noted above (p. 11) and referred to by Pietrangeli (1978: 50, 94, carta 1, I, L and e; **Fig. 1.4**). This area coincides with one of the main concentrations of late antique pottery identified during the field-walking (see below, p. 92 and **Fig. 4.8**). To its north a linear positive anomaly ([84]) runs across the slope at an angle to these structures, continuing from Area 5 and thus extending for *c.* 80 m. It perhaps represents a stretch of street that joins to the Via Flaminia.

At the northeastern end of Field 9, and separated from [83] by a quiet area, there is a further zone of surface rubble ([85]), within which is a series of walls ([86] and [87]) that connects with the revetment wall ([S]). These all follow the alignment of the valley edge, which means that they are set at an angle to the structures to their southwest. At the north, two walls ([86]) reveal a room that measures more than 10×10 m. To the south of the group is a series of narrow rooms ([87]) that extend back *c.* 18 m from a wall set along the break of slope. Further north and northeast, surface rubble masks other structures.

This group of structures continues into Field 20. Partially obscured by the boundary between the two fields is a substantial structure that is shown clearly by positive magnetic anomalies in Field 20 ([88]). It measures *c.* 16 m by more than 6 m, and was partially exposed in an illegally excavated trench beneath the hedge, which revealed two courses of well-cut tuff blocks. To its north there is a further positive anomaly ([89]) on a slightly different alignment, which may represent a further building. Ploughing in this corner of the field had brought to the surface architectural terracottas with fresh stucco still attached (Chapter 5: T12, T22 and T24), indicating the presence of a major building. Towards the San Vittore stream a series of linear anomalies associated with modern agriculture masks one possibly ancient feature ([90]), which cuts across the field at an angle to the cultivation. This perhaps may relate to the clay drainage pipe that Pietrangeli recorded in this area (1978: 50, carta 1, O; **Fig. 1.4**). A further positive linear anomaly to the west ([91]) is probably a wall foundation. This shares an alignment with a major linear anomaly ([92]) that runs across the field from a point just east of building [88] towards the junction between the boundaries of Fields 16 and 17 to the north. It continues the line of the revetment wall ([S]) exposed in Field 9 to the south, and links this to the junction of the late Roman

walls in the field boundary at the north. It thus continues the line of the late Roman wall in the boundary that separates Fields 16 and 17. It might relate to a modern boundary, but it seems more likely to be evidence for an ancient wall continuing this line and linking it to the revetment and the nymphaeum that defined the flank of the town overlooking the San Vittore stream. Two positive linear anomalies ([93] and [94]) run along the northwestern side of the field, parallel with the late Roman wall at the field edge. These seem most likely to result from the use of rubble in the construction of a modern trackway. However, they may indicate an original road line, especially given their alignment at the northern end of the field.

The area enclosed within the late Roman walls in the eastern part of Field 16 is heavily masked by surface rubble. The results of the electrical resistance survey (**Fig. 3.35**) are valuable in providing clearer detail of the structures, so it is regrettable that it proved impossible to complete this survey. The results show a clear alignment of structures with the late Roman wall at the southeastern field boundary. A substantial building ([95]) is shown clearly in the results of the electrical resistance survey, measuring *c.* 25×18 m. An area of low resistance within it appears to show a tripartite division. This building seems likely to be identified with the 'Tempio' shown in Pannini's plan (**Fig. 2.1**, no. 14), as the details of the plan are closely comparable. This building can be seen continuing to the northeast in both the magnetometer and resistance results ([96]). It is not clear whether the high-resistance feature along the southeastern edge of the area ([97]) represents a wall or is the result of the soil drying near the field edge: given the alignment, the former seems more probable. Along the northwestern flank of these structures there is a linear magnetic anomaly ([98]) that continues across Field 17 ([102]) and is probably a street. This identification is supported by the presence of a number of basalt paving blocks found dumped around the edges of Field 16. To the northwest of this, high-resistance anomalies define a large structure ([99]), *c.* 22 m wide and at least 35 m long, from the surface of which came a small marble statue ([S2]) and an altar ([S14]). Both the form and location of this suggest that it can be identified with the 'Foro' on Pannini's plan (**Fig. 2.1**, no. 17). The only structure clearly visible in the magnetometer survey results in the northern part of the field, where resistance survey was impossible, is a rectilinear set of negative anomalies ([100]), presumably walls, measuring *c.* $6 \times 7+$ m. The overgrown remains of a

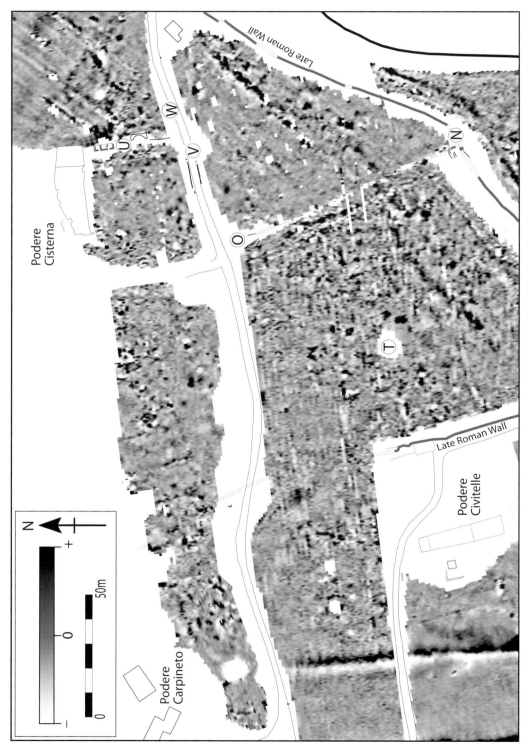

Fig. 3.39. Area 8. The magnetometry survey results in relation to the modern topography (scale 1:1,500). For the location, see Fig. 3.3; and for the geophysics scales, see Table 3.2.

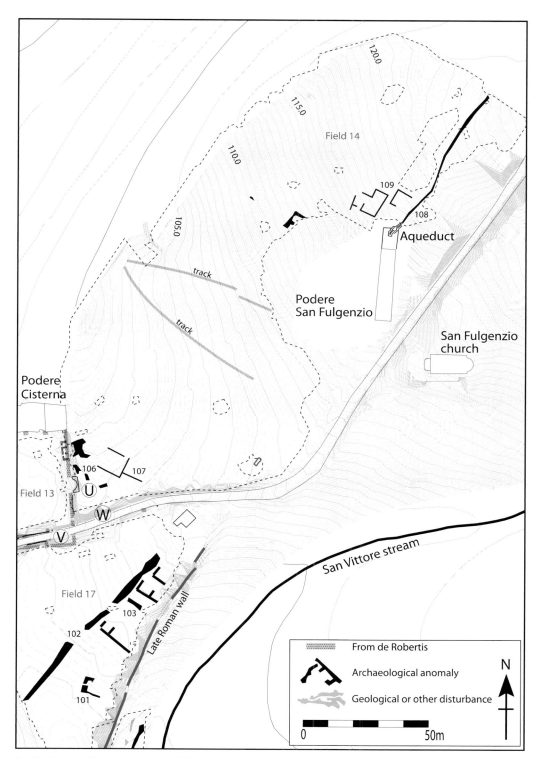

FIG. 3.44. **Area 9.** Interpretation of the magnetometry survey results in relation to the modern topography and standing monuments (scale 1:1,500). For the location, see Fig. 3.3.

the medieval or modern periods. On the other side of the track, a little to the south, the church of San Fulgenzio probably incorporates a late Roman building (**Fig. 1.9**) (see above, p. 11).

PORTO DELL'OLIO (Fig. 3.45)

In 1997, a small trial area of magnetometry was undertaken in an area immediately to the east of the Porto

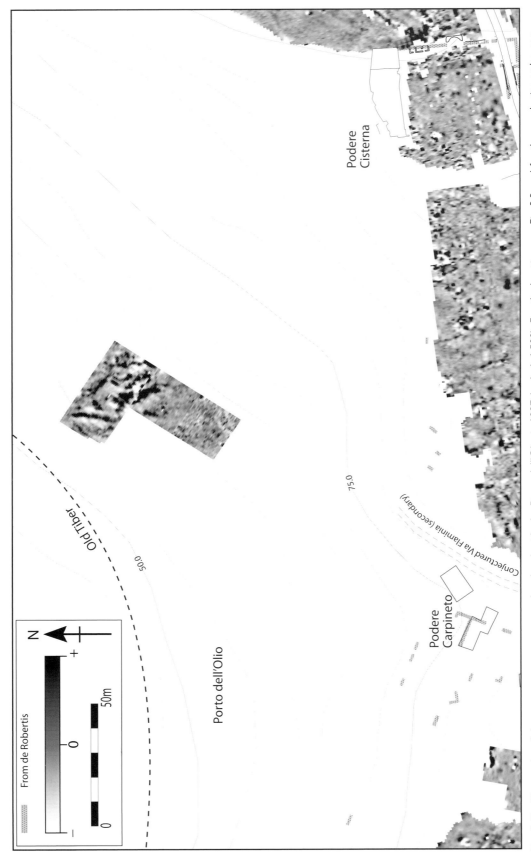

FIG. 3.45. The results of the magnetometry survey undertaken beside the Porto dell'Olio in 1997 (scale 1:1,500). For the location, see Fig. 3.3; and for the geophysics scales, see Table 3.2.

dell'Olio. This work did not reveal any significant archaeological features, with the anomalies apparently being of geological origin. In the light of later experience on the site, it is possible that the survey of a more extensive area here might reveal further archaeologically significant features.

HIGH-RESOLUTION GPR SURVEY IN THE ARCHAEOLOGICAL SITE OF OCRICULUM
Salvatore Piro

INTRODUCTION

The survey of Ocriculum was enlarged as a scientific collaboration with the Istituto per le Tecnologie Applicate ai Beni Culturali (ITABC-CNR) in 2003.

The constraints caused by the volcanic geology and depth of deposits meant that a range of geophysical prospection techniques was employed at the site. A flux-gate gradiometer survey of the entire site was undertaken to establish the extent of the buried remains. The results are variable in quality, but remain sufficiently clear to define the limits of the ancient town and to map the nature and extent of buried structures in certain parts of it. This was complemented with an electrical resistance survey undertaken with a twin-probe array of 0.5 m. In all cases, the results of resistivity survey clarified the nature and form of the responses of the buried structures visible in the magnetometer results. However, the technique remained impractical for large-scale ground coverage owing to the slow rate of data collection. In addition, both these survey techniques will rarely recognize features below a depth of 0.75–1 m.

The evident limitations of these techniques led to the important and productive collaboration between the British team and the ITABC-CNR in Rome. Using GPR it was possible to cover a relatively large open area, and the resulting 'time slices' allow analysis of features at different depths. This technique has enriched considerably our understanding of the development of particular areas of the site where the structures are buried too deeply to be understood through magneto-metry alone (Hay *et al.* 2005).

GPR DATA PROCESSING AND VISUALIZATION

One of the most useful ways of presenting the GPR datasets collected along closely-spaced parallel profiles is to display them in horizontal maps of recorded reflection amplitudes measured across the survey grid (Piro, Goodman and Nishimura 2003; Goodman *et al.* 2008; Goodman and Piro 2009). These maps, referred to as amplitude time slices, allow easy visualization of the location, depth, size and shape of radar anomalies buried in the ground. The maps can be created at various reflection time levels within a dataset to show radar structures at a specified time (depth) across a surveyed site. Mapping the energy in the reflected radar returns across a survey grid can help to create useful data that can sometimes mirror the general archaeological site plan that otherwise would have to be obtained from invasive excavation.

The raw reflection data acquired by GPR is nothing more than a collection of many individual vertical traces along 2-D transects within a grid. Each of those reflection traces, or radargrams, contains a series of waves that vary in amplitude depending on the amount and intensity of energy reflection that occurred at buried interfaces. When these traces are plotted sequentially in standard 2-D profiles, the specific amplitudes within individual traces that contain important reflection information are usually difficult to visualize and interpret. In areas where the stratigraphy is complex and buried features are difficult to discern, amplitude time-slice analysis is one of the most efficient form of post-processing that can be applied to the raw data in order to extract the 3-D shapes of buried remains (Gaffney *et al.* 2004; Gaffney, Patterson and Roberts 2004; Piro, Goodman and Nishimura 2003; Piro, Peloso and Gabrielli 2007; Piro, Ceraudo and Zamuner 2011).

INSTRUMENT CONFIGURATION AND MEASUREMENT PARAMETERS

GPR surveys were undertaken in September 2003 and September 2004, for a total of six days, in Field 8, Areas A and B (**Fig. 3.46**), and in Field 18, Areas C, D and E (**Fig. 3.47**). For the measurements, a GSSI SIR 10A$^+$ (survey 2003) and a GSSI SIR 3000 (survey 2004) equipped with a 500 Mhz bistatic antenna with constant offset were employed.

Adjacent profiles at the site were collected alternately in reversed and unreversed directions across the survey grids in 0.5 m horizontal spacing between parallel profiles. Radar reflections along the transects were recorded continuously across the ground at 80 scan s^{-1}; horizontal stacking was set to four scans. The gain control was manually adjusted to be more effective. Along each profile, markers at 1 m spacing

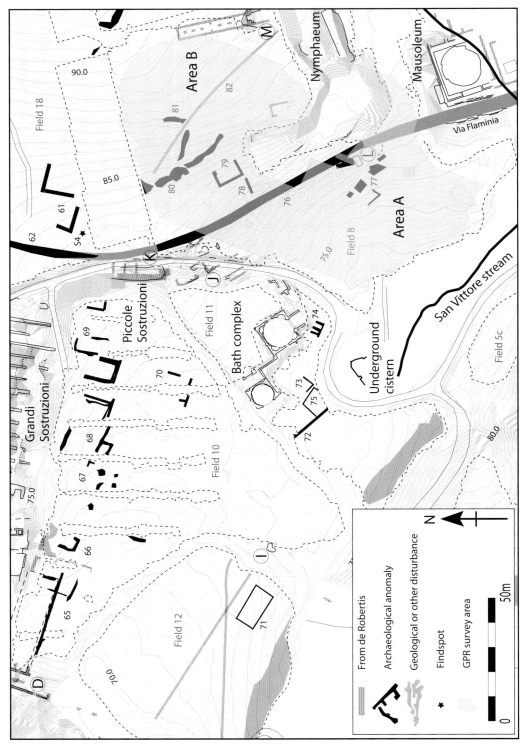

FIG. 3.46. The location of the GPR survey areas A and B in relation to Area 6. For the overall location, see Fig. 3.3.

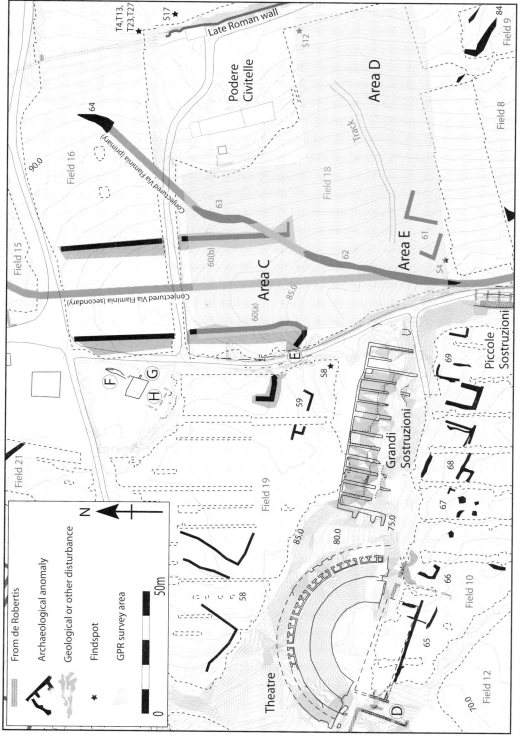

Fig. 3.47. The location of GPR survey areas C, D and E in relation to Area 5. For the overall location, see Fig. 3.3.

provided a reference. The data were later corrected for a variation in speed to a constant 30 scans per metre (or one scan per approximately 0.03 m).

All radar reflections within a 65 *ns* (two-way-travel time) and 55 *ns* time windows were recorded digitally in the field as 8 bit data and 512 samples per radar scan.

A total of 175 parallel profiles was collected in Area A, 159 parallel profiles in Area B, 135 parallel profiles in Area C, 120 parallel profiles in Area D and 135 parallel profiles in Area E.

DATA ELABORATION AND PRESENTATION

Time-slice analysis was applied to all the surveyed grids. For the five areas (A, B, C, D and E), time slices were generated at 3 *ns* intervals. The time-slice datasets were generated by spatially averaging the squared amplitude of radar reflections in the horizontal as well as the vertical. Horizontal averaging included creating spatial averages every 0.5 m along the radar transepts. The data were gridded using a krigging algorithm that included a search of all data within a 1.0 m radius of the desired point to be interpolated on the grid (Piro, Goodman and Nishimura 2003).

Band-pass filters were used to reduce the band-pass and to remove the background reflections and linear striations for each individual line in the survey grid. The low-pass filters were applied to the time-slice dataset, computing a moving window average with a filter length set by the users. The filter has a threshold amplitude setting that only allows values below these amplitudes to be included in the computation of the moving filter average. The threshold amplitude is set to a value just below the primary target signals that were strong recorded reflections from Roman walls.

The moving average is subtracted from the centre value of the filter to remove the background reflections. In addition to removing striation noise along the profile directions, the filter also has the effect of removing the mosaic pattern inherent in comprehensive maps showing adjacent areas having different background geology or slightly different ground conditions. Thresholding and data transforms were used to enhance various features detected on the time-scale maps.

ANALYSIS OF THE RESULTS

FIELD 8: AREAS A AND B
Figure 3.48 shows the time slices at the estimated depth of 0.45–0.50 m; some reflections are clearly visible in

Area B, close to the known archaeological structures. These anomalies can be interpreted as the tops of the remains of walls, characterized by large dimensions: 24×4 m (anomaly 1), 18×5 m (anomaly 2). A clear reflector (anomaly 3) measuring 15.8×1.5 m is visible in Area A, close to the boundary with Area B. In this figure it is possible to see other anomalies with low intensity that indicate the presence of deeper reflectors.

Figure 3.49 shows the time slices at the estimated depth of 0.70 m; some reflections are clearly visible in Area B, which characterized the whole investigated surface. The reflections are related to the remains of walls with different dimensions and also the presence of rubble. The anomalies shown in Figure 3.49 are more visible, having larger dimensions and rubble near to them. In Area A other clear reflectors are visible.

Figure 3.50 shows the time slices at the estimated depth of 0.90 m; some reflections are visible in Area B and characterize the whole area. The main result is that, at this depth, the GPR signal has located the deeper parts of the structures below the rubble layer. In Area B it is possible to see the plan of anomaly no. 2 more clearly, characterized by three large walls.

Figure 3.51 shows the time slices at the estimated depth of 1.1 m; at this depth the main anomalies are still present and can be considered to mark the bottom of the reflectors.

Figure 3.52 shows the time slices at the estimated depth of 1.6 m; at this depth the main individual anomalies are present only in Area B, while in Area A the isolated reflections can be related to the condition of the layer below the bottom of the reflectors.

FIELD 18: AREAS C, D AND E
Figure 3.53 shows the time slices at the estimated depth of 0.35 m. The significant anomalies have been indicated with numbers. The low-intensity anomaly (no. 1) is characterized by a very low signal and measures 90×6 m. This corresponds with a major magnetic anomaly identified in the same area, and can be correlated to the presence of road remains (see above, p. 54). Anomalies nos. 2 and 4 represent the presence of subsurface minor features beside the edges of the road. Anomaly no. 3 is characterized by linear structures, parallel with each other and at a distance of 18–19 m.

Figure 3.54 shows the time slices at the estimated depth of 0.55 m; reflections are visible in all three areas, C, D and E, although characterized by different signal intensity. Anomaly no. 1 is characterized by a

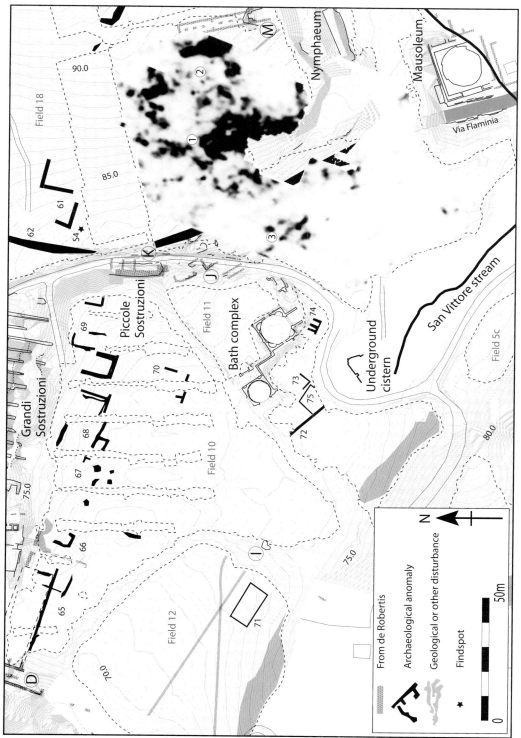

Fᴵɢ. 3.48. GPR results from Areas A and B: time-slice depth 0.45–0.50 m.

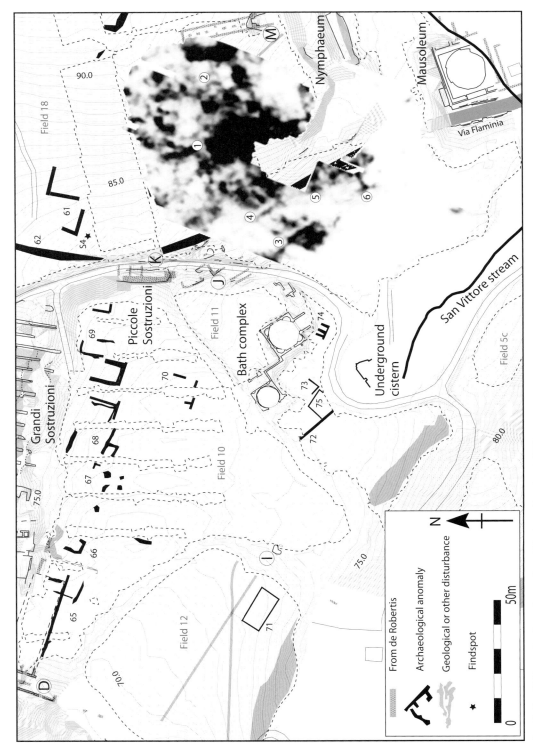

Fig. 3.49. GPR results from Areas A and B: time-slice depth 0.70 m.

FIG. 3.50. GPR results from Areas A and B: time-slice depth 0.90 m.

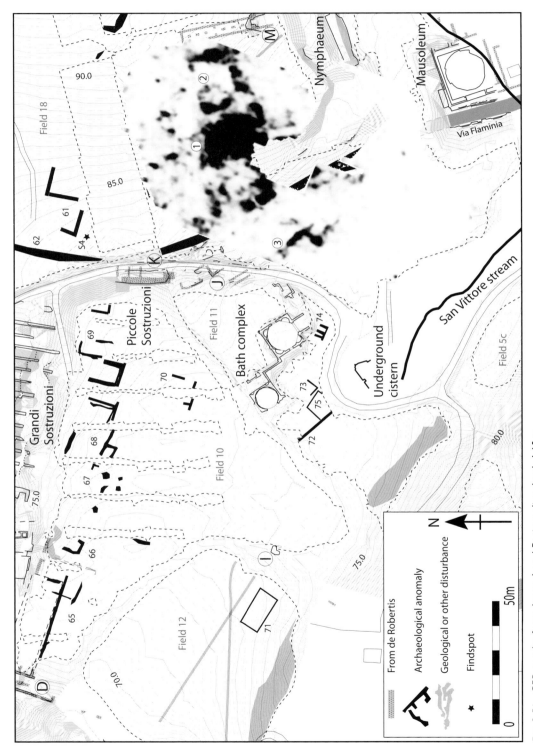

FIG. 3.51. GPR results from Areas A and B: time-slice depth 1.10 m.

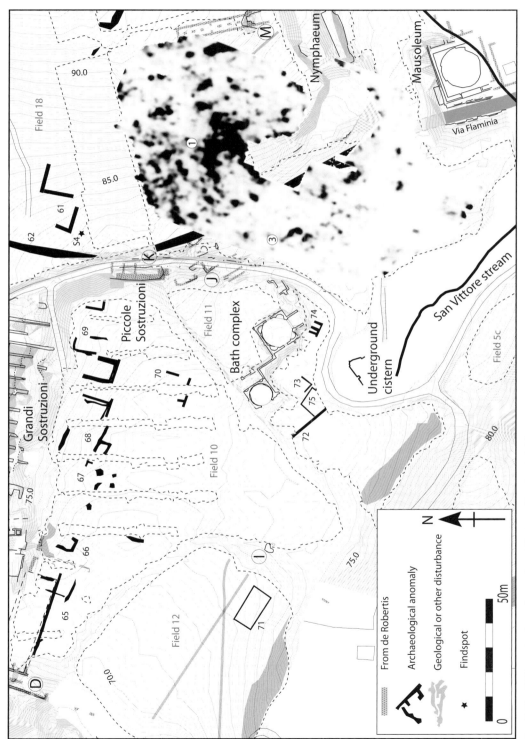

FIG. 3.52. GPR results from Areas A and B: time-slice depth 1.60 m.

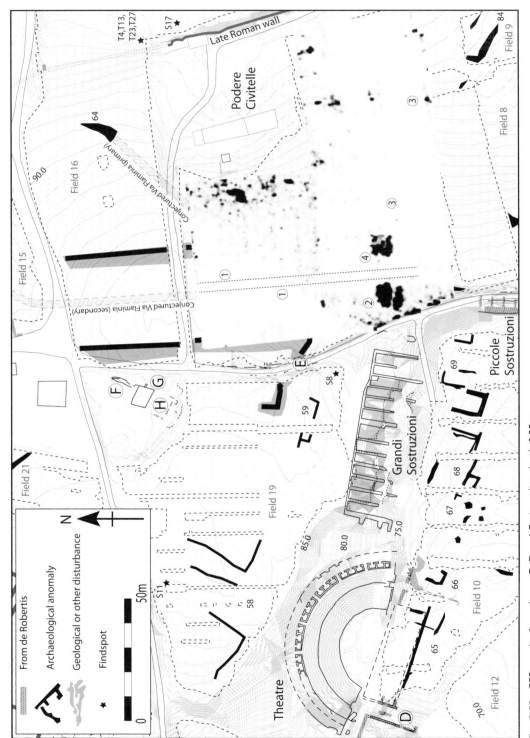

Fig. 3.53. GPR results from Areas C, D and E: time-slice depth 0.35 m.

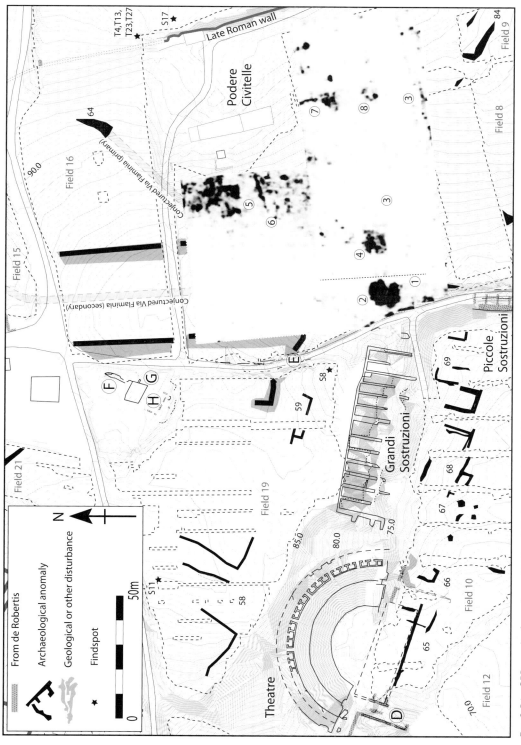

Fig. 3.54. GPR results from Areas C, D and E: time-slice depth 0.55 m.

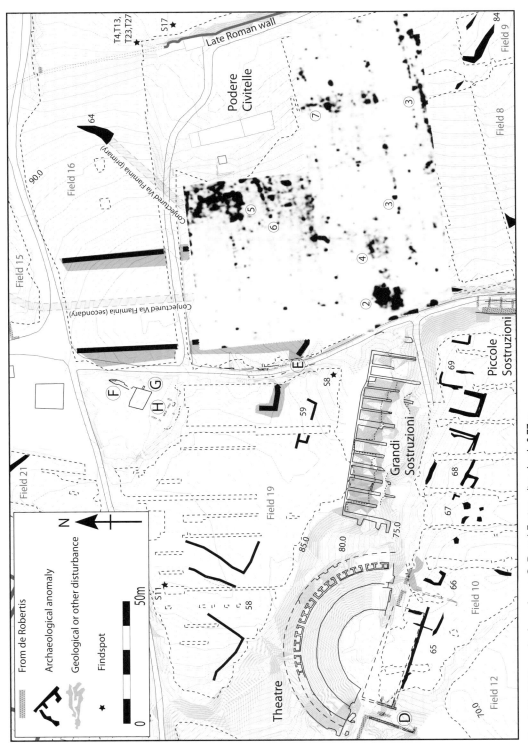

FIG. 3.55. GPR results from Areas C, D and E: time-slice depth 0.77 m.

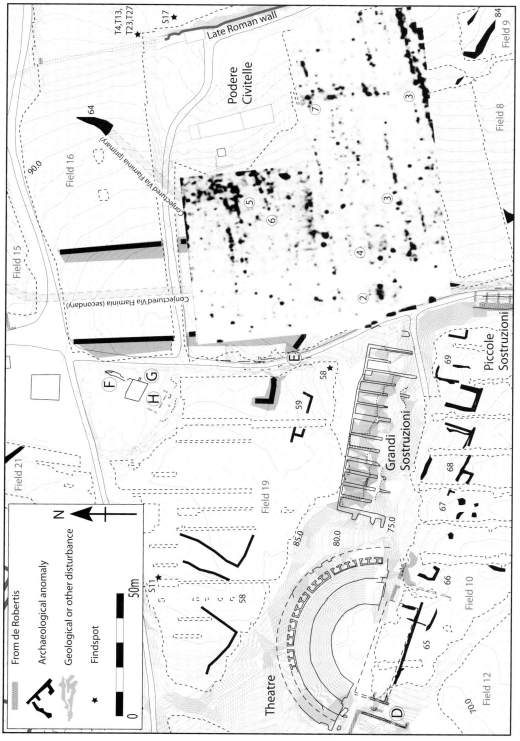

FIG. 3.56. GPR results from Areas C, D and E: time-slice depth 0.95 m.

very low signal and it is present only in Area E. Anomalies nos. 2 and 4, located beside the road, are more visible. Anomaly no. 3 is characterized by linear structures, parallel to each other and at a distance of 18–19 m. At this depth other anomalies (nos. 5 and 6), located in Area C, are also visible. These anomalies may represent walls. Anomalies nos. 7 and 8, located in Area D, measuring 14×2.5 m and 7×5 m, respectively, may indicate isolated structures.

Figure **3.55** shows the time slices at the estimated depth of 0.77 m. Anomalies nos. 2 and 4 are minor, low-intensity features located beside the road. Anomaly no. 3 is characterized by linear structures, parallel to each other and at a distance of 18–19 m. At this depth anomalies nos. 5 and 6, located in Area C, are clearly visible. These anomalies may indicate walls. Anomalies nos. 7 and 8, located in Area D, represent isolated structures with smaller dimensions.

Figure **3.56** shows the time slices at the estimated depth of 0.95 m. Anomalies nos. 2 and 4 are minor, low-intensity features located beside the road. Anomaly no. 3 is characterized by linear structures, parallel to each other and at a distance of 18–19 m. At this depth anomalies nos. 5 and 6, located in Area C, are still visible. These anomalies may represent walls. Anomalies nos. 7 and 8, located in Area D, have smaller dimensions.

CONCLUSIONS

The results of this study show that GPR is effective in mapping the remains of buried walls and floors; the locations, depths, sizes and general characteristics of the buried buildings were estimated effectively using this method.

NOTE

1. Pietrangeli's carta 1 (= Fig. 1.4) shows two locations labelled 'r', that to the north beside Podere Cisterna is evidently the find-spot, and should have been labelled 'p' to match the caption.

THE FIELDWALKING FINDS

THE FIELDWALKING RESULTS
Martin Millett

INTRODUCTION

In this chapter the results of the field-walking of Fields 7 and 9 are presented, together with summaries of the pottery and marble found. The methology used and surface conditions are summarized above (pp. 26–8). Catalogues of the other objects recovered from the field-walking of these fields, together with those collected during the geophysical survey of other areas of the site, are presented in Chapter 5. During the surface collection in Fields 7 and 9, all finds in the collection units were gathered. The pottery is fully catalogued and summaries of the distributions of other finds are provided together with distribution plots.

FIELD 7 (Fig. 4.1)

The line walking of this area revealed a widespread scatter of pottery together with a few other items, including a fragment of a sarcophagus (S9). The overall context suggests that the area lay outside the main area of settlement, in a cemetery zone. The distribution of pottery shows a main concentration in the middle of the area covered. The density of finds fell away rapidly about 30 m from the line of the Via Flaminia, hence the field-walking was limited to this zone. The overall chronology indicates that deposition of material did not start until the first century AD (see p. 112).

FIELD 9 (Figs 4.2–4.8)

The grid walking revealed a very heavy density of material. The overall distribution of pottery (Fig. 4.2) shows a consistently dense distribution across the area, with concentrations in the southwest corner and at the east, associated respectively with two buildings revealed in the magnetometry (Fig. 3.36, nos. [83] and [86]/[87]). The overall distribution of catalogued finds (Fig. 4.3) does not reveal any significant patterns, although it may be noted that T5 is a terracotta model of a bull of presumed votive significance. The distributions of marble fragments and tesserae differ from the pattern shown by the pottery. Marble fragments are spread rather thinly across the area (Fig. 4.4), but with a notable association with the areas to the east in the magnetometry (Fig. 3.36, nos. [85], [86] and [87]). By contrast, the tesserae (Fig. 4.5) show a marked concentration in the middle of the field, in an area where no clear anomalies were visible in the results of the magnetometry (cf. Fig. 3.36).

The overall chronology of the pottery from this field demonstrates a range from the fourth century BC to the seventh century AD (see below, pp. 111–12). A comparison of the distributions of dated sherds (Figs 4.6–4.8) reveals a series of patterns. Although sherds of all periods were found across the whole area, Republican material (Fig. 4.6) shows a concentration on the highest part of the field at the northeast, perhaps as a result of deposits here having been eroded by ploughing, thus revealing more evidence of the earliest phases. This conclusion is perhaps supported by the comparative absence of later pottery from this part of the site. Early Imperial pottery (Fig. 4.7) is distributed more evenly, and generally reflects the overall density of pottery finds (cf. Fig. 4.2). However, its distribution is somewhat thinner than the overall density pattern in the eastern part of the field. The distribution of late antique pottery (Fig. 4.8) more generally reflects the overall density of pottery, implying that the structures revealed in the magnetometry (Fig. 3.36, nos. [85], [86] and [87]), probably continued in occupation into this period.

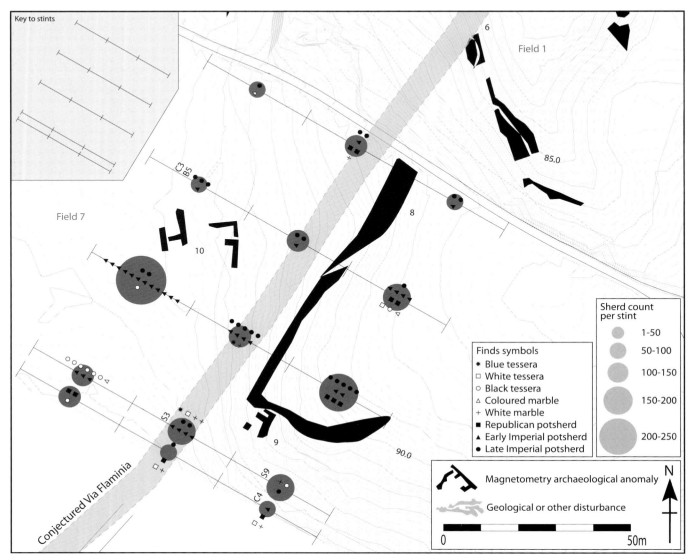

FIG. 4.1. **Overall distribution of the finds from the field-walking in Field 7.**

THE POTTERY

Sabrina Zampini[1]

The pottery collected in Fields 7 and 9 was listed by grid square or line stint, with sherds identified to fabric and form, and dates suggested where possible. The distribution evidence is shown by date in a series of distribution maps (**Figs 4.6–4.8**), while the fabrics and forms are summarized by field in **Tables 4.1–4.13**.

During the fieldwalking survey of Fields 7 and 9, 6,555 pottery sherds were collected. Kitchen-ware is the best represented ceramic class in the assemblages, followed by amphorae and both table- and

storage-wares. As regards the fine-wares, African red slip ware sherds are the most common.

Abbrevations used:

A.C. (anfora cretese) = Marangou Lerat 1995.
Agora = Robinson 1959.
Atlante = Pugliese Carratelli 1981.
Bailey = Bailey 1980.
Camulodunum = Hawkes and Hull 1947.
Esquiline type = *CIL* XV 782–4 and tab. II.
Conspectus = Ettlinger 1990.
Curia II = Morselli and Tortorici 1989.
Dressel = Dressel 1899.

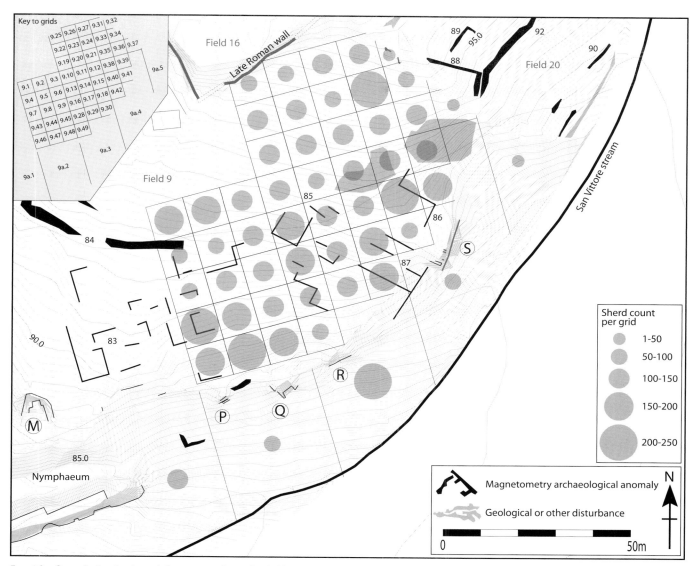

FIG. 4.2. Overall distribution of the pottery from the field-walking in Field 9.

Empoli, A. di = Cambi 1989.
Forlimpopoli = Aldine 1978.
Hayes = Hayes 1972.
Kapitän = Kapitän 1961.
Keay = Keay 1984.
LR (Late Roman, amphora) = Hayes 1976.
Maña = Maña 1951.
Mau = Mau 1898.
Morel = Morel 1981.
Ostia I = Carandini *et al.* 1968.
Ostia II = Berti *et al.* 1970.
Ostia III = Carandini and Panella 1973.
Ostia IV = Carandini and Panella 1977.
Pascual = Pascual Guasch 1962.

Pélichet = Pélichet 1946.
Ricci = Ricci 1987.

FINE-WARES

REPUBLICAN AND EARLY IMPERIAL PERIODS

Occupation of the site during the Orientalizing and Archaic periods is documented by a few sherds of coarse-wares and bucchero, which are not referable to precise typologies as they are highly fragmented and worn (Table 4.1).

The Hellenistic phase is far better represented (see also the sections on amphorae and kitchen-ware, below, pp. 102–5, 106–10) as 140 sherds of black-gloss

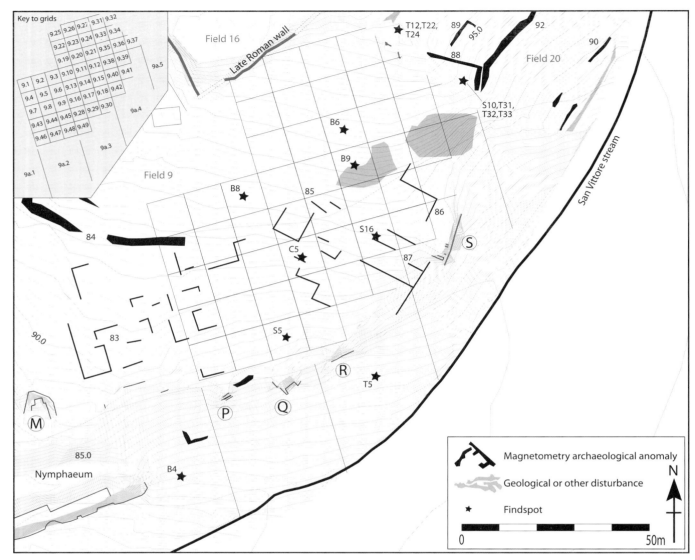

FIG. 4.3. Distribution of coins, brick stamps, terracottas and sculpture from the field-walking in Field 9.

wares were collected (Table 4.2). Fifteen fragments are attributed to a specific shape, while a further two can be assigned to a generic form. Most of the identified vessels derive from a production that is similar to that of the *atelier des petites estampilles*, a production that involved several workshops in Latium, southern Etruria and the Faliscan area between the end of the fourth and the first half of the third centuries BC.

The most common type (represented by five fragments) is the hemispherical bowl with incurving rim belonging to the series Morel 2783 and 2784, typical of the first phase of this production, while only one bowl type Morel 2538b was identified, which is again typical of the initial phase of production (Brecciaroli Taborelli 2005: 67). In addition, the everted rim of a patera of the series Morel 1323, a fish-plate of the series Morel 1124 and a jug with rounded and everted rim Morel 5226 were documented.

The patera of the series Morel 1647c, documented by two vessels, can be dated between the third and the beginning of the second centuries BC, whilst the bowl with almond-shaped rim Morel type 2534c and the bowl with flaring walls Morel 2653 are datable to the second century BC, as is a Morel 2252 patera with a poorly-defined rim; all these types are documented by a single sherd. Finally, a rim of a Morel 2862 bowl was found; it dates to 175–50 BC.

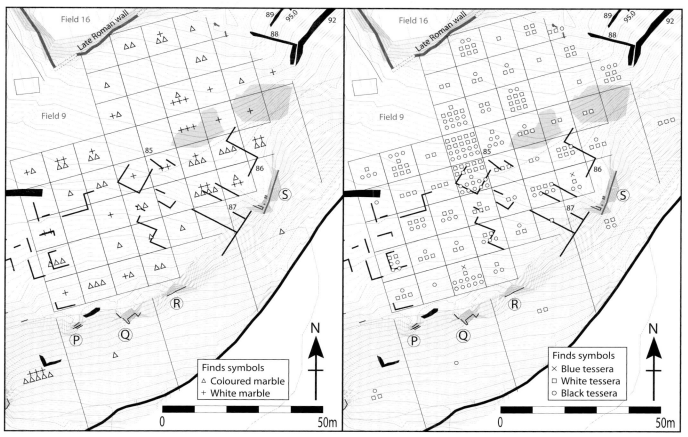

FIG. 4.4. Distribution of marble fragments from the field-walking in Field 9.

FIG. 4.5. Distribution of tesserae from the field-walking in Field 9.

In addition, only one fragment (a base of an unidentified plate) attributable to the Campana A production was found. This production derives from the area of Naples and was typical of the period between the second and first centuries BC.

In the early Imperial period, Arretine *sigillata* is the most common fine-ware, with as many as 113 fragments (Table 4.3). Twelve of them can be assigned to a precise shape, while an additional four can be related to generic forms. Cups are the most common vessels: the earliest identified type — *Conspectus* 7 — is characterized by flaring walls and a poorly-defined rim; it dates to the early to mid-Augustan period. A date in the first half of the first century AD can be suggested for the cup with vertical walls *Conspectus* 28.3.1, whilst the type with a carinated wall documented in our assemblage with variants *Conspectus* 27.1.1 and 27.1.2 dates between the Tiberian and Flavian periods. Finally, a more generic date between the end of the first century BC and the end of the first century AD can be ascribed to the hemispherical bowl *Conspectus* 36.

Plates are less common, and mostly documented by the type with flaring walls and a small everted rim comparable to *Conspectus* 3, which dates it to between the Claudian/Tiberian period and the first half of the second century AD. Another plate, *Conspectus* 4.6, characterized by a shallow and convex wall, is documented by a single fragment; its date is Tiberian–Claudian. Finally, a base fragment bearing an unreadable *in planta pedis* stamp is documented, as well as a body sherd with a graffito.

Thin-walled pottery is attested by 42 fragments (Table 4.4), but their very poor state of preservation allowed for the identification of only two beakers and two cups. The type Ricci 1/27, with an ovoid body and everted rim, is earliest and dates to the third quarter of the first century BC. The type Ricci 1/29, also attested, lacks a precise date and looks quite similar to the previous one, though it is characterized by a slightly larger rim (Ricci 1987: 250).

As regards the cups, there is a fragment of type Ricci 2/412 with slightly incurving wall, produced in the Augustan period, whilst another fragment with

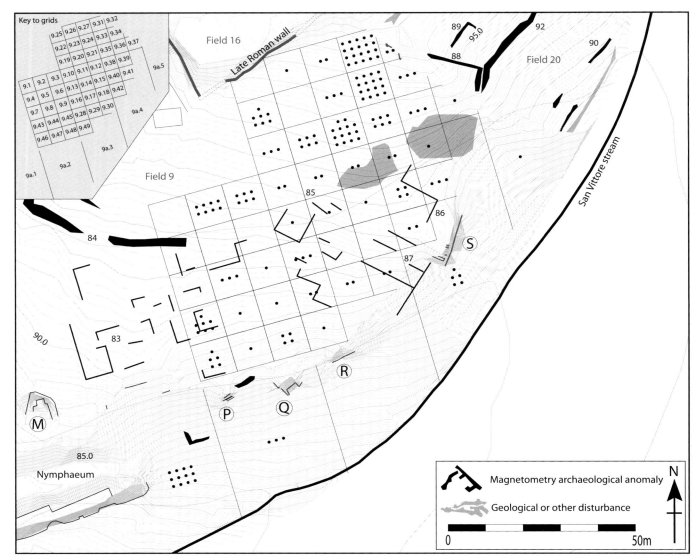

FIG. 4.6. Distribution of pottery sherds dated to the Republican period from the field-walking in Field 9.

a hemispherical wall, type Ricci 2/407, dates to between the Tiberian period and the end of the first century AD.

Most fragments are not decorated, although it is worth noting a wall fragment that bears *en barbotine* decoration with small spines (Ricci 2) typical of the first century BC, and three wall sherds with rusticated decoration (Ricci 63), very common in the first two centuries of the Imperial period.

MID- AND LATE IMPERIAL PERIODS

African red slip ware is the most common fine-ware, being attested by 269 fragments; 55 of them were attributed to a known type (Table 4.5). ARS A is the most frequent (103 fragments); it is also characterized by a wide typological variety. The identified specimens date to between the Flavian period and the mid-third century AD, hence they cover the full chronological range during which the workshops located in Zeugitana produced this class of fine-ware. The two bowl types Hayes 2 and Hayes 8a, as well as the uncommon jug Hayes 137, nos. 1–2 (*Atlante* I: 40), date to the first phase of production. Production A2 is also well documented through the carinated bowl Hayes 14; the large dish with flattened rim Hayes 6, with variants 6b and 6c; the carinated dish with a poorly-defined rim Hayes 16; and the dishes with a slightly incurving rim Hayes 26 and 27.

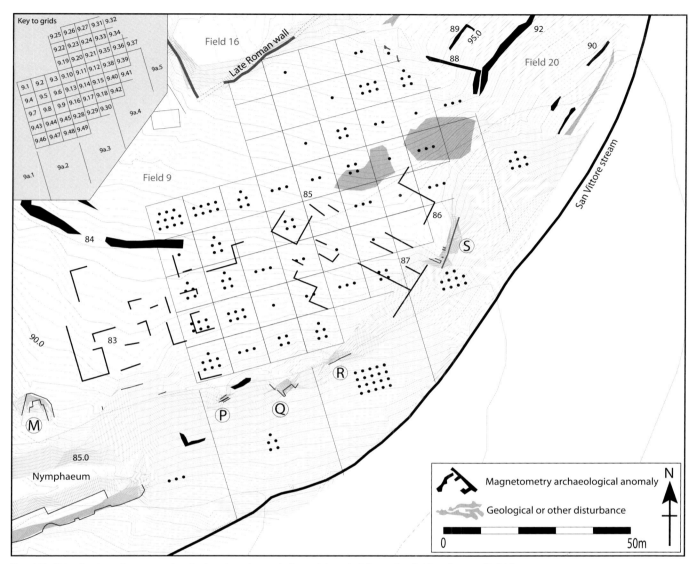

FIG. 4.7. Distribution of pottery sherds dated to the early Imperial period from the field-walking in Field 9.

Finally, the Hayes 3c dish, with everted rim, is attested by one fragment.

Production A/D is documented by just one fragment of dish Hayes 31, nos. 1–4, whilst 76 fragments can be attributed to production C, whose workshops, located in the area of ancient Byzacena in central-eastern Tunisia, were in operation between the early third and the early decades of the sixth centuries AD. In the assemblage, only two types are documented: the bowl Hayes 45a and dish Hayes 50 — one of the most common types belonging to this production, which is documented here with variants a and b (*Atlante* I: 65).

Eighty-nine fragments were attributed to production D; the types identified are those that occur more commonly between the mid-fourth and the end of the

fifth centuries AD, which coincides with the greatest development of the northern Tunisian workshops. The highest number of rims belongs to a type of flat-based dish with incurving rim, type Hayes 61, documented by variants a and b, immediately followed by the flanged bowl Hayes 91. Some of the identified types were produced during the fifth century AD. This is the case with the large bowls and dishes, Hayes 76, 80a and 87a, whilst the survey did not recover any type whose production started after the end of the fifth century AD.

It is worth noting the presence of two fragments attributable to *sigillata medio-adriatica* (Fontana 2005: 260) (Table 4.6). These are the rim of a plate or dish with flattened lip, identifiable with the type

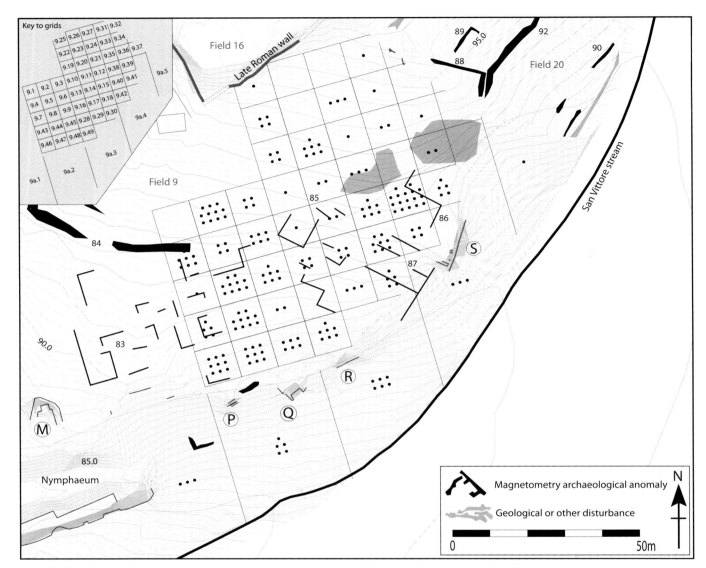

FIG. 4.8. Distribution of pottery sherds dated to the late Imperial period from the field-walking in Field 9.

Brecciaroli Taborelli 12b (Brecciaroli Taborelli 1978: 19–22), dating to the second and third centuries AD, and a wall sherd that is likely to belong to the same vessel.

TABLE 4.1. The bucchero from the survey in Fields 7 and 9.

Fabric	Form	Field 7	Field 9
Bucchero	open form	–	2
Bucchero	unidentified	–	2
Impasto bruno	unidentified	–	3
Impasto rosso	*testo da pane*	–	1

It is also important to note the 53 fragments of Roman red slip ware, a production that is documented between the second and fifth centuries AD (**Table 4.7**). This is so widespread in Umbria that it has been suggested that the workshops specializing in this ceramic class may have been located in the middle and upper Tiber valley (Fontana 2005: 265). Among the collected sherds, thirteen can be attributed to a generic shape, although only in four cases has it been possible to find a precise published parallel. Most of the fragments derive from open vessels: nine bowls and a plate were identified, as well as two fragments belonging to unidentifiable open vessels. The only closed vessel is a type of jug that could not be identified. A plate with a poorly-defined rim and

TABLE 4.2. The black-gloss wares from the survey in Fields 7 and 9.

Form	Form type	Date range	Field 7	Field 9
Plate	unidentified	200–1 BC	–	1
Bowl	Morel 2534c	200–150 BC	1	–
Bowl	Morel 2538b	300–250 BC	–	1
Bowl	Morel 2653	200–100 BC	–	1
Bowl	Morel 2783/4	305–265 BC	–	4
Bowl	Morel 2784	305–265 BC	–	1
Bowl	Morel 2862	175–50 BC	–	1
Bowl	unidentified	350–1 BC	–	1
Jug	Morel 5226	305–265 BC	–	1
Plate	Morel 1124	305–265 BC	–	1
Plate	Morel 1323	305–265 BC	–	1
Plate	Morel 1647c	270–190 BC	1	1
Plate	Morel 2252	180–100 BC	–	1
Plate	unidentified	350–1 BC	–	1
Unidentified	unidentified	350–1 BC	8	114

TABLE 4.3. The Arretine *sigillata* from the survey in Fields 7 and 9.

Form	Form type	Date range	Field 7	Field 9
Cup	*Conspectus* 27.1.1	AD 14–68	–	1
Cup	*Conspectus* 27.1.2	AD 14–68	–	1
Cup	*Conspectus* 28.3.1	AD 1–50	–	1
Cup	*Conspectus* 36	20 BC–AD 100	–	1
Cup	*Conspectus* 7	10 BC–AD 14	–	1
Cup	*Conspectus* B 3.13	27 BC–AD 150	–	1
Cup	unidentified	40 BC–AD 100/150	–	4
Plate	*Conspectus* 3	AD 20/41–100/150	–	1
Plate	*Conspectus* 3.3.1	AD 20/41–100/150	–	1
Plate	*Conspectus* 3.3.2	AD 20/41–100/150	1	–
Plate	*Conspectus* 4.6	AD 14–40	–	1
Plate	*Conspectus* B 2.5	AD 1–37	–	2
Unidentified	unidentified	40 BC–AD 140/150	8	89

TABLE 4.4. The thin-walled pottery from the survey in Fields 7 and 9.

Form	Type	Decoration	Date range	Field 7	Field 9
Cup	Ricci 2/407		AD 14/37–100	–	1
Cup	Ricci 2/412		27 BC–AD 14	–	1
Beaker	Ricci 1/27		50–25 BC	–	1
Beaker	Ricci 1/29		–	1	–
Unidentified	unidentified	Ricci 2	100–1 BC	–	1
Unidentified	unidentified	Ricci 63	27 BC–AD 200	–	3
Unidentified	unidentified		–	1	33

carinated wall (Monacchi 1999: fig. 193.97), a flanged bowl (Monacchi 1999: fig. 189.58) and two bowls with a poorly-defined rim and a more and less deep body (Monacchi 1999: fig. 188.28 and fig. 187.1) are documented.

LAMPS

Only 23 lamp fragments were collected during the field survey (Table 4.8), and given the low level of preservation only three of them have been identified to a particular type. The three identifiable lamps relate to completely different periods. The first one is a lip belonging to a cylindrical type as from the Esquiline (*CIL* XV 782–84 and tab. II), characterized by an anvil-shaped lip and dating between the second half of the second and the mid-first centuries BC. The second identified fragment is the disk of a lamp type Bailey B, with two grooves and a handle on the disk itself (type Bailey Q956), dating to the second half of the first century AD (Bailey 1980: 183). The last is the base of a north African lamp, the preserved fragment of which does not allow for a precise identification of the type, hence it is only generically referable to types *Atlante* VIII–X, whose production dates between the mid-fourth and the end of the sixth centuries AD.

COMMON-WARES

This definition includes all ceramic vessels used on a daily basis for food preparation and consumption, as well as for the cooking and preservation of food. As many as 3,980 fragments from the survey belong to this broad category; unfortunately, the high level of fragmentation of the sherds allowed for the

identification of only a small proportion of them. Kitchen-ware is, by far, more common, accounting for just over 65% of the analysed coarse-wares. Macroscopic analysis of the fabrics showed the vast majority of sherds to have derived from a local production, although some kitchen vessels were produced in Campania and northern Africa.

TABLE- AND STORAGE-WARES

There are 1,363 fragments assigned to this class, 314 of them characterized by a very thin coloured slip that very often was spread unevenly and covers only the outer surface of the vessel up to the rim. Only eighteen fragments could be assigned to a specific shape — seven bowls, three basins, three lids, two mortaria, two jugs and one bottle: the only identifiable types date to between the early and late Imperial periods (Table 4.9). Two closed forms were identified: a bottle with a small everted and rounded rim that finds a parallel among the materials from the Domus delle Pareti Gialle in Ostia (Pohl 1970: fig. 84.171), in a context dating to the Trajanic period, and a jug with a funnel-shaped rim that finds a parallel again from the same site at Ostia but in a Hadrianic context (Pohl 1970: fig. 117.80). Among the open vessels, too, only two rims were identified: the first is a basin with a band-shaped rim, very common in contexts dating to the early Imperial period and with a precise parallel from the Curia in Rome, datable to the mid-first to mid-second centuries AD (*Curia* II: fig. 254.82). The other one is a colour-coated bowl characterized by a small flattened and slightly hanging rim, whose upper surface is decorated with a series of *ovoli*: it is comparable to a vessel from Santo Stefano Rotondo in Rome, in a context dating to the beginning of the fifth century AD (Martin 1991: abb. 3.12).

TABLE 4.5. The African red slip ware from the survey in Fields 7 and 9.

Fabric	Form	Form type	Date range	Field 7	Field 9
A1	bowl	Hayes 2	AD 60–90	1	–
A1	bowl	Hayes 8a	AD 80–160	–	3
A	jug	Hayes 137	AD 90–160	–	1
A2	bowl	Hayes 14	AD 150–250	–	2
A2	bowl	Hayes 14a	AD 150–200	–	1
A2	dish	Hayes 3c	AD 100–75	–	1
A2	dish	Hayes 6	AD 90–200	–	1
A	dish	Hayes 6b	AD 175–200	–	2
A2	dish	Hayes 6c	AD 150–200	1	–
A2	dish	Hayes 16	AD 150–250	1	1
A2	dish	Hayes 26	AD 150–210	–	1
A2	dish	Hayes 27	AD 160–220	1	2
A	unidentified	unidentified	AD 90–250	10	74
A/D	dish	Hayes 31, nos. 1–4	AD 200–50	–	1
C2	bowl	Hayes 45a	AD 230–350	–	2
C	dish	Hayes 50	AD 230–400	–	10
C1	dish	Hayes 50a	AD 230–350	–	1
C3/4	dish	Hayes 50b	AD 350–400	–	2
C	unidentified	unidentified	AD 230–400	11	50
D	bowl	Hayes 80a	AD 400–500	–	3
D	dish	Hayes 59	AD 320–420	–	1
D	dish	Hayes 61	AD 325–450	1	–
D	dish	Hayes 61a	AD 325–420	1	3
D	dish	Hayes 61b	AD 400–50	–	1
D	dish	Hayes 64	AD 380–450	–	1
D	dish	Hayes 76	AD 425–75	–	2
D2	dish	Hayes 87a	AD 450–500	–	2
D	flanged bowl	Hayes 91	AD 350–600	–	3
D	flanged bowl	Hayes 91a–b	AD 350–530	–	1
D2	large bowl	Hayes 67	AD 360–470	–	1
D	unidentified	unidentified	AD 300–650	9	60

TABLE 4.6. The *sigillata medio-adriatico* from the survey in Fields 7 and 9.

Form	Form type	Date range	Field 7	Field 9
Plate	Brecciaroli Taborelli 1978: F. 12b	AD 100–300	–	1
Unidentified	unidentified	–	–	1

TABLE 4.7. The Roman red slip ware from the survey in Fields 7 and 9.

Form	Form type	Date range	Field 7	Field 9
Bowl	Monacchi 1999: fig. 187, 1 + D31	AD 100–500	–	1
Bowl	Monacchi 1999: fig. 189, 58	AD 100–500	1	–
Bowl	unidentified	AD 100–500	–	6
Jug	unidentified	AD 100–500	–	1
Open form	unidentified	AD 100–500	1	1
Plate	Monacchi 1999: fig. 193, 97	AD 100–500	–	1
Bowl	Monacchi 1999: fig. 188, 28	AD 100–500	–	1
Unidentified	unidentified	AD 100–500	5	34

KITCHEN-WARES

This is the most common ceramic class among those analysed: the total number of sherds of local kitchen-ware is 2,562. Again, the number of identifiable shapes and types is not very high, but in order to make their presentation clearer, they have been divided into different groups of forms summarized in Table 4.10 following a chronological sequence.

Casseroles are the most common, with 92 examples, 44 of which can be paralleled with published examples. The identified types cover the Imperial period as a whole, from the first up to the sixth centuries AD, based on the typological evolution of their shapes.

The oldest casseroles are those characterized by a flattened rim similar to types *Ostia* II: 477–8 and *Ostia* III: 49, which circulated during the first two centuries of the Imperial period. The most common casseroles at Ocriculum are those with a flattened and thinner rim than the ones previously described; they are also characterized by a hook on the underside of the rim and a sharp junction between the underside of the rim and the wall. These vessels are well documented from the third century AD (*Ostia* I: 398, 399). From the mid-fourth century AD the flattened rims tend to become narrower, very often incurving, with a hook on the underside and reeded upper surface (Broise and Scheid 1987: fig. 220a.47, 48 a–b, 49, 217), and finally they get bigger, losing their original shape almost completely (Staffa 1986: fig. 399.201–2; Roberts 1997: fig. 236.178a, 180 a–b). In order to complete the analysis of casseroles, it is worth noting a fragment with an internally thickened rim, clearly a local imitation of the Tunisian type Hayes 23b.

The jar is the second most common shape after the casserole, with 62 fragments, 54 of which were identified. In this case, the largest number of documented specimens date to the mid- and late Republic, and almost all of them are of the same type: the cooking pot with almond-shaped rim, both in the earlier versions with an ovoid body and a rough almond-shaped rim (Dyson 1976: CF 24, 27 and 32), and in the later type, with a well-made almond-shaped rim, which continued to be produced up until the beginning

TABLE 4.8. The lamps from the survey in Fields 7 and 9.

Form type	Date range	Field 7	Field 9
Atlante I, type VIII–X	AD 350–600	–	1
Bailey B (Q956)	AD 50–90	–	1
Esquiline cylindrical	150–50 BC	–	1
Unidentified	–	3	17

TABLE 4.9. The table- and storage-wares from the survey in Fields 7 and 9.

Fabric	Form	Form type	Date range	Field 7	Field 9
Plain ware	basin	*Curia* II, fig. 254.82	AD 50–150	–	1
Plain ware	basin	unidentified	–	–	2
Plain ware	bottle	Pohl 1970: fig. 84.171	AD 40–140	–	1
Plain ware	jug	Pohl 1970: fig. 117.80	AD 100–200	–	1
Plain ware	jug	unidentified	–	–	1
Plain ware	lid	unidentified	–	–	2
Plain ware	mortarium	unidentified	–	–	2
Plain ware	unidentified	unidentified	–	168	871
Thin coloured slip ware	bowl	Martin 1991: abb. 3.12	AD 400–500	1	–
Thin coloured slip ware	bowl	unidentified	–	–	6
Thin coloured slip ware	lid	unidentified	–	–	1
Thin coloured slip ware	unidentified	unidentified	–	19	287

of the Imperial period (*Ostia* II: 507). The early Imperial types are less frequent, although some of them are documented: there are specimens with a small thickened rim (Dyson 1976: 22II71 and *Ostia* III: 630), those with a flattened and rounded rim (*Ostia* II: 483; Pohl 1978: fig. 158.239), and those with a straight flat rim (Pohl 1978: fig. 110.1597).

The few late antique types are characterized by a straight flat rim more or less oblique and thickened (Roberts 1997: fig. 235.170a, 174; fig. 236.176), or by rounded and thickened rims (Roberts 1997: fig. 236.177).

Lids are represented by 50 examples, 23 of which were identified to type. The only Republican type is that with a poorly-defined rim (Dyson 1976: CF 57). The type with a slightly upturned and rounded rim is well documented (*Ostia* II: 513–14); its production started in the late Republican period and continued until the second century AD, whilst in the Imperial period the most frequent type has a triangular-section rim, which is more or less well articulated (Carta 1978: fig. 131.254–5, 258; Pohl 1970: fig. 87.273–4).

There were nine cooking dishes, seven of which could be identified to type. They cover a long chronological range from the third century BC until the mid-fifth century AD. The type with a poorly-defined rim, internally marked by a deep step, is the earliest (Dyson 1976: CF 12); it is followed by a type with everted rim and seat for the lid (Duncan 1965: fig. 6,

F.24). A cooking pan, whose production started in the Republican period and continued into the Imperial period, is that characterized by a bifid rim (Dyson 1976: V-D 5). Finally there is one specimen dating to the late antique period, which is characterized by an incurving and thickened rim (Martin 1991: abb. 7.44). There is also a base fragment of a tripod skillet, not identified to a specific form.

POMPEIAN RED WARE
There are only eight fragments of the typical Campanian fabric rich in red inclusions (volcanic glass) and with an internal red slip (Table 4.11). Among them it is worth noting the base of an unidentified cooking dish and the rim of another cooking dish with a shallow body and a poorly-defined rim (Goudineau 1970: tav. 1.15–16), produced between the Augustan period and the mid-first century AD. The other pieces are wall sherds that cannot be assigned to a specific shape.

AFRICAN COOKING-WARES
African cooking-wares are not very well documented here, with only 38 fragments belonging to this ceramic class (Table 4.12). The identified types are those widely distributed between the Flavian period and the fourth century AD. Plates/lids are the best documented: three have a poorly-defined rim, two of them of type *Ostia* I: 18, which dates between the first and mid-third centuries AD, the other is type *Ostia* II: 302, documented

TABLE 4.10. The kitchen-wares from the survey in Fields 7 and 9.

Form	Form type	Date range	Field 7	Field 9
Casserole	*Ostia* II: 477	AD 1–140	–	2
Casserole	*Ostia* II: 478	AD 1–140	1	–
Casserole	*Ostia* III: 49	AD 50–200	2	5
Casserole	Pohl 1970: fig. 86.238	AD 90–130	1	–
Casserole	*Ostia* III: 435	AD 90–140	–	1
Casserole	*Ostia* I: 398	AD 240–420	1	5
Casserole	*Ostia* I: 399	AD 240–420	–	11
Casserole	Broise and Scheid 1987: fig. 220a.48b	AD 340–550	–	1
Casserole	Broise and Scheid 1987: fig. 220a.47	AD 350–420	–	1
Casserole	Broise and Scheid 1987: fig. 220a.49	AD 360–450	–	2
Casserole	Broise and Scheid 1987: fig. 220a.217	AD 360–450	–	1
Casserole	Broise and Scheid 1987: fig. 220a.48a	AD 360–450	–	2
Casserole	Staffa 1986: fig. 399.202	AD 360–450	1	–
Casserole	Roberts 1997: fig. 236.178a	AD 360–550	–	2
Casserole	Roberts 1997: fig. 236.180a	AD 360–550	1	1
Casserole	Roberts 1997: fig. 236.180b	AD 360–550	–	1
Casserole	Staffa 1986: fig. 399.201	AD 360–550	1	–
Casserole	imitation of Hayes 23b	–	–	1
Casserole	unidentified	–	7	41
Jar	Dyson 1976: CF 24	300–100 BC	–	5
Jar	Dyson 1976: CF 27	300–100 BC	–	1
Jar	Dyson 1976: CF 32	275–150 BC	–	1
Jar	Duncan 1965: fig. 10, F. 34	275–1 BC	–	2
Jar	Duncan 1965: fig. 10, F. 34a	275–1 BC	–	1
Jar	Dyson 1976: V-D 23	275–1 BC	–	1
Jar	Duncan 1965: fig. 12, F. 38b, A89	275 BC–AD 50	–	1
Jar	Dyson 1976: FG 35	275 BC–AD 50	–	1
Jar	*Ostia* II: 507	275 BC–AD 50	2	21
Jar	Dyson 1976: PD 45	200–30 BC	–	1
Jar	Duncan 1965: fig. 12, F. 38a, A 85	150–1 BC	–	1
Jar	Duncan 1965: fig. 12, F. 38a, A 88	150–1 BC	–	1
Jar	Duncan 1965: fig. 12, F. 38b, A92	150–1 BC	–	1
Jar	Duncan 1965: fig. 12, F. 38b, A94	150–1 BC	–	1
Jar	Dyson 1976: V-D 50	150–1 BC	–	1

TABLE 4.10. **Continued.**

Form	Form type	Date range	Field 7	Field 9
Jar	Dyson 1976: PD 40	100–30 BC	–	1
Jar	Dyson 1976: PD 39	100 BC–AD 40	–	1
Jar	Dyson 1976: 221171	AD 1–100	–	1
Jar	*Ostia* II: 483	AD 40–140	–	2
Jar	*Ostia* III: 630	AD 40–140	–	1
Jar	Pohl 1978: fig. 110.1597	AD 40–140	–	1
Jar	Pohl 1978: fig. 158.239	AD 100–50	–	1
Jar	Roberts 1997: fig. 236.176	AD 390–550	–	1
Jar	Roberts 1997: fig. 236.177	AD 390–550	–	1
Jar	Roberts 1997: fig. 235.170a	AD 390–550	–	1
Jar	Roberts 1997: fig. 235.174	AD 390–550	–	1
Jar	unidentified	–	1	7
Lid	Dyson 1976: CF 57	275–100 BC	–	2
Lid	*Ostia* II: 513	100 BC–AD 200	–	6
Lid	*Ostia* II: 514	100 BC–AD 200	–	1
Lid	*Ostia* II; 516	AD 1–200	–	1
Lid	*Curia* II: fig. 257.128	AD 40–120	–	2
Lid	Carta 1978: fig. 131.255	AD 40–200	–	2
Lid	*Ostia* II: 511	AD 50–150	–	1
Lid	Carta 1978: fig. 131.254	AD 70–200	–	5
Lid	Pohl 1970: fig. 87.274	AD 70–200	1	–
Lid	Carta 1978: fig. 131.258	AD 90–120 (?)	–	1
Lid	Pohl 1970: fig. 87.273	AD 90–120 (?)	–	1
Lid	unidentified	–	–	27
Cooking dish	Dyson 1976: CF 12	300–100 BC	–	1
Cooking dish	Duncan 1965: fig. 6, F. 24	150–1 BC	–	1
Cooking dish	Dyson 1976: V-D 5	100 BC–AD 100	–	2
Cooking dish	Dyson 1976: LS 46/47	AD 90–230	–	2
Cooking dish	Martin 1991: abb. 7, 44	AD 360–450	–	1
Cooking dish	unidentified	–	–	2
Incense burner	unidentified	–	–	1
Tripod skillet	unidentified	150–1 BC	–	1
Unidentified	unidentified	–	299	2,048

TABLE 4.11. The Pompeian red ware from the survey in Fields 7 and 9.

Form	Form type	Date range	Field 7	Field 9
Cooking dish	Goudineau 1970: tav. I.15–16	15 BC–AD 50	–	1
Cooking dish	unidentified	–	–	1
Unidentified	unidentified	–	–	6

during the first two centuries of the Imperial period; two more fragments are, in turn, characterized by a thickened rim and can be identified with type *Ostia* I: 261, which circulated between the second and early fifth centuries AD, whilst the last plate/lid has a hanging rim, type Hayes 182, dating to AD 150–250. The only documented cooking dish, to which two rims were attributed, is that with a quarter-round wall, Hayes 181, dating to between the second half of the second and the end of the fourth centuries AD. Finally two casseroles are documented: one with a poorly-defined rim, type Hayes 23a, produced between the Flavian period and the mid-third century AD; the second characterized by an applied rim, type *Ostia* III: 267, typical of the second through to the first quarter of the fifth centuries AD.

AMPHORAE

A total of 1,933 amphora sherds was collected: this is the most common ceramic class in the assemblage from the Ocriculum survey after kitchen-ware (**Table 4.13**). The amphorae cover a wide chronological range from the mid-third century BC to the seventh century AD. The amphorae were divided into production groups and their presentation follows a chronological order.

ITALIC AMPHORAE
Italic amphorae are represented by 173 sherds. They were exclusively wine amphorae and the so-called Spello type is the most common (*Ostia* II: 369). This is a small flat-based amphora, produced in several different workshops of central Italy (Panella 2001: 195; Fontana 2003: 169) between the Tiberian/Claudian period and the end of the second century AD. Far less frequent, although documented in the assemblage, are the two other types of small wine amphorae produced in central Italy: the Forlimpopoli type, dating between the end of the first and end of the second centuries AD, produced in some workshops in Aemilia, and the later Empoli type, produced in Empoli as well as in other workshops of inland Etruria, from the third up to the fifth centuries AD.

The occupation of the site in the Hellenistic period, which was attested by black-gloss ware, is confirmed by the amphora evidence. Indeed, in addition to a rim of a late Greco-Italic type, whose production occurred in several workshops of Latium, Etruria and Campania from the last quarter of the third century BC, there are

TABLE 4.12. African cooking-wares from the survey in Fields 7 and 9.

Form	Form type	Date range	Field 7	Field 9
Casserole	Hayes 23a	AD 75–250	–	1
Casserole	*Ostia* III: 267	AD 100–425	1	–
Cooking dish	Hayes 181	AD 150–400	–	2
Plate/lid	Hayes 182	AD 150–250	–	1
Plate/lid	*Ostia* I: 18	AD 100–250	–	2
Plate/lid	*Ostia* I: 261	AD 100–425	–	2
Plate/lid	*Ostia* II: 302	AD 1–200	–	1
Unidentified	unidentified	–	–	28

and eastern Mediterranean commodities are scarcely documented in the surface assemblage. The presence of Roman pottery does not definitively go beyond the sixth century AD.

THE OVERALL POTTERY CHRONOLOGY
Martin Millett

Using the information of the individual dated sherds collected from the two fields, the overall dating range of the pottery is presented in **Figure 4.9**. To produce this graph a value of 1.0 was given to each individual dated sherd, and this number was divided between the centuries it spanned. Thus, a sherd dated AD 50–200 scored 0.5 for both the first and second centuries AD, whilst one dated AD 100–500 scored 0.25 for each of the second, third, fourth and fifth centuries. This method of data presentation has the advantage of representing the evidence evenly, without giving undue emphasis to sherds that can be dated only to very broad time ranges (Millett 2000).

The bulk of the dated pottery comes from Field 9, near the centre of the site. The analysis of the pottery

from this field shows that it has a basic chronological range that starts in the fourth century BC and continues to the seventh century AD, with the main concentration between the first century BC and the sixth century AD. Although the number of Republican sherds is relatively modest, there appears to be evidence for activity from the fourth century BC onwards. We should note that the number of dated sherds is a function both of the intensity of occupation and the rate of pottery supply. In this context, it is useful to compare the Ocriculum graph with information from the recent restudy of the Tiber valley pottery (Patterson, Di Giuseppe and Witcher 2004: fig. 3). This shows that the overall shape of the Ocriculum graph is very similar to that for the number of sites dated by pottery in South Etruria. The exception is at the beginning of the period, when sites of 350–250 BC are more common in the Tiber valley. An analysis of the dates of the earliest sherds from Field 9 shows that most that have a date range including the fourth century BC actually are dated only to a broad Republican range, and occupation did not certainly start until the first half of the third century BC. It should be observed that the same is true also at the other end of the range, with

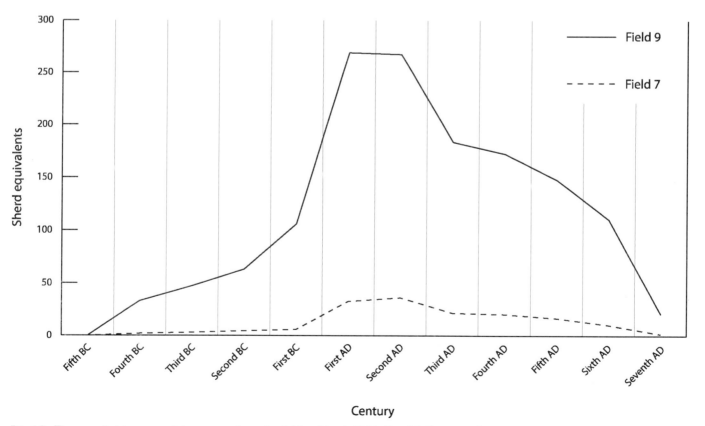

FIG. 4.9. The overall date range of the pottery from the field-walking in Fields 7 and 9. For an explanation, see the text.

the latest date of the latest sherds being AD 650, but most of these pieces may date earlier, with the cessation of ceramic supply being more likely in the sixth rather than the seventh century.

There are fewer dated sherds from Field 7, and here there is no more than a scatter of material dated to before the first century AD. By comparison, the peak of dated sherds is less pronounced and the fall off towards the late antique period is also less marked. This suggests that ceramic deposition in this marginal area of the site was confined largely to the Imperial period. A date for its commencement in the first century AD would be broadly consistent with the date suggested for the construction, and thus subsequent use, of the amphitheatre (see p. 34).

A NOTE ON REGIONAL COMPARISONS
Simon Keay and Martin Millett

It is notable that the pottery catalogued and discussed above represents the first quantified assemblage of Roman pottery from an urban site in this part of the Tiber valley. This makes any systematic comparative comment on the assemblage almost impossible. A fuller discussion of this assemblage will become possible when full details of the pottery from rural sites in the valley, restudied as part of the Tiber Valley Project, are published fully. This should make it possible to explore differences between urban and rural sites, as well as between the towns on the Tiber, like Ocriculum, and those located at a distance from it.

For the moment, only a few observations can be made with reference to studies of the pottery from the region that have been published, although it should be noted that Ocriculum lies on the very northern margin of the area included in the Tiber Valley Project. The comparatively small amounts of Republican material from our survey do not allow any systematic comparisons with the material published by Helga Di Giuseppe and her colleagues (2008), although the overall pattern of supply is not obviously divergent. The much larger range of Imperial and late antique material allows us to be much more confident that the range of pottery and amphora types present is very similar to that recorded elsewhere (Bousquet, Felici and Zampini 2008; Fontana 2008). However, it seems most likely that any variations will relate to the proportions of types represented, rather than their presence or absence, and such data must await fuller publication of pottery from comparative sites.

NOTE

1.   Translated by Emmanuele Vaccaro.

THE OTHER FINDS

THE COINS
Simon Keay

C1. Area 1, Field 1, Grid 02
AE, diameter 21 mm
Illegible.

C2. From an unsurveyed field to the south of the Podere Casa Nuova, along the line of the Via Flaminia
AE, diameter 16 mm
Obv: bust r faintly visible in part
Rev: twin parallel markings
Date uncertain.

C3. Area 1, Field 7, Line 7.4 (**Fig. 4.1**)
AE, maximum diameter 18 mm
Perhaps a pre-Roman issue.

C4. Area 1, Field 7, Line 7.15 (**Fig. 4.1**)
AE, maximum diameter 21 mm
Obv: bust visible — but no details clear
Rev: lettering visible but not legible: perhaps *spes reipublicae* or *gloria romanorum*. Figure standing (l) holding a spear/sceptre in the left hand, a ?globe in the right hand
Mint: unclear; letters *in exergue* — but illegible
Comment: later fourth century AD.

C5. Area 7, Field 9, Line 9.16 (**Fig. 4.3**)
AE, maximum diameter 9 mm
Quite a thick flan. Illegible.

C6. Area 1, Field 1, Grid 15
AE, flan incomplete, maximum diameter 20 mm
Illegible.

THE MARBLE AND OTHER STONE

FRAGMENTS OF MARBLE SCULPTURE
Sophy Downes

The marble sculptures collected during the survey appear to date primarily from the early Imperial period, when the site was occupied intensively, and they bear witness to the range of private and civic activity at Ocriculum during that period. The locations of the findspots are shown on the figures of the relevant area in Chapter 3.

S1. Herm of (?)Dionysus (**Fig. 5.1**)
Findspot: Area 8, Field 15, near boundary with Field 13 (**Fig. 3.40**) (inventory no. 7).
Height: 115 mm
Width: 130 mm
Depth: 65 mm
Width of face: 80 mm
Material: Carrara marble.

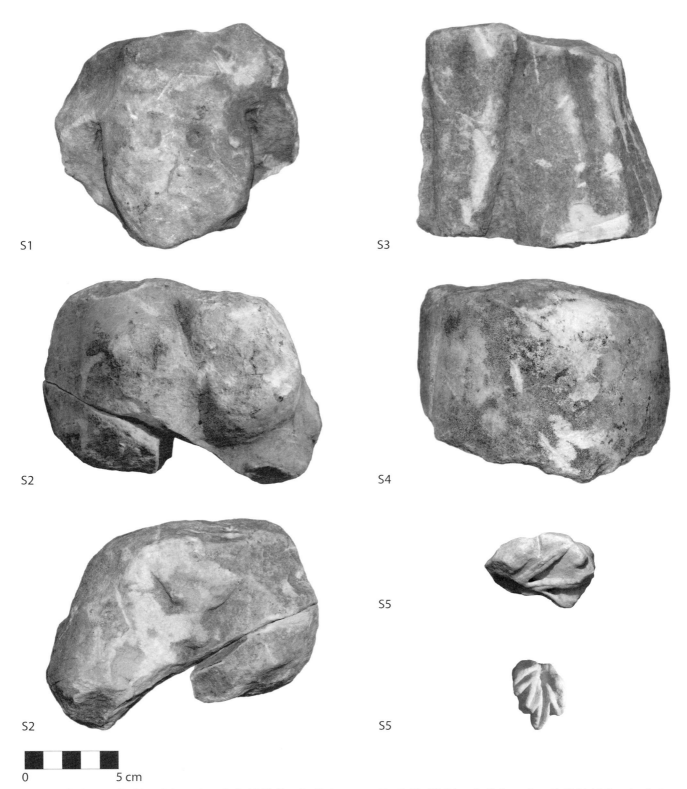

FIG. 5.1. Sculpture: S1 (Herm) from Area 8, Field 15 (for the findspot, see Fig. 3.40); S2 (Heracles?) from Area 7, Field 16 (for the findspot, see Fig. 3.36); S3 (sarcophagus fragment) from Area 1, Field 7, Line 7.11 (for the findspot, see Figs 3.7 and 4.1); S4 (arm fragment) from Area 5, Field 18 (for the findspot, see Fig. 3.19); and S5 (fragment of floral decoration — two views) from Area 7, Field 9 (for the findspot, see Figs 3.36 and 4.3). *(Photos: Sophie Hay and Martin Millett.)*

The head is small, about a third life-size. It has suffered severe damage and erosion, and is broken above chin level by an irregular, slanting cut. Nevertheless, the outline of the face can be distinguished, as can a substantial mass around the forehead and sides of the face. The head has a flat back, from which the face emerges symmetrically and looks straight forward. The features of the face have been destroyed almost completely. The traces that do survive are the slight indentations at each side of the face, the outside edges of widely-spaced eye sockets, and the curve of the cheeks, heavy, soft and smooth. On the top of the head, the hair is etched as neat, shallow runnels repeated in a zigzag pattern. Around this, and standing out wide at the sides of the head, is a substantial and irregular mass of marble. The detail of a veined leaf, which survives at the very left extremity, confirms that this was a wreath. The sides of the face are framed by a further mass of hair, shallower and set back from the cheeks, which gives the head much of its width. The moulding is firm, and two drill holes are visible, positioned slightly asymmetrically on each side, between the hair and the face. Finally, there is a shallow rectangular hollow in the flat surface of the back, which may be the remains of an attachment process.

The head corresponds well to the customary spatial dispositions of herms, one of the most common pieces of Roman domestic sculpture. A herm typically consists of a naturalistically sculpted bust, placed upon a pillar to which male genitals are attached at the front and, sometimes, arm-stumps at the sides. It is a distinctive variant in a tradition that privileged naturalistic representation, as its version of the body is truncated and constrained, symbolic rather than realistic. In keeping with this, the head is usually carved, not in the round, but with a flat back, and with shallower dimensions than the true proportions of a human head. In the case of a double herm, the flattened back merges into a second head, facing in the opposite direction; in a single herm it forms the back of the sculpture. In herms the head is positioned squarely, staring straight ahead, as opposed to the angled neck and evasive gaze common elsewhere in classical sculpture. It also often carries elaborate hair and headgear, which can make it, on its own, appear top-heavy, but, when the herm is complete, balance the weight of the pillar below.

Our head has the flat back, squared face and massy stone headgear overshadowing the face that are associated with herms. However, as it is broken off at the chin, it is impossible to be certain that it was a true herm, complete with pillar and genitals. Moreover,

considered as a herm, the head is unusual in some respects. Firstly, it is very small. Miniaturization is a common feature of Roman domestic sculpture (Bartman 1992: 17, 45), but even compared to herm heads from private garden contexts in Pompeii, our head is diminutive. It is half the size of those from the Casa di Marco Lucrezio (Dwyer 1982: 43), the closest parallel, and those from the Casa dei Vettii (Ministero per i Beni Culturali e Ambientale 1990: nos. 181 and 182, inv. 690 and 691). Secondly, the flat back is undecorated, whereas the single herms from Sperlonga (Iacopi 1963: figs 118–21) and Pompeii (Ministero per i Beni Culturali e Ambientale 1990: 186, inv. 2914), both close iconographic parallels and both in marble, have ornate reverse sides. It is possible, therefore, that the head is not strictly a herm, but rather a decorative head in the same style, maybe deliberately referencing hermic sculpture. The hollow in the flat surface of our head may be later damage; however, it also may show where the head was attached to a wall or similar surface, in which case it could not be a true herm.

The earliest Greek herms, from which the genre originates, were specifically religious objects, depicting the god Hermes and found in sanctuaries and liminal zones such as street corners and doorways. However, by Roman times their status was less specific. From the fourth century BC onwards they started to depict other deities, and in the Hellenistic period portrait herms of athletes, writers, philosophers and politicians became commonplace (for a summary of the development, see: Harrison 1965: 108–41). Under Roman influence, the categories became fluid, and it is not always easy to distinguish between their function as objects of cult or as decoration (Jashemski 1979: 121). There are examples of heads with very close typological similarities to known herms in non-hermic settings: a marble circular relief plaque in the Metropolitan Museum of Art depicts a head so close to the Mahdia and Getty herms that they are thought to be using the same model (Mattusch 1994: 439); the Pompeii herm has a finely smoothed base and, despite its hermic appearance, may never have been attached to a pillar at all (Mattusch 1994: 440). Our head, therefore, plausibly may be within the hermic tradition, without strictly being a herm.

The two features of our head that significantly have survived are the trace of a wreath at the left temple and the beardless chin, soft and archaic in line. The wreath, an important part of sympotic paraphernalia, suggests a Dionysiac theme. Dionysus himself is a very common subject for Roman herms (Farrar 1998: 117). However, it is a somewhat problematic identification: our head is beardless and, although in other genres of Roman sculpture Dionysus was frequently depicted as a youth, as a herm he customarily was portrayed bearded. There are examples of youthful, beardless Dionysus herms; however, they form one half of a double herm consisting of a young and old Dionysus back to back. The most striking examples are three herms from the Casa di Marco Lucrezio at Pompeii (Dwyer 1982: figs 36, 39 and 52), which share our head's heavy cheeks. However, rather than a wreath, they have hair arranged into heavy archaic ringlet fringes, or elaborate waves, so they are not close enough to demonstrate that they are all one type and thus, conclusively, that our head is a Dionysus.

One possibility is that our head had a companion piece, an old Dionysus to balance it. It is even possible that, if it was a true herm, it was part of a double herm and that the flat and hollowed back was attached to a second head, although this would be unusual as herms usually were carved from one piece of stone (Farrar 1998: 123). Alternatively, it may simply have been a single beardless Dionysus. There is considerable variation in iconography among the Dionysus herm types. There are some very close copies, such as the Mahdia and Getty herms, which have allowed precise typologies to be created (cf. Mattusch 1994: 438: 'we are tempted to think of them as having been mass-produced'): some herms clearly do come from the same originals and, in some cases, the copying process is extremely accurate. However, there are plenty of herms that do not fit into these groups, and, while clearly inspired by the genre, are idiosyncratic in the details (River God — Jashemski 1979: fig. 278; Heracles — Jashemski 1979: fig. 336). Our head is most probably one of these.

This being so, however, the wreath does not prove the Dionysiac subject. Although it is the most likely association, wreaths can be found also on statues of athletes or Heracles, both of which are possible subjects for herms (Harrison 1965: 127; Jashemski 1979: fig. 336; Dwyer 1982: figs 52–4).

These pieces were produced to similar archaizing designs over a long period of time from the Classical era onward (Harrison 1965: 108). It therefore is difficult to assign a date to the sculpture, particularly as so much of its stylistic identity has been obliterated. Carrara (Luna) marble, from which the head is made, of suitable quality for sculpture, was available in Rome from *c*. 30 BC (Kleiner 1992: 5). It was used most extensively under Augustus and the Julio-Claudian dynasty (that is,

27 BC–AD 68). A date within this period would correspond well to the history of the site at Otricoli.

The plans suggest that the area where the head was found was on the edge of a public space, perhaps a temple temenos (see p. 73). This is somewhat surprising, as herms, decorative or otherwise, are found most often in a domestic garden setting. Possibly this suggests that the head was indeed a purely decorative attachment to some public building, but more probably it has simply been displaced.

S2. Part of a miniature statuette of (?)Heracles (**Fig. 5.1**)
Findspot: Area 7, Field 16, adjacent to boundary with Field 17 (**Fig. 3.36**) (inventory nos. 14 and 15).
Height: 120 mm
Width: 155 mm
Depth: 95 mm
Material: Carrara marble.

Most of the statue has been lost: only the section from the waist to mid-thigh survives. Additionally, a piece of the left thigh has been broken off recently: the two pieces were found together and can be joined along the clean diagonal break. The sculpture is a miniature: the full height of the statue would have been about half a metre. The surface is abraded, with numerous nicks and slashes in the stone. The underlying curves of the buttocks and thighs can be seen clearly, however, as well as the outline of pubic hair and male genitals. The musculature is heavy, even exaggerated. The weight is on the left leg and the left hip is pushed out to the side; the right leg is slightly slackened.

At the top of the right thigh a circular bump protrudes, about 30 mm in diameter. This could be either the remains of a support, perhaps one of the tree stumps frequently found in Roman sculpture, or the remains of the statue's hand resting on the leg. The latter disposition is seen in a statue of Heracles from garden II.viii.6 in Pompeii (Jashemski 1979: fig. 192), which has close parallels to our statue. The left thigh has a ridge all along its length, varying from 20 to 30 mm in extent, and thus a sizeable proportion of the statue's total width. This also could be a support: the Pompeii Heracles has folds of cloth falling against the leg in a similar position. However, there the extrusion of the cloth is visible from both sides, whereas in our statue there is a misalignment between the front and back of the sculpture, such that the ridge only exists at the back — at the front the space is simply taken up in the thigh. A number of statues of Heracles, notably the Farnese Heracles (Moreno 1995: 421 (for a rear view)), exaggerate the musculature to the extent that such a ridge appears. Our statue cannot be exactly a Farnese Heracles type: the Farnese Heracles has the weight on the right leg and the ridge on the left, whereas our statue has both weight and ridge on the left. However, it is possible that it is a similar treatment of the muscle that creates this effect.

The statue, although a miniature, does not appear to mimic the pose of any known piece of large-scale sculpture. Rather, like the Pompeii Heracles, it seems to be an innovative variation within the genre of miniature sculpture. This makes its subject difficult to identify with any certainty. Heracles is a likely subject for a muscular nude, particularly if the ridge theory above is correct, and many miniatures of the hero in different poses survive (for surveys, see: Jashemski 1979: 121–3; Moreno 1995: 347–79). However, the statue also could plausibly be Poseidon (Bartman 1992: figs 62–71), a satyr (Bartman 1992: figs 46–7), or a particularly burly athlete (Harrison 1965: 127), all known subjects for miniature sculpture.

Miniature sculpture is associated most frequently with private contexts: it is often displayed in naturalistic garden settings, or placed on ornamental tables to form the focal point of a room (Bartman 1992: 39–42). However, it is known also in the public sphere and could appear alongside life-sized sculpture with apparent disregard for unity of scale (Bartman 1992: 42; Pliny, *Historia Naturalis* 34.11.24). Field 16 at Ocriculum was central within the town, with evidence for both public and private structures (see above, p. 69, 72). The statue's display context, and indeed function, are therefore ambiguous. It could have come either from a private house or from the forum or temples, and, in either case, its display could be votive or aesthetic. Both Bartman (1992: 43–8) and Jashemski (1993: 121–2) noted that it is difficult to distinguish between the art historical and religious functions of miniature sculpture in private settings. Jashemski considered that the Heracles discussed above, found in a Pompeian garden, was paid cult, as it was discovered along with an altar, but without such context it is hard to be sure. The role is no clearer in the public sphere. In general there is a shift from the religious to the decorative in the late Hellenistic period; however, it is more that the decorative aspect is emphasized — the religious function can still remain. The fact that our statue does not seem to copy a cult statue may suggest that its status was primarily aesthetic, but it is not definitive proof.

As with the Herm head, both the marble type and the part of the city in which the statue was found suggest an early Imperial date. However, Roman miniaturization continued until at least the third century AD (Bartman 1992: 31) and the findspot is within the late Roman walls, so the date potentially could be significantly later.

S3.   Fragment of a sarcophagus (**Fig. 5.1**)
Findspot: Area 1, Field 7, Line 7.11 (**Figs 3.7** and **4.1**) (inventory no. 39).
Dimensions: 110–20 × 105–30 × 30–45 mm
Material: Carrara marble.

This square piece of marble is broken off on all sides. The back is flat and roughly worked, the front is sculpted as a relief. The relief consists of slightly off-vertical runnels separating different depths of stone, most plausibly interpreted as folds of hanging cloth. The piece was found in the south of Ocriculum, close to where the Via Flaminia enters the city. This is a prime area for funerary monuments; indeed a number of mausolea still stand there today (Pietrangeli 1978: 90). The thinness of the stone, and the roughly worked back, suggest that it was part of a sarcophagus. Reliefs are found on a number of funerary monuments from Ocriculum (Pietrangeli 1978: 90, figs 173–84). These are all non-figured; however, figured relief is extremely common on Roman sarcophagi in general (Amedick *et al.* 1998; McCann 1978: 21). Stone sarcophagi appear suddenly in the Roman world in the mid-second century AD (McCann 1978: 19), a date that coincides nicely with the period of greatest occupation of Ocriculum, from the mid-second to mid-third centuries (Pietrangeli 1978: 20). During the Severan age, from AD 192 to 235, relief becomes increasingly deeply drilled and undercut (McCann 1978: 22); the shallowness of our relief therefore suggests a date in the second half of the second century.

S4.   Arm piece (**Fig. 5.1**)
Findspot: Area 5, Field 18 (**Fig. 3.19**) (inventory no. 23).
Height: 105 mm
Width: 135 mm
Depth: 70 mm
Material: Pentelic marble.

The stone has a curved surface, smoothed to a high finish, although subsequently abraded and discoloured, and a flat surface left rough and irregular. A small rectangular indentation cut out at the upper edge of the flat surface is probably the remains of joining apparatus. The semicircular section at that end of the piece is fairly smooth, though curved, and may be the original surface; the semicircular section at the other end is clearly broken off.

The piece was almost certainly originally part of a relief; the curved shape suggests that it was part of a human limb. It was made separately and then attached to the flat surface. It may well, therefore, have been a repair or addition, rather than part of the original work. The hollow for the joining insert is very shallow; it will not, therefore, have been a strong support, which again suggests that the piece may have been an addition to the original design, inserted and in part supported by the stone already in place round it. The position of the joint suggests that the limb was an arm, rather than a leg. If the piece was positioned horizontally, as an arm plausibly could be, the weight would fall on the metal joint such as to secure it further; vertically, as a leg usually would be, it would have very little strength.

Human figures are ubiquitous in Roman relief, so there is no way of determining what scene the piece comes from. It is most likely that it derives from a piece of monumental public architecture, either a temple or a commemorative arch. If it is an arm, the scale of the relief would have been somewhat above life-size. Field 16 is close to the path of the ancient Via Flaminia and the civic centre of Ocriculum (Pietrangeli 1978: carta 1), which makes an architectural context entirely plausible. The main buildings of this part of the city were erected in the early Empire (Pietrangeli 1978: 26), so a date around then is likely for the creation of the relief, although, if it is a subsequent repair, our piece of marble would have a later date than the initial construction. The importation of Pentelic marble is not unusual, but the material probably marks the setting as high status.

S5.   Piece of floral decoration (**Fig. 5.1**)
      Findspot: Area 7, Field 9, Grid 9.48 (**Figs 3.36** and **4.3**) (inventory no. 106).
      Dimensions: 60 × 40 × 20–30 mm
      Material: Carrara marble.
This small piece of marble, broken off at the base from its original setting, is carved in the round into a floral design. The curved tongue forms a leaf with deep runnels demarcating the veins. It is flanked on each side by a flat surface, the two of which meet in a gentle point below. One side is now worn away almost to nothing; the other still retains high-quality work and deep carving, including drill holes between the raised leaf veins. There is a slightly inexact correspondence between the two sides and the tongue: the veins meet, but only approximately, along the

shared edge. The piece is thus unified in three dimensions, although the planes seem to have been envisaged separately. The effect is a stylized naturalism.

The outwards curving movement of the leaf is similar to the acanthus florals at the base of a Corinthian column capital. The piece is too small to be from a public architectural setting; however, miniature columns are sometimes used in domestic contexts, either in internal peristyles, or, on an even smaller scale, to support sculpture, as in the Casa dei Vetti (Ministero per i Beni Culturali e Ambientale 1990: figs 181 and 182), where the columns are 1.685 m and 1.687 m high respectively. However, acanthus capital leaves are usually flattened scrolls, whereas our piece of marble is solid and triangular in section. Although there are exceptions to this, such as the corner acanthus leaves on the squared Corinthinan capital from the Casa del Fauno (Spinazzola 1928: 29), it is more probable that the piece belongs to a marble candelabrum or other piece of ornamental furniture. Vegetalizing motifs are common throughout Roman interior decoration; the marble plausibly could come from an ornamental table or *kline* support. However, they are most commonly in use in candelabra, which, indeed, often deliberately reference column decoration (Yerkes 2005: 157), and it is likely that this is from where our piece of marble originally came. The curlicues on the three marble candelabra from the Mahdia shipwreck are a close match (Cain and Dräger 1994: figs 1–3 and (details) 4–6, 10, 11, 13), as are the tiered acanthus leaves on the stems of three candelabra in Rome (Cain 1985: Taf. 37). The findspot of the piece supports a domestic context: recent geophysical survey and surface collection there found considerable domestic material (see above, pp. 67–9, 91).

The stone is Carrara marble, so the piece of furniture must have been Italian, not imported. The marble type also dates it to post 30 BC. It is perhaps most plausibly dated to around the turn of the millennium: the area also contains what are thought to be early Imperial structures (see above, p. 91), and the early Imperial period was a high point in the production of ornate marble candelabra (Cain 1985: 5–6).

OTHER SCULPTURE

S6.   Republican head from a funerary monument (Fig. 5.2)
      Findspot: Area 1, Field 1 (**Fig. 3.7**) (museum inventory no. 402542).
      Dimensions: 280 × 240 × 140 mm
      Material: vesicular travertine limestone.

FIG. 5.2. Sculpture: S6 (head) from Area 1, Field 1 (for the findspot, see Fig. 3.7). *(Photo: Soprintendenza per i Beni Archeologici dell'Umbria. Reproduced courtesy of the Soprintendenza per i Beni Archeologici dell'Umbria.)*

This piece was found in the plough-soil during the survey in 2002 and is now on display in the Antiquarium on site. It has been published (Cenciaioli 2006: 116–17) and the following description is a translation:

'Fragment from a larger-than-life-size male head, lacking its upper part and showing evidence of considerable abrasion and erosion to the surfaces. The piece consists of the head and part of the neck. It has a well-modelled right ear, which stands well proud of the side of the head, has a heavy margin and prominent lobe and hole. Allowing for its state of conservation, one may note the anatomical details, its large almond-shaped and heavily underscored eyes, the prominent eyebrows and bridge of the nose; the nose is largely missing, but the lips are fleshy and the cheeks slightly hollow. The chin is cut sharply. The back of the head is flattened, suggesting that this was a frontal funerary bust'.

It is datable to the late Republican period. A parallel is drawn with another bust in a similar style from a funerary monument at Palombara, beside the via Flaminia to the north of the modern village of Otricoli and dated to 60–50 BC. This piece also is carved from travertine limestone and has a similar flattened back to the head (Pietrangeli 1978: 170, fig. 194; Giuliano 1987: 72–4, R41; Cenciaioli 2006: 116, no. 2).

S7. Findspot: Area 3, Field 2 (**Fig. 3.13**) (inventory no. 76).
Dimensions: $95 \times 50 \times 95$ mm
Material: white marble, Carrara?
This is a small curved piece suggestive of drapery from a statue. (Not illustrated.)

THE MARBLE ARCHITECTURAL ORNAMENT
Martin Millett

S8. Small fragment, perhaps from an entablature, with a finely carved *calyx* (?) above a stepped border with a plain zone beneath (**Fig. 5.3**). Total height *c.* 135 mm.
Area 5, Field 19 (**Fig. 3.19**) (inventory no. 32).

S9. Fragment of cornice moulding, *c.* 80 mm tall, with cyma recta above the bead and cyma reversa below. (Not illustrated.)
Area 1, Field 7, Line 7.12 (**Figs 3.7** and **4.1**) (inventory no. 10).

S10. Fragment of cornice moulding, *c.* 75 mm tall, with cyma recta above a broad quarter-round moulding with a cavetto below. (Not illustrated.)
Area 7, Field 20 (**Fig. 3.36**) (inventory no. 12).

S11. Piece from the shaft of a semi-engaged column with a plain polished shaft. Estimated diameter *c.* 200 mm. (Not illustrated.)
Area 5, Field 19 (**Fig. 3.19**) (inventory no. 24).

S12. Large fragment from the lower block of a high-quality Corinthian capital, apparently from a square pilaster (**Fig. 5.3**). The style of the acanthus is comparable with those from the Temple of Mars Ultor (Ungaro 2007: fig. 177). It is deeply carved, with drill holes at the terminals of the grooves.
Area 5, Field 18 (**Fig. 3.19**) (inventory no. 13).

S13. Fragment of a table top (?) with a circular surface set on top of a hexagon, total thickness *c.* 25 mm (**Fig. 5.3**). Each side of the hexagon has an estimated length of *c.* 200 mm, and its edge has a cavetto moulding.
Area 3, Field 2 (**Fig. 3.13**) (inventory no. 75).

FIG. 5.3. Sculpture and inscriptions: S8 (fragment of architectural ornament) from Area 5, Field 19 (for the findspot, see Fig. 3.19); S12 (fragment of a column capital) from Area 5, Field 18 (for the findspot, see Fig. 3.19); S13 (fragment of a table top) from Area 3, Field 2 (for the findspot, see Fig. 3.13); S16 (fragment of an inscription) from Area 7, Field 9, Grid 9.18 (for the findspot, see Figs 3.36 and 4.3); and S17 (fragment of an inscription) from Area 7, Field 16 (for the findspot, see Fig. 3.36). *(Photos: Sophie Hay and Martin Millett.)*

LIMESTONE ALTAR
Martin Millett

S14. Uninscribed altar (Fig. 5.4)
Findspot: Area 7, Field 16 (Fig. 3.36) (museum inventory no. 402537).
Dimensions: 1.12 m × 600 mm × 370 mm
Material: local white limestone.

This item was found on the ploughed surface during the survey in 2005 and is now on display in the Antiquarium on site. It has been published (Cenciaioli 2006: 42–3) and the following description is derived from that publication.

Damaged. Top, upper and lower corners broken. Surfaces abraded and eroded plus evidence of several scrapes caused by ploughing. Cut from a rectangular block with a socle on the front and two sides comprising a chamfer delimited by torus mouldings. A pair of closely-spaced torus mouldings divided by a narrow groove also define the upper margins. Plain flat front, sides carved with reliefs of a *patera ombelicata* (right) and an *urceus* (left). The back of the altar is flat and unworked. In the absence of an inscription, the type is only approximately datable to the first century AD.

THE INSCRIPTIONS
Martin Millett

S15. Fragment of a white marble panel from Area 1, Field 1 (Fig. 3.7). Probably from a funerary plaque (Fig. 5.5).
]ELI [
]A • [

S16. Fragment of a marble slab 45 mm thick. Serifs from two large letters survive at the lower margin (Fig. 5.3).
Area 7, Field 9, Grid 9.18 (Figs. 3.36 and 4.3) (inventory no. 79).

S17. Fragment of a marble slab 70 mm thick, with one roughly dressed face and the other highly polished. The roughly dressed face has a crude 'A' cut on it, 35 mm tall (Fig. 5.3).
Area 7, Field 16 (Fig. 3.36) (inventory no. 69).

S18. Edge of a 25 mm thick plaque for an inscription, with a moulded border and a fixing hole in its edge. No text survives. (Not illustrated.)
Area 1, Field 1 (Fig. 3.7) (inventory no. 50).

FIG. 5.4. **Altar, S14, from Area 7, Field 16 (for the findspot, see Fig. 3.36).** *(Photo: Soprintendenza per i Beni Archeologici dell'Umbria. Reproduced courtesy of the Soprintendenza per i Beni Archeologici dell'Umbria.)*

FIG. 5.5. **Inscription S15 from Area 1, Field 1 (for the findspot, see Fig. 3.6).** *(Photo: Soprintendenza per i Beni Archeologici dell'Umbria. Reproduced courtesy of the Soprintendenza per i Beni Archeologici dell'Umbria.)*

THE TERRACOTTAS
Rose Ferraby and Martin Millett

FREE-STANDING SCULPTURE

T1. Amorphous fragment (Fig. 5.6). One side smoothed and curved with red paint decoration. Finely-tempered, light orange fabric, coated in places with a thin layer of deep red paint. $65 \times 65 \times 30$ mm.
Area 4, Field 3 (Fig. 3.17) (inventory no. 151).

T2. Human torso with folds of drapery hanging from the shoulder (Fig. 5.6). Coarse, heavily-tempered fabric at the core, with a finely-tempered terracotta surface layer. Possible traces of paint in the folds of the fabric. $150 \times 100 \times 70$ mm.
Area 4, Field 3 (Fig. 3.17) (inventory no. 158).

T3. Fragment of a human torso with drapery (Fig. 5.6). Coarsely-tempered fabric, with a rich orange colour. $115 \times 105 \times 20$ mm.
Area 5, Field 16 (Fig. 3.19) (inventory no. 163).

T4. Thin leg of an animal, probably a horse (Fig. 5.6). Coarsely-tempered fabric, showing evidence of smoothing on the surface. Very light orange, almost white, colour. $180 \times 50 \times 50$ mm.
Area 7, Field 16 (Fig. 3.36) (inventory no. 174).

T5. Miniature sculpture of the torso and part of the rear legs of a bull (Fig. 5.6). Finely-tempered, red fabric. The surface is a richer red, showing possible evidence of paint. $60 \times 35 \times 35$ mm.
Area 7, Field 9, Grid 9a.3 (Figs 3.36 and 4.3) (inventory no. 175).

T6. Amorphous sculptural fragment (Fig. 5.6). Coarsely-tempered, crude piece. Light orange fabric. $65 \times 45 \times 25$ mm.
Area 4, Field 3 (Fig. 3.17) (inventory no. 177).

ARCHITECTURAL ORNAMENT

T7. Fluting from a column shaft above a torus moulding (Fig. 5.6). Finely-textured, light-coloured fabric. Surface evidence for stucco. $80 \times 70 \times 20$ mm.
Area 4, Field 3 (Fig. 3.17) (inventory no. 148).

T8. Very damaged fragment of cavetto moulding with anthemion decoration (Fig. 5.7). Coarsely-textured, rich orange fabric. $115 \times 65 \times 45$ mm.
Area 4, Field 3 (Fig. 3.17) (inventory no. 152).

T9. Top of the fluted shaft of a semi-engaged column (Fig. 5.7). On the front, there is a torus moulding above the terminals of three flutes. The reverse is flat. It has a coarsely-textured core, with a smooth surface. There is evidence of stucco on the surface. $130 \times 70 \times 60$ mm.
Area 4, Field 3 (Fig. 3.17) (inventory no. 160).

T10. Fragment from a perforated cornice plaque (Fig. 5.7) similar to examples found in the theatre (Stopponi 2006: 63, nos. 2–3). Very light orange, finely-tempered fabric on the surface, with a more coarsely-tempered core. $110 \times 60 \times 30$ mm.
Area 4, Field 3 (Fig. 3.17) (inventory no. 149).

T11. Free-standing arch-shaped bar from a perforated cornice plaque (Fig. 5.7) similar to examples found in the theatre (Stopponi 2006: 63, nos. 2–3). It has a dense fabric with some visible inclusions. The core is light orange, whereas the surface is orange/grey, especially in the clefts of the decoration. $80 \times 80 \times 30$ mm.
Area 4, Field 3 (Fig. 3.17) (inventory no. 161).

ANTEFIXES

T12. Antefix with a relief trefoil palmette decoration (Fig. 5.7). Coarsely-tempered core, with a finer surface texture. Light orange in colour, with a grey tinge to the surface. $90 \times 80 \times 20$ mm.
Area 7, Field 20 (Fig. 3.36) (inventory no. 168).

T13. Antefix with scroll decoration (Fig. 5.7). Coarsely-tempered, dark red fabric throughout. Reverse shows evidence of smoothing during manufacture.
Area 7, Field 16 (Fig. 3.36) (inventory no. 172).

T14. Elaborate trefoil palmette antefix (Fig. 5.7). Coarsely-textured, light orange fabric, with a relatively smooth surface. Some parts of the relief decoration are hollow in the core. $65 \times 45 \times 25$ mm.
Area 3, Field 2 (Fig. 3.13) (inventory no. 178).

TERRACOTTA PLAQUES

T15. Top edge of a plaque showing reversed 'S' motifs (Fig. 5.7). Coarsely-textured and coarsely-tempered, in mid-orange fabric at the surface, with a deeper red core. $110 \times 60 \times 30$ mm.
Area 4, Field 3 (Fig. 3.17) (inventory no. 150).

T16. Plaque with a beaded margin between panels, with one containing a medallion that uses a swag of drapery and figure (?) within (Fig. 5.8). Coarsely-textured, coarsely-tempered core in mid-orange. Surface is smooth and a lighter orange than the core. $115 \times 65 \times 45$ mm.
Area 4, Field 3 (Fig. 3.17) (inventory no. 153).

T1

T2

T3

T4

T5

T6

T7

FIG. 5.6. Terracottas: T1, from Area 4, Field 3 (for the findspot, see Fig. 3.17); T2, from Area 4, Field 3 (for the findspot, see Fig. 3.17); T3, from Area 5, Field 16 (for the findspot, see Fig. 3.19); T4, from Area 5, Field 16 (for the findspot, see Fig. 3.36); T5, from Area 7, Field 9, Grid 9a.3 (for the findspot, see Figs 3.36 and 4.3); T6, from Area 4, Field 3 (for the findspot, see Fig. 3.17); T7, from Area 4, Field 3 (for the findspot, see Fig. 3.17). *(Photos: Rose Ferraby.)*

0   5 cm

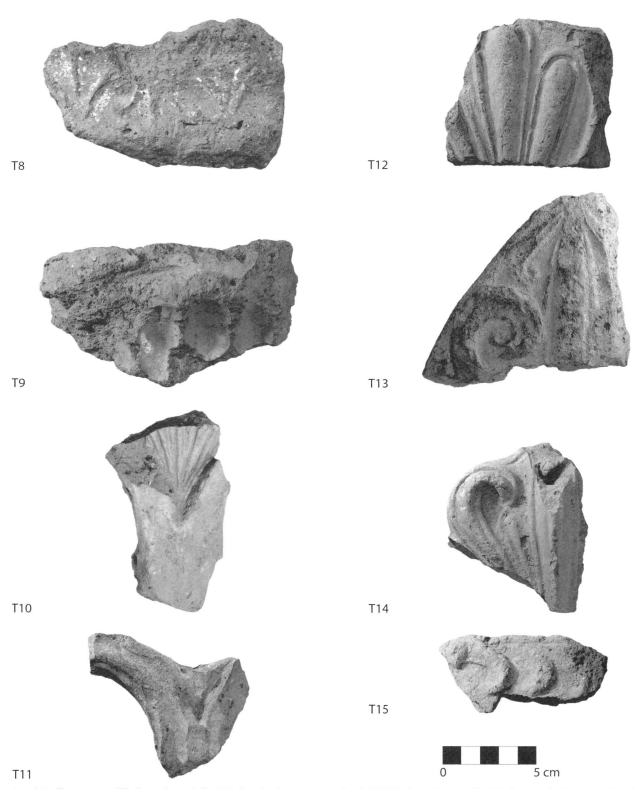

FIG. 5.7. Terracottas: T8, from Area 4, Field 3 (for the findspot, see Fig. 3.17); T9, from Area 4, Field 3 (for the findspot, see Fig. 3.17); T10, from Area 4, Field 3 (for the findspot, see Fig. 3.17); T11, from Area 4, Field 3 (for the findspot, see Fig. 3.17); T12, from Area 7, Field 20 (for the findspot, see Fig. 3.36); T13, from Area 7, Field 16 (for the findspot, see Fig. 3.36); T14, from Area 3, Field 2 (for the findspot, see Fig. 3.13); and T15, from Area 4, Field 3 (for the findspot, see Fig. 3.17). *(Photos: Rose Ferraby.)*

T17. Upper margin with an ovolo of egg and dart (**Fig. 5.8**). Light orange fabric, tempered with fine sand, forming a smooth surface. 130 × 150 × 20 mm.
Area 4, Field 3 (**Fig. 3.17**) (inventory no. 154).

T18. Low relief plaque (**Fig. 5.8**) showing the torso of a female dancer with drapery hanging from her shoulder and bare belly (cf. Stopponi 2006: 67, no. 2). Light orange fabric, tempered with very fine sand. The surface has a red tint, which may be evidence of paint. 50 × 35 × 35 mm.
Area 4, Field 3 (**Fig. 3.17**) (inventory no. 155).

T19. Beaded panel margin and part of the beaded edge to a medallion (?) (**Fig. 5.8**). Coarsely-tempered, mid-orange fabric. The surface shows evidence of stucco. 120 × 70 × 20 mm.
Area 4, Field 3 (**Fig. 3.17**) (inventory no. 156).

T20. Egg and dart ovolo (**Fig. 5.8**). Mid-orange core, with a light orange surface. The fabric includes fine temper. 70 × 40 × 20 mm.
Area 4, Field 3 (**Fig. 3.17**) (inventory no. 157).

T21. Lower margin of a plaque with a stylized scroll (?) (**Fig. 5.8**). The style is similar to an example described by Stopponi (2006: 63, no. 1). The fabric is generally finely-tempered, with some larger inclusions. The core is mid-orange, but the surface is whitened with a possible layer of stucco. 130 × 70 × 60 mm.
Area 4, Field 3 (**Fig. 3.17**) (inventory no. 162).

T22. Fragment of a large plaque in white clay (**Fig. 5.8**). The rear is flat, and the front decorated with vertical fluting and fillet on the arris between each pair of flutes. It is generally finely-tempered, but with some larger inclusions. It has a very smooth, white stucco surface. The core is also a very light orange. 160 × 80 × 30 mm.
Area 7, Field 20 (**Fig. 3.36**) (inventory no. 165).

T23. Engaged fluted column with a torus above, and a broad fillet on the arris between the flutes (**Fig. 5.8**). Coarse fabric of light orange/grey colour. 90 × 60 × 30 mm.
Area 7, Field 16 (**Fig. 3.36**) (inventory no. 167).

T24. Fragment of a plaque decorated with a vegetal scroll below a beaded upper margin (**Fig. 5.8**). Finely-tempered fabric in a light reddish orange. Evidence of a stucco surface. 90 × 80 × 20 mm.
Area 7, Field 20 (**Fig. 3.36**) (inventory no. 169).

T25. Upper margin with an attachment hole above (**Fig. 5.9**). Border beading above a rectangular inset frame. Coarsely-tempered, greyish orange fabric. 80 × 55 × 15 mm.

Area 4, Field 3 (**Fig. 3.17**) (inventory no. 170).

T26. Horizontal torus above egg and dart (**Fig. 5.9**). A moderately coarsely tempered, mid-orange fabric, with some large inclusions. 90 × 80 × 30 mm.
Area 4, Field 3 (**Fig. 3.17**) (inventory no. 171).

T27. Torus above arched niches springing from an indistinct column capital (**Fig. 5.9**). Coarsely-tempered, reddish orange fabric. The surface has a whitish sheen. 90 × 110 × 30 mm.
Area 7, Field 16 (**Fig. 3.36**) (inventory no. 173).

T28. Plaque in fine white clay showing drapery (?) (**Fig. 5.9**). Generally medium- to finely-tempered fabric, with some larger inclusions. The surface is very smooth with a suggestion of white stucco coating. 60 × 35 × 35 mm.
Area 4, Field 3 (**Fig. 3.17**) (inventory no. 176).

MISCELLANEOUS

T29. Top of a triangular piece with the front surface showing incised decoration (**Fig. 5.9**). The back surface is smoothed and with the stub of a probable handle. The decoration is somewhat crude, using a linear style that resembles the vegetal patterns used on antefixes. This may perhaps be a crude antefix. However, the use of incision and the presence of a handle on the reverse suggest that it may be a stamp or perhaps a mould. It is in a finely-tempered fabric, with the colour changing from reddish orange at the bottom, to a more yellow-white at the top. White specks of mortar are concentrated in one area of the surface. 150 × 10 × 70 mm.
Area 4, Field 3 (**Fig. 3.17**) (inventory no. 159).

T30. Fragment of a disc with a plain back and edge (**Fig. 5.9**). A relief-decorated front shows curved features, perhaps a scroll or a large trefoil. It is possibly from a large antefix. It is in a medium-tempered fabric, with dark brown-black inclusions. It is a pinkish orange colour throughout. There is some evidence of stucco in the clefts of the decoration. 115 × 105 × 20 mm.
Area 5, Field 19 (location unrecorded) (inventory no. 164).

THE STUCCO
Martin Millett

T31. Fragment of entablature with a figured frieze above a torus moulding with an egg and tongue border below (**Fig. 5.9**). It is in very battered

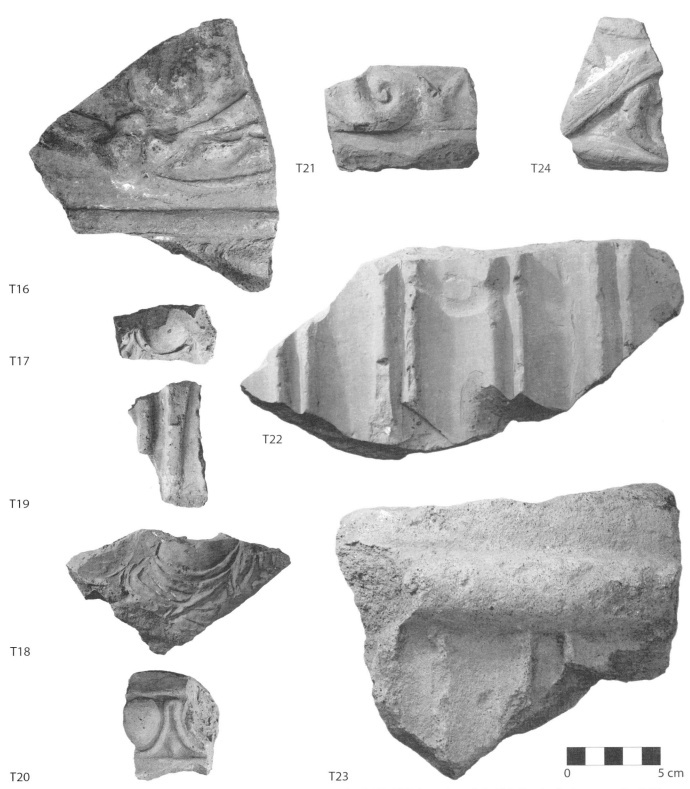

FiG. 5.8. **Terracottas:** T16, from Area 4, Field 3 (for the findspot, see Fig. 3.17); T17, from Area 4, Field 3 (for the findspot, see Fig. 3.17); T18, from Area 4, Field 3 (for the findspot, see Fig. 3.17); T19, from Area 4, Field 3 (for the findspot, see Fig. 3.17); T20, from Area 4, Field 3 (for the findspot, see Fig. 3.17); T21, from Area 4, Field 3 (for the findspot, see Fig. 3.17); T22, from Area 7, Field 20 (for the findspot, see Fig. 3.36); T23, from Area 7, Field 16 (for the findspot, see Fig. 3.36); and T24, from Area 7, Field 20 (for the findspot, see Fig. 3.36). *(Photos: Rose Ferraby.)*

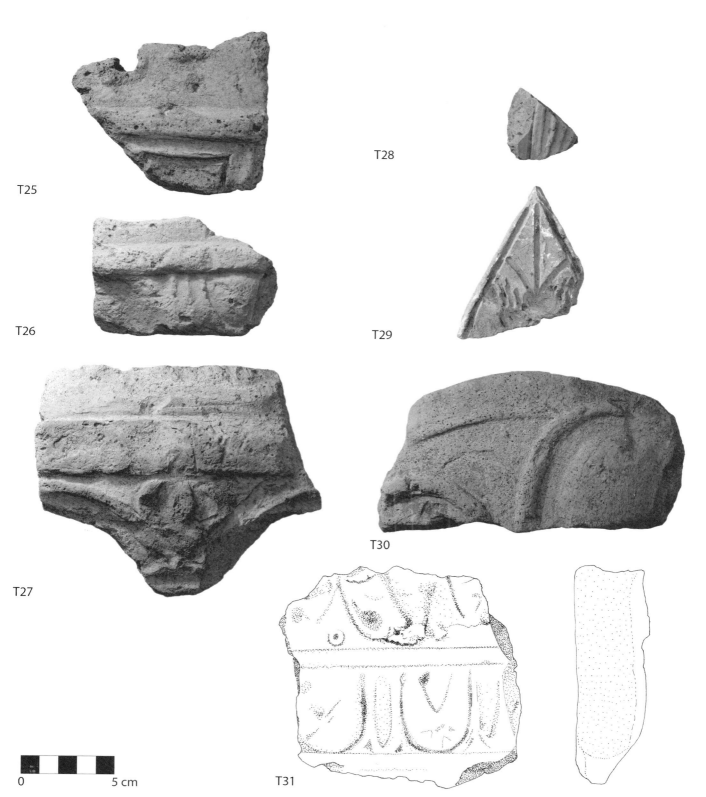

T25

T26

T27

T28

T29

T30

T31

0   5 cm

FIG. 5.9. Terracottas and stucco: T25, from Area 4, Field 3 (for the findspot, see Fig. 3.17); T26, from Area 4, Field 3 (for the findspot, see Fig. 3.17); T27, from Area 7, Field 16 (for the findspot, see Fig. 3.36); T28, from Area 4, Field 3 (for the findspot, see Fig. 3.17); T29, from Area 4, Field 3 (for the findspot, see Fig. 3.17); T30, from Area 5, Field 19 (findspot unrecorded); and T31, from Area 7, Field 20 (for the findspot, see Fig. 3.36). *(Photos and drawing: Rose Ferraby.)*

condition, but the frieze appears to show the legs of a human figure to the right and the tail of an animal above a ring to the left. The frieze appears to have been from a curved entablature. Height 150 mm, width 130 mm.
Area 7, Field 20 (Fig. 3.36).

T32. Five pieces of fluting from a large column (not illustrated). The flutes are *c*. 80 mm wide, separated by a plain fillet, *c*. 15 mm in width.
Area 7, Field 20 (Fig. 3.36).

T33. Fragment of rectangular stepped moulding, possibly from an entablature of the composite order (not illustrated). Height *c*. 55 mm.
Area 7, Field 20 (Fig. 3.36).

These three pieces, all from the same area, indicate the presence of a finely-decorated building of some scale. It is not possible to estimate the size of the fluted columns, but their substantial size perhaps indicates a public structure.

THE BRICK STAMPS
Shawn Graham

CATALOGUE

B1. (Fig. 5.10)   [........]PR M AVRELI ANTO
                 [........]PORT LIC
= *CIL* XV 408; variant determined by *signum*, which does not survive on this example
           OP DOL EX PR M AVRELI ANTO
                 NINI AVG N PORT LIC
Date: AD 212–17 (Steinby 1974: 74)
Area 4, Field 3 (Fig. 3.17) (inventory no. 188).
The variant *signa* of *CIL* XV 408 point to an origin in different *figlinae*. The *signum* of the first variant, 408a (*mars dextrorsum respicins, s. clipeo humi posito innititur, elevato d. brachio hastam manu tenet; superne sertum*), appears in the stamps of C. Casinius Numidianus in the *figlinae Publilianae* in the years AD 212–17, with *Aemilia Severa* as *domina*. The second and fourth variants, 408b and 408d, likewise may be connected to the *figlinae Publilianae*, though with different *officinatores*. The *signum* in 408c (*aries dextrorsum, superne caduceus, infra ad dextram crumena*) was used by Fulvius Primitivus alone in the *figlinae Domitianae Minores* (Steinby 1974: 74).
    These linkages, as well as the movement of *officinatores* between the *figlinae* concerned, led Steinby to argue that, during the Severan period, the *Portus Licini* functioned as a warehouse for the old *figlinae* belonging to the *gens Domitia* (Steinby 1974: 73–4).

The *Portus Licini* was mentioned by Cassiodorus (*Variae* 1.25) and so was still operational during the reign of Theodoric. Janet DeLaine (1997: 90–1) argued that the actual location of the *Portus Licini* ought to be somewhere along the Farfa river.
    A fragment of *CIL* XV.1 408b (tied to the *figlinae Publilianae*) was found at the site of a furnace near Bomarzo at the Valle del Fosso del Rio (a complex of sites tied, on the evidence of brick stamps, to the *gens Domitii*), which suggests that it was made there (site no. 7; Gasperoni 2005: 117). Other *figlinae* in evidence at this complex include *Caninianae*, *Domitianae Minores*, *Domitianae Veteres*, *Fulvianae*, *Terentianae* and *Ponticulanae* (Gasperoni 2005: 105).
    It should be noted that the question of where bricks found at Ocriculum were actually made cannot be answered from the information provided in the stamps themselves, since bricks made from different fabrics sometimes carry the same stamp. Similarly, the presence of wasters at the site near Bomarzo does not demonstrate conclusively that that was the only site at which bricks carrying that particular stamp were made (cf. Graham 2006: 28–54).

B2. (Fig. 5.10)   [.........]RA AVG N FIGL [...]
                 [.........]NGEN[...]
= *CIL* XV 203 OP DOL EX PRA AVG N FIGL NOV
           SABINIA INGENVA
              ramus palmae
Date: AD 212–17 (Steinby 1974: 40)
Area 4, Field 3 (Fig. 3.17) (inventory no. 189).
Officinatores known in this *figlinae* also appear in the *figlinae Domitianae Minores*. Sabinia Ingenua began her career during the reign of Septimius Severus (Steinby 1974: 40).

B3. (Fig. 5.10)   OPVS DO[---]
                 FIGL[---]
= ?*CIL* XV 195 or 196
CIL XV 195: OPVS DOL DE PRAED AVGG NN EX
           FIGL VET CAECIL AMANDA
Mulier sinistrorsum respiciens, s. Cornu copiae, d. Palmae ramum tenet (Hilaritas)
CIL XV 196: OPVS DOL DE PRAED AVGG NN EX
           FIGL VET CAECIL·AMANDA
              DE
              LIC
Mulier sinistrorsum respiciens, s. Cornu copiae, d. Palmae ramum tenet (Hilaritas)
Date: AD 198–211 (Steinby 1974: 39)
Area 4, Field 3 (Fig. 3.17) (inventory no. 190).

FIG. 5.10. Brick stamps: B1, from Area 4, Field 3 (for the findspot, see Fig. 3.17); B2, from Area 4, Field 3 (for the findspot, see Fig. 3.17); B3, from Area 4, Field 3 (for the findspot, see Fig. 3.17); B4, from Area 7, Field 9, Grid 9a.1 (for the findspot, see Figs 3.36 and 4.3); B5, from Area 1, Field 7, Line 7.4 (for the findspot, see Figs 3.7 and 4.1); and B6, from Area 7, Field 9, Grid 9.21 (for the findspot, see Figs 3.36 and 4.3). *(Photos: Rose Ferraby.)*

Caecilia Amanda began her career under Septimius Severus. Her stamps appear at each stage in the ownership history of the *figlinae Domitianae Veteres* (including the interlude where C. Fulvius Plautianus owned the *figlinae*). In two of her stamps, *CIL* XV 194 and 196, the phrase 'de lic' is used, which probably refers to the *Portus Licini* (given all the various connections between the *portus* and the *figlinae* tied to the *gens Domitia*), but it possibly could refer to the *pr. Lic(iniana)* (Steinby 1974: 39). The interpretation then becomes that the *figlinae Veteres* was situated in the *praedia Liciniana*, as was the *portus* (Steinby 1974: 48).

B4. (Fig. 5.10)   [--- TO]NNEIANÆ
                          ISA[---]
= ?

This semicircular stamp appears to be a new one belonging to the *figlinae Tonneianae*; the second line, ISA[---] might be restored as 'Isaurica'. If that is correct, it might refer to Flavia Seia Isaurica, a known *domina* of the *Tonneianae*, *c.* AD 115–41. A problem with this hypothesis is the shape of the stamp, which would indicate a date in the latter half of the first century; known stamps of Flavia Seia Isaurica from *Tonneianae* have an orbiculus.
Area 7, Field 9, Grid 9a.1 (**Figs 3.36** and **4.3**) (inventory no. 191).

B5. (Fig. 5.10)   OPVS DOLIARE·EX P[............]
                          DOMI[............]
                          NVM[......]
= *CIL* XV 176:
OPVS DOLIARE·EX PRAED·AVG·N ·FIGLIN·
      DOMITIANAS·MINORES·
            NVMERI·IVSTI
      gallus dextrosum, ante eum globus
Date: AD 180–92 (Steinby 1974: 38)
Area 1, Field 7, Line 7.4 (**Figs 3.7** and **4.1**) (inventory no. 192).
L. Numerius Iustus began his work under Marcus Aurelius, in the *figlinae Domitianae Minores* and continued under Commodus. He was still active under C. Fulvius Plautianus, to whom control of the *figlinae* was transferred by Septimius Severus (Steinby 1974: 38).

B6. (Fig. 5.10)   [---]SARIVS[---] + A + D [---]
= ?
The stamp appears to be semicircular with an orbiculus, which would date it somewhere in the second century. The letter combination 'sarius' does not seem to appear

FIG. 5.11. Brick stamps: B7, from Area 8, track to south of Field 15 (findspot not recorded); B8, from Area 7, Field 9, Grid 9.3 (for the findspot, see Figs 3.36 and 4.3); and B9, from Area 7, Field 9, Grid 9.12 (for the findspot, see Figs 3.36 and 4.3). *(Photos: Rose Ferraby.)*

in any other brick stamp. A dubious connection could be made to Arrius Antoninus (later Antoninus Pius), who is known in brick stamps, or alternatively to his mother Arria Fadilla.
Area 7, Field 9, Grid 9.21 (**Figs 3.36** and **4.3**) (inventory no. 193).

B7. (Fig. 5.11)   MI DMI ON [---]
= ?
This rectangular, bordered stamp would seem to be unknown hitherto. Based on its shape, it would seem to date to the early to mid-first century AD.
Track to the south of Area 8, Field 15 (location not recorded) (inventory no. 194).

B8. (Fig. 5.11)   [---] PR[A---]
                      [---] AVG [---]
= *CIL* XV 721 or 722:
CIL XV 721:   OP·DOL·EX·PRAED
                FAVST·AVG·N
                   nux pinea
CIL XV 722:   OPVS DOLIARE·EX PRAED
                FAVSTINAE·AVG
Date: AD 138–41
Area 7, Field 9, Grid 9.3 (**Figs 3.36** and **4.3**) (inventory no. 195).
Faustina Augusta was *domina* of the *figlinae Domitianae Novae* at this time (Steinby 1974: 40).

B9. (Fig. 5.11)   NO[---]
= ?*CIL* XV 1768 NOVAS
Date: first century AD?
Area 7, Field 9, Grid 9.12 (**Figs 3.36** and **4.3**) (inventory no. 196).
The earliest securely dated stamp of the *figlinae Novae* is a Trajanic stamp of Atimetus, slave of Vibia (S. 49 (Bloch 1947; 1948), *CIL* XV 200). Vibia might have been an *officinatrix* of the *Domitii*, or she could have been a *domina* in her own right. The *Novae* at this period is probably the same *figlinae* later known as the *figlinae Domitianae Novae* (Steinby 1974: 40, 69). It is not possible to tie this example to these *figlinae* securely, though the number of other stamps from *gens Domitii* connected stamps recovered in this survey would seem to suggest that the *Domitii* had some control over the provisioning of brick to Ocriculum.

GENERAL DISCUSSION

While the ownership of the estates from which brick was produced in the Tiber valley became concentrated in imperial hands over the course of the second century, the pattern apparent from this collection of stamped brick at Ocriculum suggests a particular provisioning from the estates that historically had belonged to the *Domitii* before they attained the purple. This suggests that this particular collection of stamps is associated with a building (or buildings) especially connected to

the *Domitii*. Similar connections between the person who commissioned a building and the provisioning of the building materials are attested at Ostia (DeLaine 2002). Whether this tie is through chains of patronage or direct intervention it is impossible to say on this evidence.

Integration and discussion

Martin Millett, with a contribution from Lacey M. Wallace

The survey has provided a range of new information about Ocriculum that complements and extends that from previous studies. A series of conclusions that have been drawn about specific monuments in the preceding text is brought together here, together with a consideration of broader aspects of interpretation. The first sections deal with issues concerning particular aspects of the interpretation of the site, suggesting a reconstruction of its historical and topographic development, and highlighting subjects deserving further research. In the later parts of the chapter broader conclusions are drawn together and more speculative suggestions made, with the intention of stimulating further debate about this key site.

RECONCILIATION WITH PANNINI'S PLANS (Fig. 6.1)

No new discussion of Ocriculum would be complete without an attempt to review the important plan drawn by Giuseppe Pannini and published by Giuseppe Guattani in 1784 (Fig. 2.1) since this image has dominated understanding of the site ever since. It is clear that the work by Pannini, recorded in this plan, is based on the common eighteenth-century convention of rationalizing observations in relation to idealized views based on contemporary understanding of the canons of Classical architecture. In the case of Ocriculum, this process involved two different levels of idealization.

First, we have its impact on the presentation of individual buildings. This is seen most clearly at the amphitheatre, where the published reconstruction (Fig. 2.3) takes no account of the rock-cut structure of its southern half. The theatre (Fig. 2.2) equally was presented in the context of contemporary understanding of other extant examples. By contrast, the records of less canonical building types, like the baths (Figs 2.1 and 2.6) and the 'Quartiere d' Soldati' (no. 9) — more commonly known as the 'Grandi Sostruzioni' — (Fig. 2.5), are less obviously idealized. In the case of the latter, it remains difficult to assess how far the fore-work shown in the 1784 plan is real or a result of idealization. Despite these problems, the illustrations of these buildings mostly seem sufficiently reliable in general outline and detail to allow them to be used to help interpret the surviving remains.

Second, a degree of idealization clearly was applied to the overall topography of the town plan (Fig. 2.1). This is clear both from the strong orthogonal element in the plan as drawn, which deployed two grid axes despite the absence of any such scheme in the actual topography, and from the relationship shown between the individual buildings. The plan shows clearly, if schematically, the layout of olive groves on the site, and it is possible that, given the difficult topography of the landscape, the eighteenth-century surveyors were misled into believing that the town plan was more regular than it is. Indeed, they may have used the tree lines as a basis for some of their survey. However, details of the plan suggest that a more systematic and deliberate rationalization was imposed. We may note, in particular, the square enclosure containing three buildings (nos. 13, 14 and 17) towards the top of the plan. This can be identified with the late Roman enclosure towards the east of the settlement in Fields 16 and 17 (Fig. 3.36). The whole area enclosed is basically triangular in shape, although a wall following the boundary dividing the two modern fields forms a trapezoidal enclosure to the west, which we can surely identify with the square shown by Pannini. Both this enclosure and the terraces to its north, at the Podere Cisterna (Fig. 3.40), which clearly can be related to the 'Ninfeo' (no. 22) and 'Conserua d'Acqua' (no. 23) on the 1784 plan, evidently was presented according to an assumed rationale rather than on the basis of any accurate survey. This rationale seems to have sought to relate the buildings to an orthogonal grid, even if it required moving their relative positions in relation to one another or 'correcting' their plans to make them more rectilinear. Where the standing remains were sufficiently close together and preserved well

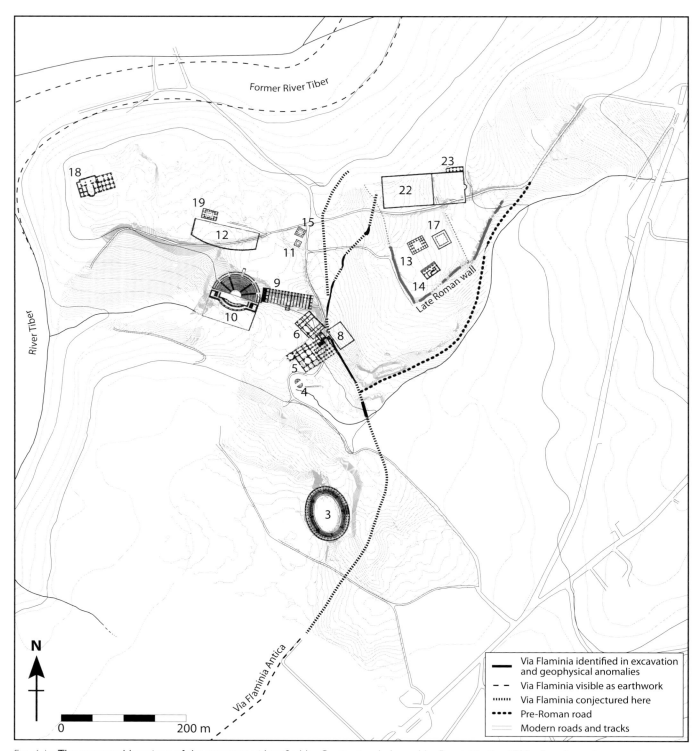

FIG. 6.1. The suggested locations of the structures identified by Guattani and planned by Pannini in the 1780s. For discussion, see the text.

enough to discourage any such rationalization, as in the case of the 'Grandi Sostruzioni' (no. 9) and the baths (nos. 5 and 6), a more accurate representation of their relationship was presented. However, the angle of the

baths was then used to project a second grid axis, which was then extended to the right-hand portion of the plan, bringing the amphitheatre (no. 3) onto the same alignment.

On the basis of this analysis of Pannini's presentation of the evidence, it seems reasonable to attempt to identify individual extant structures with those shown on his plan, although one should be very cautious about using a location on the plan alone as evidence for any individual identification. Most of the structures recorded on the plan can be related to modern features without difficulty, as shown in Table 6.1.

The only structures over which there is significant debate about identification are nos. 11 (Foro) and 15 (Tempio) on Pannini's plan. Both lie towards the centre of the site, and no. 15 generally is referred to as the basilica. This particular building is of considerable significance, as a group of imperial statuary was excavated there and the building has more recently been reinterpreted as an Augusteum (Dareggi 1982), although we should note the recent questioning of such a term (Wallace-Hadrill 2011: 153). As noted above (p. 19), Pietrangeli (1978: 48–9) concluded that it was located at the Podere Civitelle, a situation that certainly makes sense on a straightforward reading

TABLE 6.1. Correlation between the principal features shown on Pannini's plan of 1784 (Fig. 2.1), Pietrangeli's identifications (Fig. 1.4), and those suggested in this volume.

Key feature on Pannini's plan (Fig. 2.1)	Identification in Pietrangeli 1978: carta 1 (= Fig. 1.4)	Location and suggested identification (Chapter 3 and Fig. 6.1)	Reference to our plans
1. Via Flaminia	–		
2. Sepolcri	–		
3. Anfiteatro	V, anfiteatro	amphitheatre, Areas 1 and 2	Figs 3.7 and 3.10, amphitheatre
4. Conserua d'Acqua	m	Area 6, cistern in valley floor	Fig. 3.27, underground cistern
5. Terme	Z in key, N on plan	Area 6, baths	Fig. 3.27, baths
6. Terme Hiemali	h in key, not shown on plan	Area 6, baths	Fig. 3.27, baths
7. Gran Muro	D	–	–
8. Magnifico Palazzo	I in key, not shown on plan	–	–
9. Quartiere d' Soldati	AA, 'Grandi Sostruzioni'	Area 5, 'Grandi Sostruzioni'	Fig. 3.19, 'Grandi Sostruzioni'
10. Teatro	T, teatro	Area 5, theatre	Fig. 3.19, theatre
11. Foro	BB	see discussion	
12. Stadio	o in key, not shown on plan	Area 4, Field 3 and Area 5, Field 19	Figs 3.17 and 3.19
13. Colleggio	u	Area 7, Field 16 [T]	Fig. 3.36, [T]
14. Tempio	s in key, not shown on plan	Area 7, Field 16 [95]	Fig. 3.36, [95]
15. Tempio (also 'Basilica')	b, Podere Civitelle	Area 5, Field 19	Fig. 3.22, [F]
16. Pozzi	t	not identified	–
17. Foro	r	Area 7, Field 16 [99]	Fig. 3.36, [99]
18. Palazzo Publico	z	Area 4, Field 3 [37]	Fig. 3.17, [37]
19. Nobile Abitazione	V, Podere Scorga	Podere Scorga, Area 4, Field 3	Fig. 3.17, Scorga
22. Ninfeo	CC, Podere Cisterna	Area 8, Podere Cisterna	Fig. 3.40
23. Conserua d'Acqua	DD, Podere Cisterna	Area 8, Podere Cisterna	Fig. 3.40

of its location on the eighteenth-century plan. Similarly, Carlo Pietrangeli identified structure no. 11 shown on Pannini's plan, and labelled as 'Foro', with what he described as the remains of a rammed limestone floor and mosaic with *opus reticulatum* walling (1978: carta 1, BB = Fig. 1.4). This location corresponds to the structures we recorded in the northeast corner of Field 19 (Fig. 3.22; p. 51). Pietrangeli's identification of the Podere Civitelle with the basilica has been accepted in all subsequent accounts of the site.

As noted above (pp. 51–4), there are two problems with Pietrangeli's identifications. First, our survey did not reveal major structures in the vicinity of the Podere Civitelle, and although they may lie in the area beneath the house and under the farmyard behind it, the fragments of walling visible in this area are not easy to reconcile with the plan published by Pannini. Second, the major structures we recorded in the corner of Field 19 clearly suggest two major buildings, one with an apse (Fig. 3.22, [F]), the other with marble walls and external niches on the south side (Fig. 3.22, [H]). The features of the former cannot be reconciled with the plan of the 'Foro' on Pannini's main illustration (Fig. 2.1, no. 11), where a square building with internal colonnade is shown. It is possible that they do relate to the marble walls to the south (Fig. 3.22, [H]), although there are no specific features to support this suggestion. By contrast, the apse we recorded closely resembles the form of that shown on Pannini's published plan of the basilica ('Tempio' no. 15), so it probably should be identified with the Augusteum excavated in the eighteenth century. This would make good sense in relation to the supposed temenos in the area of the 'Grandi Sostruzioni' and the large enclosed area immediately to the east (Fig. 3.19), which is best understood as a forum through which the Via Flaminia passed (see pp. 54 and 140).

This identification creates a problem with the overall interpretation of Pannini's plan. On the one hand, if the two buildings we have identified can be correlated with both the 'Foro' and 'basilica', they are immediately adjacent, much closer together than Pannini indicates (that is no. 15 *c.* 150 m east/northeast of no. 11 on the same alignment). However, his plan certainly does not show the relative position of other buildings correctly. It is perhaps more likely that the marble wall with niches (Fig. 3.22, [H]), is not to be identified with the 'Foro', and his plan simply transposed nos. 15 and 11. These issues could perhaps be resolved with further GPR survey or some small-scale excavation at the two locations.

The various elements of the eighteenth-century plan and results from our survey are integrated in the overall interpretative plan (Fig. 6.1 and Table 6.2). This work shows clearly that although the eighteenth-century plan was published at a scale of *c.* 1:4,350 (its scale bar of 500 Roman feet printed at a length of 34 mm), it contains a series of inconsistencies of scale, with the buildings generally shown larger than they should have been. Although most of the buildings can be reconciled with the standing remains if reduced to 75%, this is not universally the case. It may be noted, however, that the median (75%) and mean (75.9%) both lie remarkably close to this figure, suggesting a general consistency in the original survey. Equally, the adjustment to the orientation of the structures varies from 210° to 287°, with a median of 238° and a mean of 246°, again suggesting a reasonable consistency in the original work. It is uncertain whether these variations relate to the original survey, or to the production of the published plans, but they are not immediately comprehensible in relation to any systematic conversion. There is evidently scope for further analysis that might shed light on the methods used in the original survey of the site, but this lies beyond the remit of the present study.

Our overall plan reconciles the eighteenth-century work with the present survey (Fig. 6.1) and provides an important new framework for understanding the site. This is drawn upon in the discussion that follows.

THE VIA FLAMINIA WITHIN OCRICULUM (Figs 6.2 and 6.3)

It is clear, from both its historical context and the evidence of this survey, that the development of the river port and town of Ocriculum was related closely to the history of the Via Flaminia. In this context, it is paradoxical that our knowledge of its precise route through the town remains comparatively poor. As noted above (p. 35), this is partly a result of the depth of its burial in parts of the site. Thomas Ashby and Roland Fell (1921: 163–5) believed that the road's original route was focused on the hilltop where the medieval village stands, passing to the east of the riverside site of Ocriculum. This conclusion is entirely understandable, given the common belief that the development of a settlement beside the Tiber came comparatively late, with Ed Bispham most recently suggesting its establishment came only in the middle of the first century BC (2007: 319–21). As this chronology, and therefore Ashby and Fell's presupposition,

TABLE 6.2. Notes on the adjustments made to reconcile Pannini's plan with the structures revealed by our survey (based on work by Lacey M. Wallace). Note: positive angles indicate anticlockwise rotation, negative angles indicate clockwise rotation.

Building	Adjustment to orientation	Adjustment to scale	Notes
3. Amphitheatre	rotated −60°	scaled 75% to match remains	
4. Conserua d'Acqua	rotated −35°	scaled 84.5% to match remains	
5. Terme, 6. Terme Hiemali, and 8. Magnifico Palazzo	rotated −35°	scaled 84.5% to match remains	see also Fig. 3.30
9. Grandi Sostruzioni	rotated −28°	scaled 75% to match remains	
10. Theatre	rotated −38°	scaled 75% to match remains	
11. Foro	rotated −46° to match alignment of 15 Tempio/basilica and the apse [F] and its opening	scaled 50% to match marble structure [H]	see also Fig. 3.22
12. Stadio	rotated −32° to align with [57]	scaled 87.5% to match field boundary at the western side and the end of [57]	
13. Colleggio	rotated 9° as a hypothesis based on 17 Foro and [99]	scaled 70% as a hypothesis to match 17 Foro and [99]	
14. Tempio	rotated 17° to match alignment of [95]	scaled 85% to approximate to the surviving remains	
15. Tempio or basilica	rotated −46° to match alignment of apse [F] and its opening	scaled 85% to approximate to the surviving remains	
17. Foro	rotated 9° to match alignment of [99]	scaled 70% to approximate to the surviving remains	
18. Palazzo Publico	rotated −60°	scaled 112.5% to approximate to the surviving remains	
19. Nobile Abitazione	rotated −35°	scaled 75% as a hypothesis based on the theatre	
22. Ninfeo, and 23. Conserua d'Acqua	rotated −35°	scaled 75% to approximate to the surviving remains	

can now be shown to be wrong with the identification of a settlement beside the Tiber from the pre-Roman period, and intensive settlement from the first half of the third century BC (see below, p. 141), it is as well to reconsider the evidence for the Via Flaminia in the vicinity of the town.

The most recent accounts of the Via Flaminia (Pineschi 1997: 29–30, plan on p. 75; Bertacchini 2006: fig. 1) do not discuss its route through the site, but show a course that basically follows the modern trackways, entering from the south by the amphitheatre and exiting to the north along the track that passes the church of San Fulgenzio, thence climbing the hill to the

site of the present village (Fig. 6.2). Pietrangeli (1943: 106–18, fig. 15; 1978: 165–72, fig. 191) differed, and distinguished three routes (Fig. 6.2), one he considered to have been ascertained, the other two hypothetical. None of his proposed routes is entirely consistent with the evidence from our survey. It is therefore worth systematically considering the line of the road through the town, allowing both for the ambiguities of the survey evidence and for the likelihood that no single course was maintained throughout the history of the town.

The *agger* of the Via Flaminia is clearly visible running across the flat ground in the fields to the

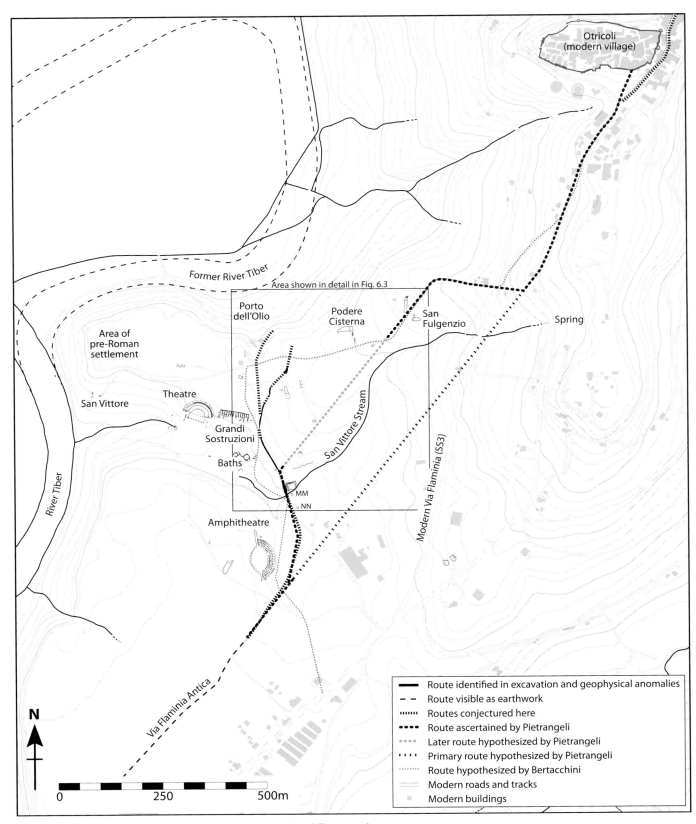

FIG. 6.2. The various routes of the Via Flaminia proposed by different authors.

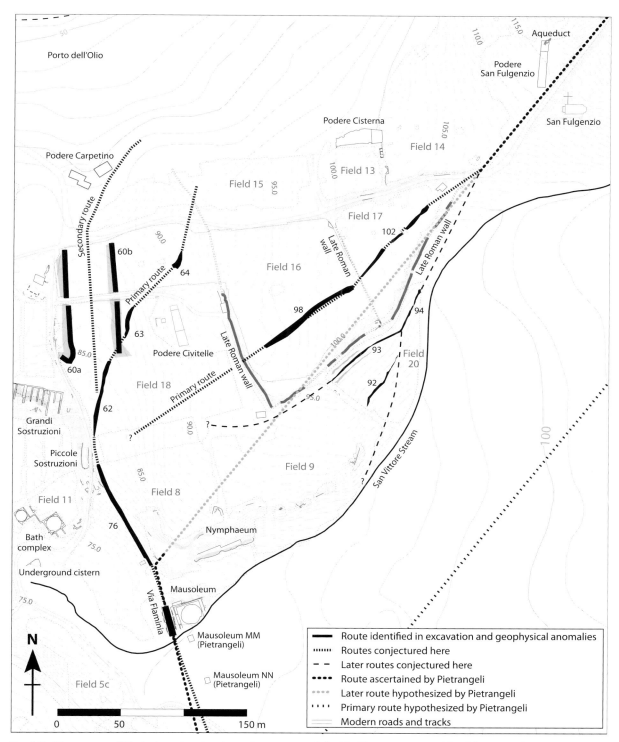

FIG. 6.3. The centre of Ocriculum showing the various routes of the Via Flaminia proposed by different authors.

south of the amphitheatre, where a series of funerary monuments is extant beside it (Fig. 1.2). It then runs across Field 7, with a quarry defining its southeastern side (Fig. 3.7). It must continue northwards into Field 1, perhaps skirting close to the eastern side of the

amphitheatre, where some magnetic anomalies may indicate its course. It is more likely, however, that it descended and ran along the floor of the small valley a little to the east (see p. 35). This route is more consistent with the course suggested slightly further north. In either case, the proximity of a line of probable funerary monuments that flank its eastern side confirms its general course (Fig. 3.7, [1] and [2]). Equally, the positioning of the amphitheatre immediately beside it is significant (see p. 146).

The basalt surface of the road has been exposed by excavation to the west of the circular mausoleum in the southern part of Field 8, just north of the point where it crosses the San Vittore stream (Figs 3.27 and 3.32). Its course to the south of this is indicated by the location of two extant funerary monuments in a field that lay outside our survey area (Figs 1.4 and 6.3, MM, NN). These two monuments would have stood directly by the eastern side of the road if it followed the more easterly route suggested in Field 1. If the more westerly course had been taken, the Via Flaminia would have curved in from further west, passing a little to the west of the more southerly monument. The former course seems the more likely, especially given the alignment of funerary monuments in this stretch as the road approached the town. The excavated stretch of road (Fig. 3.32) lies at a point immediately west of the present crossing of the San Vittore stream, near where the stream turns to the west, and close to the beginning of the sector of the valley that was artificially filled and levelled in the Roman period (see pp. 149–51). Although the depth of the natural valley at this point is uncertain, it seems probable that it was chosen deliberately for ease of crossing, although a small bridge or causeways and culvert anyway must have been needed. It is notable that elsewhere spectacular bridges formed an important feature of the Via Flaminia (Ballance 1951), so some more elaborate crossing perhaps may have existed here before the infilling of the valley.

The route as the road then climbs the ridge is clear, both from the geophysical survey (Fig. 3.27) and from a stretch previously exposed in agricultural work near the ridge top (Pietrangeli 1978: fig. 42). To the north, the survey shows that it continued across the ridge, most likely with a change of course at some stage in the town's development. Evidence for the route in the earlier phase is visible in the results of the magnetometry (Figs 3.19 and 6.3, [62], [63] and [64]), heading north/northeast across Field 18 and into Field 16, but not traceable any further. In a later phase, this route was cut through by a terrace and one of the major retaining walls (Figs 3.19 and 6.3, [60b]), which defined the piazza on the ridge top through which the road then passed.

The route taken by the Via Flaminia from the ridge top in both phases is uncertain. Three possible courses

have been suggested previously, although they are not mutually exclusive. Two envisage that the Via Flaminia climbed eastwards following along the ridge upon which Ocriculum was built to join the route followed by the modern road.

In the first alternative, shown as 'ascertained' by Pietrangeli (1942: fig. 15; 1978: fig. 191), instead of following the route northwards up the slope past the circular mausoleum and on to the ridge, it is shown as a line that turns northeastwards to follow the western side of the San Vittore stream, joining the existing track by the eastern end of Field 17 (Figs 6.2 and 6.3). From there, it follows the present trackway past the church of San Fulgenzio, crossing the line of the modern road and following an extant route up to the hilltop, where it coincides with the present road through the village of Otricoli, passing to the east of the walled enceinte. There are two pieces of evidence from the survey to support the idea that a road followed this general course through the town, although it would appear to be a secondary route, not that of the Via Flaminia itself. The road visible running through Fields 16 and 17 (Figs 3.36 and 6.3, [98] and [102]) lies on this line, although it was clearly blocked at the southwest by the construction of the later Roman enclosure wall, and there is no evidence to show how it earlier linked with the Via Flaminia in Field 18. As suggested below (p. 147), there appears to have been a phase of terracing of the slope in this area, perhaps associated with the alteration of the main route of the Via Flaminia and the construction of the retaining walls ([60a] and [60b]) discussed above (p. 54). It is thus likely that the street in Fields 16 and 17 originally continued down the slope to the south, to intersect with the primary course of the Via Flaminia in Field 18. When this route was cut with the construction of the terraces on the slope, an alternative route would have been required, and there is perhaps evidence for such a route in Field 20 (Figs 3.36 and 6.3, [94]). This route ran to the east of the late Roman wall, alongside the San Vittore stream, although its route further to the southwest is uncertain. It might have either followed round the outside of the wall, cutting across to a junction with the Via Flaminia at the back of the 'Grandi Sostruzioni' in Field 18 (Fig. 6.3, [93]), or, more likely, continued close beside the stream, passing in front of the 'Nymphaeum' (Figs 3.36 and 6.3). These suggestions, although speculative, would provide a solution to the continuing need to connect the town to the hilltop, whilst also providing access along the ridge top throughout the occupation of the town.

Secondly, Pietrangeli's plan also shows a hypothetical route for the Via Flaminia that bypasses the Roman town altogether, joining the straight section of road known from earthworks to the south of the town with a stretch on the same alignment that runs from the modern road northeast of San Fulgenzio up to the hilltop south of the village (Fig. 6.2). Such a route may have been useful to traffic wishing to bypass the town, but we know of no evidence to support the idea, which may simply be based on the unverified account given by Ashby and Fell (1921).

Finally, the routes shown by Milena Bertacchini (2006: fig. 1[1]) and Igino Pineschi (1997: 75) both show the Via Flaminia following the modern trackway eastwards along the ridge to join the route proposed by Pietrangeli where it passes the church of San Fulgenzio. This route is impossible, given that the present trackway cuts though a series of ancient structures, including the pair of late Roman walls between Fields 16 and 18 (Fig. 3.40), as well as the cistern beside Field 17 (Fig. 3.40, [V]).

The route indicated by our evidence has the Via Flaminia continuing northwards across the ridge in Field 18, running through the piazza defined by retaining walls [60a] and [60b] (Figs 3.19 and 6.3). At the north it then would have cut down across the slope, following a line to the northeast past the standing structure in the Podere Carpentino, to reach the Porto dell'Olio (Figs 3.40 and 3.45). We have no evidence for its course beyond this, but it may well have run beside the former meander in the Tiber before climbing to rejoin the present road to Narni further north. Such a route would have provided a link between the river port and the town, but would have bypassed the hilltop *enceinte*. Given our evidence that this represents a secondary stage in the road's development, it is likely that the earlier route seen in the geophysics results a little further east (Figs 3.19 and 6.3, [63] and [64]) also cut across the ridge, and then descended across the slope to the northeast to pass the Porto dell'Olio; we certainly have no evidence for any route running up the northern side of the ridge to the east.

The route we are suggesting for the Via Flaminia, which also linked the river port, would make good sense in terms of the chronology of Ocriculum as now established, since when the road was laid out in 220 BC, the riverside settlement was well established. This disproves past hypotheses that have been predicated on the assumption that the *enceinte* on the hilltop under the present village was the main settlement in occupation at this time, so that the road must have headed there first,

with the later diverticulum to the riverside settlement needing to be connected back to the hilltop. The route, we are suggesting, had as its primary focus our site and the Porto dell'Olio. This path for the Via Flaminia also makes sense in relation to the earlier topography, as it passes across the ridge immediately to the east of the core of the pre-Roman settlement, which now appears to have been surrounded by a rampart (below, Figs 6.4 and 6.5). Following this hypothesis, the route up to the hilltop, although needed, may be viewed as having been secondary in functional terms. It probably first followed the route visible in Fields 16 and 17, and was diverted to the east through Field 20 at a later date. Both these routes join the modern track past San Fulgenzio and run up to the present village.

It is clear that there remains legitimate uncertainty about the road network in the immediate vicinity of Ocriculum. It is equally certain that the resolution of these uncertainties can be found only with further fieldwork, particularly around the Porto dell'Olio and in the area to its northeast.

HISTORICAL AND TOPOGRAPHICAL DEVELOPMENT OF THE TOWN
(Figs 6.4–6.7)

PRE-ROMAN ORIGINS AND EARLY DEVELOPMENT (Fig. 6.4)

The pottery collected from Fields 7 and 9 provides new and independent evidence for the chronology of the occupation of Ocriculum that modifies previous understanding (see above, pp. 92–112). Previous work has provided strong evidence for occupation covering an area of c. 4 ha at the western end of the ridge, in the vicinity of the San Vittore chapel, from the eighth century BC (Cifani 2003: 126–31; Cenciaioli 2006: 18–20; Cenciaioli 2008: 813–15). There is also a sixth-century BC terracotta from the Podere Cisterna (Dareggi 1978; Pietrangeli 1978: 24, fig. 6; Cenciaioli 2006: 20), a little further east along the ridge. Our survey has added significantly to knowledge of this period by identifying what is probably an earthen rampart defining the northern side of the ridge in this area (Figs 3.17 and 6.4, [47], [48] and [49]). Although this feature remains undated, there must be a strong possibility that it relates to the pre-Roman phase, and this possibility should be tested by excavation. If it is of this period, it would suggest that the settlement was rather more extensive than previously thought, covering the whole of the ridge to the west of the

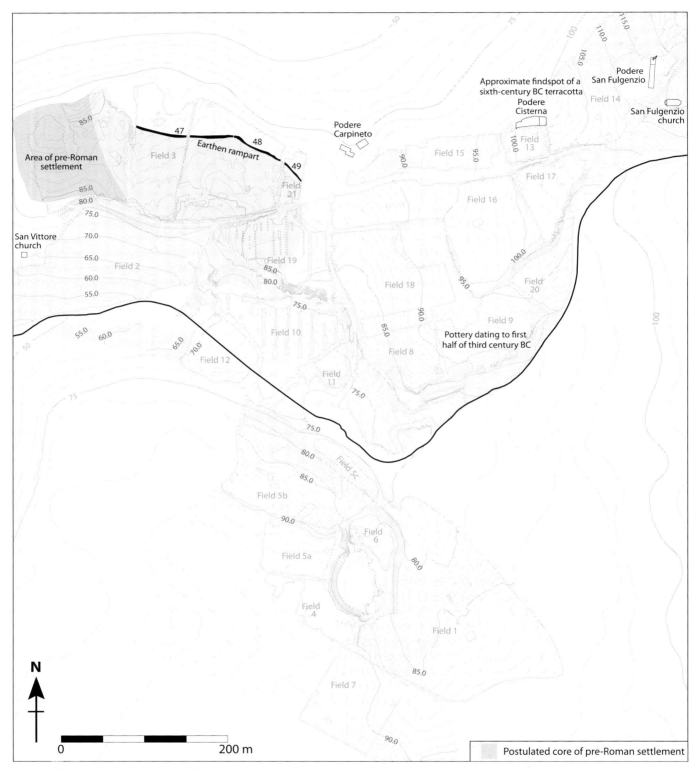

FIG. 6.4. The suggested topography of the site in the pre-Roman period.

modern crossroads. The pattern of its growth from the eighth-century BC nucleus to occupation of the whole ridge is uncertain, but its position commanding an important landing-place on a bend in the Tiber immediately to the north is surely significant.

The ceramic evidence from Field 9, near the centre of the site but beyond the suggested pre-Roman core, certainly indicates continuous occupation from the first half of the third century BC, with the possibility of some activity in the fourth century (see above, pp. 111–12). This shows that the core of the settlement on the ridge had expanded before the alliance with Rome in 308 BC, and certainly much before the construction of the Via Flaminia c. 220 BC (see above, p. 5). Given the uncertainty about the date and status of the hilltop *enceinte* under the modern village, it is not possible at present to establish whether the two sites were occupied consecutively or contemporaneously during this period, although future work should be able to resolve this if ceramics from the hilltop can be studied fully. However, the chronology provided here shows that by the time the Via Flaminia was constructed, there was an important settlement here that was on the planned route that may have been designed to pass in front of the entrance to the historic core (see above, p. 141).

We have comparatively little evidence for the structure of the settlement in these early phases and, aside from the sixth-century BC terracotta noted above, perhaps associated with a temple, there is no evidence of any public buildings.

THE REPUBLIC AND EARLY PRINCIPATE
(Figs 6.5 and 6.6)

The construction of the Via Flaminia at the end of the third century BC will have had a significant impact in changing the nature of Ocriculum, integrating it more effectively both with Rome and with places further to the north in Italy. There seems little doubt that the junction of road and river was also significant in enhancing the importance of Ocriculum, as emphasized by the suggested route of the Via Flaminia running beside the Porto dell'Olio. The epigraphic evidence shows a thriving municipality by the later first century BC (Pietrangeli 1978: 29–30; Bispham 2007: 319–21 — although it should be noted that the latter's dating for the town's magistracies is based on the incorrect assumption that the town was not established beside the Tiber until the middle of the first century BC).

The character of the town remains obscure until the first century BC, when a series of major buildings was constructed. The only evidence for any earlier Republican public building comes from a fragmentary architectural terracotta, perhaps derived from a temple pediment, found near the church of San Fulgenzio and dated stylistically to the second century BC (Pietrangeli 1978: 11, 22; Stopponi 2006: 57). It shows a nude Apollo-type figure in full relief, with drapery around the lower body. Although the context is uncertain, and it lies outside the core of the occupied area, this may suggest the presence of a temple at this date.

In terms of planning, the extent of relatively level ground for building on the ridge was constrained by the Tiber to the north and west, the San Vittore stream to the south, and the uphill slope to the east. The total area available for settlement thus amounted to no more than c. 10 ha, while its elongated and slightly irregular shape determined the layout of the settlement and constrained its development. It is along the southern cliff of the ridge that the earliest surviving public buildings were constructed (Fig. 6.6).

The 'Grandi Sostruzioni' appear to have been built in order to extend building space on the ridge to the south, probably in the first century BC or the early first century AD. It is arguable that they were constructed in several phases, and they are best interpreted as a platform that supported a temenos, with the temple in the centre, either facing north across the ridge, or facing south across the valley (see pp. 49–51). In either case, as it was constructed before the infilling of the valley of the San Vittore stream to the south, the enormous platform would have created a massive and impressive façade, dominating the approach up the Via Flaminia from the south, and arguably also visible when approaching along it coming south from Narnia. Indeed, it seems probable that the temple also would have been visible on the skyline of the ridge to those passing along the Tiber from both north and south. Although there is a rich variety of epigraphic and sculptural evidence from the site, there is no firm evidence to suggest what the dedication of the temple might have been. It has been associated with both the famous head of a statue of Jupiter (Pietrangeli 1978: 116–18), and thus with a Capitolium, and with the goddess Valentia, recorded on a third-century AD inscription from the site (*CIL* XI 4082; Pietrangeli 1978: 11, 32, fig. 24). In the absence of good evidence for their findspots, neither suggestion can be confirmed.

The theatre (see above, pp. 55–6), which lies immediately to the west, is probably Augustan in origin and the

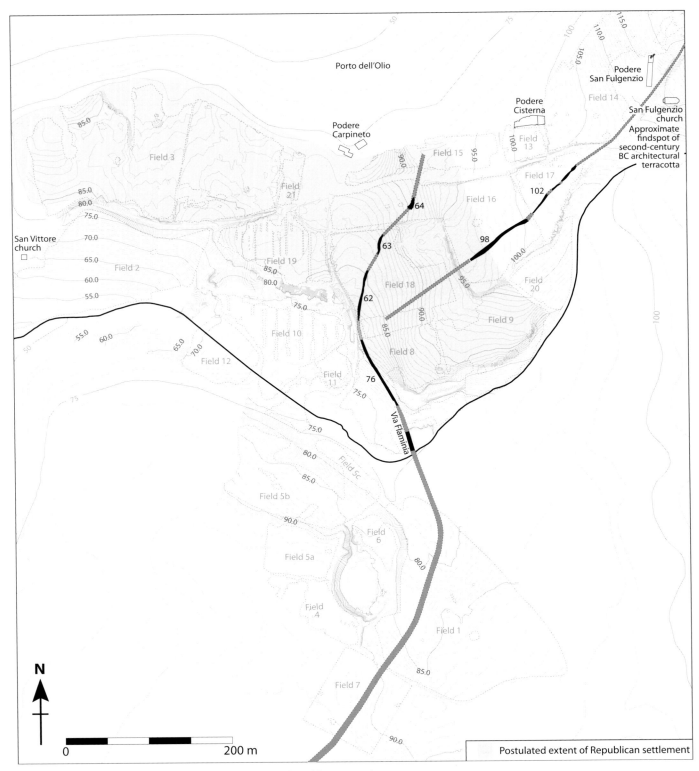

Porto dell'Olio

Podere San Fulgenzio

Field 14

San Fulgenzio church

Podere Cisterna

Approximate findspot of second-century BC architectural terracotta

Podere Carpineto

Field 15

Field 13

85.0

Field 3

Field 21

Field 16

Field 17

102

90.0

95.0

100.0

64

98

100.0

85.0

80.0

75.0

70.0

63

San Vittore church

65.0

Field 19

Field 2

60.0

85.0

55.0

80.0

62

Field 18

95.0

Field 20

90.0

Field 9

55.0

60.0

65.0

70.0

50

75.0

Field 10

85.0

Field 8

Field 12

Field 11

76

75.0

Via Flaminia

75

Field 5c

80.0

85.0

Field 5b

90.0

Field 6

Field 5a

Field 4

Field 1

N

Field 7

85.0

0   200 m

90.0

Postulated extent of Republican settlement

Fig. 6.5. The suggested topography of Ocriculum in the Republican period.

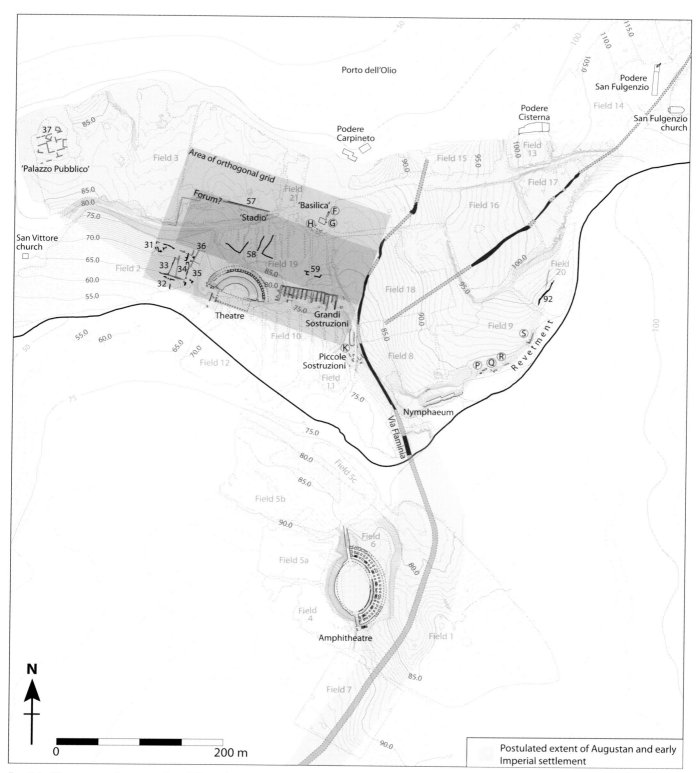

Porto dell'Olio

Podere
San Fulgenzio

Field 14

San Fulgenzio
church

Podere
Cisterna

37

85.0

'Palazzo Pubblico'

Field 3

Area of orthogonal grid

Podere
Carpineto

Field 15

95.0

Field 13

100.0

Field 17

Field 21

Forum?   57

'Basilica' F

Field 16

85.0
80.0
75.0

'Stadio'

H   G

San Vittore
church

70.0

31   36

65.0

58

Field 19

100.0

Field 20

Field 2

33 34 35

85.0

59

92

60.0

32

80.0

55.0

Theatre

Grandi
Sostruzioni

75.0

80.0

Field 18

95.0

90.0

85.0

Field 9   S

50 55.0 60.0

Field 10

Piccole
Sostruzioni

K

P Q R

Revetment

65.0 70.0

Field 12

Field
11

Field 8

75.0

100

75

Nymphaeum

Via Flaminia

75.0

80.0

Field 5c

85.0

Field 5b

90.0

Field 6

Field 5a

Field
4

Field
3

Amphitheatre

Field 1

85.0

N

Field 7

90.0

0   200 m

Postulated extent of Augustan and early
Imperial settlement

FIG. 6.6. The suggested topography of Ocriculum in the early Imperial period.

scaenae frons is dated by epigraphy to the early first century AD. It seems most likely to have been built as part of the same programme as the 'Grandi Sostruzioni', as the theatre too would have provided a magnificent frontage to those arriving at the town. As noted above, its frontage is aligned with that of the 'Grandi Sostruzioni', while the misalignment at the rear of the latter is probably a result of the course of the rock-face (see p. 50). When taken with the other buildings that once continued this façade further to the west beyond the theatre (Area 3, Fig. 3.13, [32]–[36]), we appear to have evidence for the wholesale redevelopment of this aspect of the site at this period. Given the similarity in masonry technique between the 'Piccole Sostruzioni' (see pp. 60–2; Fig. 3.27, [K]) and the central vaults of the 'Grandi Sostruzioni', it is tempting to associate the construction of the two. In this case, the 'Piccole Sostruzioni', which formed a revetment to support the Via Flaminia as it climbed up to the ridge, may have been designed to provide a view from the road across the urban façade to the west.

These building works fit into a broader phase of urban development, although the exact sequence of building over a period of perhaps a hundred years is uncertain at present. Further to the east, on the southern flank of the ridge, the nymphaeum (Figs 3.27 and 3.37) must date to broadly the same period, arguably representing a more modest continuation of the frontage overlooking the southern approach along the Via Flaminia. It is clear that the lack of space for expansion on the ridge top repeatedly led to the construction of revetments and platforms that extended the space for building outward beyond the edges of the ridge. This is seen most clearly in the constructions noted above, but there is also evidence for a series of similar remains on the southeast side overlooking the San Vittore stream (Fig. 6.6, [P]–[S] and [92]), and to the north above the former course of the Tiber. These all appear to have fulfilled a similar function in providing space upon which to build by creating artificial platforms that extended beyond the ridge edge. It seems likely that this development was taking place from the end of the first century BC onwards, and it seems highly probable that those along the northern flank of the ridge also created a monumental frontage designed to dominate the view of the city from both the Tiber and the Via Flaminia. The terraced complex, which includes the buildings surviving at the Podere Cisterna (Fig. 3.40), would have dominated the view of the eastern part of the ridge from the Tiber, the river port and the southwards approach along the Via Flaminia.

In the central area there are remains incorporated in the standing buildings at the Podere Carpineto (Fig. 3.41), and behind this it seems very likely that both the central piazza and the temple standing on the 'Grandi Sostruzioni' would have been clearly visible on top of the ridge. Finally, to the west, the large building labelled as 'Palazzo Pubblico' on Pannini's plan (Fig. 2.1, no. 18; Fig. 3.17, [37]) has a dominant ridge-edge position overlooking the river.

The amphitheatre (see above, pp. 31–4) appears to have been constructed marginally later than the theatre, probably in the first half of the first century AD, but its characteristic location in a funerary area on the southern edge of the town was also carefully designed both to dominate the approach from the south along the Via Flaminia, and also to be visible clearly when looking south down the road from the town centre. The stone façade of the amphitheatre probably had at least three storeys and used rusticated masonry along the side that flanked the road as it descended into the valley of the San Vittore stream. Since it was cut into the steep side of the natural slope, this will have meant that it was hardly visible to the traveller arriving by road from the south, so the architecture of the complex only gradually will have been revealed as one began to descend, dominating the curve of the road, with its visual effect being enhanced with the slope. Such a visual impact was reflected also in the construction of the series of funerary monuments that lined this stretch of the road. This re-emphasizes in material form the way in which the Via Flaminia was fundamental to the city.

Although the pattern of elaboration of urban monuments is commonplace at this period, it may be that there are particular reasons in the case of Ocriculum. We might first consider the commonly supposed association between urban monumentalization and the development of towns as political centres. In this context we may note that Bispham (2007: 371–2) has commented on the close links between the urban élites at Ocriculum and Caesar's faction at Rome, perhaps providing a context for the town's development. Second, it is notable that Augustus claimed to have restored the Via Flaminia in 27 BC (*Res Gestae* 20.5), a circumstance that might have encouraged the subsequent construction of the monuments at Ocriculum forming a façade overlooking the newly-restored road.

There is also evidence for the development of an orthogonal planning grid across part of the ridge behind the theatre at the same period (Fig. 6.6). Its date is indicated by the incorporation of the theatre within the scheme, suggesting that it was laid out in the later first century BC or early first century AD. The grid was bounded to the east by the primary phase of the Via Flaminia, prior to the cutting of the revetted piazza through the ridge top. This might suggest that the centre of the town was replanned at the stage when the Via Flaminia was restored under Augustus in 27 BC. Its limited extent is surely a function of the tight topographical constraints, although we should note how it was focused on the historic core of the town.

At the centre of this planned area lies the area identified by Pannini as a 'Stadio' (Fig. 2.1). This is defined in our survey by a terrace wall to the north (Fig. 3.17, Area 4 [57]) and by a terrace beneath a modern boundary to its west. Its eastern side presumably originally lay along the edge of the Via Flaminia. The southern side was defined by the theatre and 'Grandi Sostruzioni'. The foundations on the slope to the west of the theatre in Area 3 (Fig. 3.13, [31]–[36]) may represent its southwest corner. It thus forms a rectangle, c. 230 m long by 70 m, which may have formed a monumental focus for the town. This perhaps can be labelled as a forum, although it is remarkably large and was occupied by a series of large structures (Fig. 3.19, [58]–[59]). Immediately to its north lay the surviving remains interpreted as the 'basilica' or Augusteum (see above, pp. 51–4), supporting the suggestion that it was a forum. Its size and position in relation to the Via Flaminia are comparable with the Augustan layout, incorporating the theatre, at Carsulae (Morigi 1997: fig. 76). Given its evident importance, further investigation of the area must be a priority for the future.

The early Imperial period saw not only the construction of an extraordinary group of public buildings, but also their elaboration with a remarkable collection of statuary — including a number of pieces discovered during the current survey. This emphasis on public monuments should not detract from the clear commercial significance of the site. Although the area of known residential occupation is relatively modest (see p. 151), there is little reason to doubt that it was a thriving town that drew considerable wealth from its control of river and road communications. This view is reinforced by the evidence of the pottery from the survey of Fields 7 and 9, which illustrates a very strong series of widespread trade connections (see above, pp. 110–11). This pattern is reflected also in the historical evidence for the growth of a series of large rural estates under the control of a group of wealthy landowners who were closely networked with the imperial household under Vespasian, and some of whom can be shown to have been engaged in the supply of materials like bricks to Rome (J. Patterson 2006: 272–4; 2008: 491–3). A similar pattern is indicated by the ownership of brickworks in the area under Trajan.

It is notable also how the epigraphy from the site includes dedications from a comparatively small group of families down into the late Imperial period (Pietrangeli 1978: 29–34), suggesting that the patronage that led to the elaboration of the urban centre was the work of a limited urban élite. In this sense the prosperity and architectural elaboration demonstrated in the early Imperial period may be seen largely as a function of its role in relation to Rome itself.

URBAN REPLANNING (Fig. 6.7)

The evidence from the survey and earlier work provides clear evidence for two major developments in the planning of the site. One, on the ridge top, is difficult to date; the other, involving the area of the San Vittore valley, can be dated to the second decade of the second century. The development on the ridge top is probably somewhat earlier, and involved the realignment of the Via Flaminia as it crossed the ridge (see above, p. 140). This was achieved by the creation of a cutting through the ridge revetted by a pair of retaining walls to east and west (Fig. 3.19, [60a] and [60b]). This created a piazza c. 38 m wide that extended for c. 100 m across the ridge, with the Via Flaminia running through it. Since this feature is cut at an angle to the earlier orthogonal grid, which incorporated the structures immediately to its west (Fig. 3.19, [F], [G] and [H]), it is presumed to post-date them, and thus probably dates to the later first century AD or later.

Further up the slope to the east of the Via Flaminia is a group of structures recorded by Pannini (see above, pp. 20, 135; Figs 2.1 and 6.1), in Fields 13, 15, 16 and 17, later enclosed by the late Roman wall (see above, p. 64; Fig. 3.36). It is notable that the alignment of both the western side of this enclosure and the wall beside the Podere Cisterna is similar to the new route of the Via Flaminia and the associated piazza (Fig. 3.40), arguably suggesting that they were all laid out as part of the same plan. If this were the case, then the terracing of this hillslope, seen so clearly in the results of the contour survey (Figs 6.8 and 6.9), might be seen as part of the same phase of urban planning, and necessitated the realignment of the road providing access along the ridge to the east (see

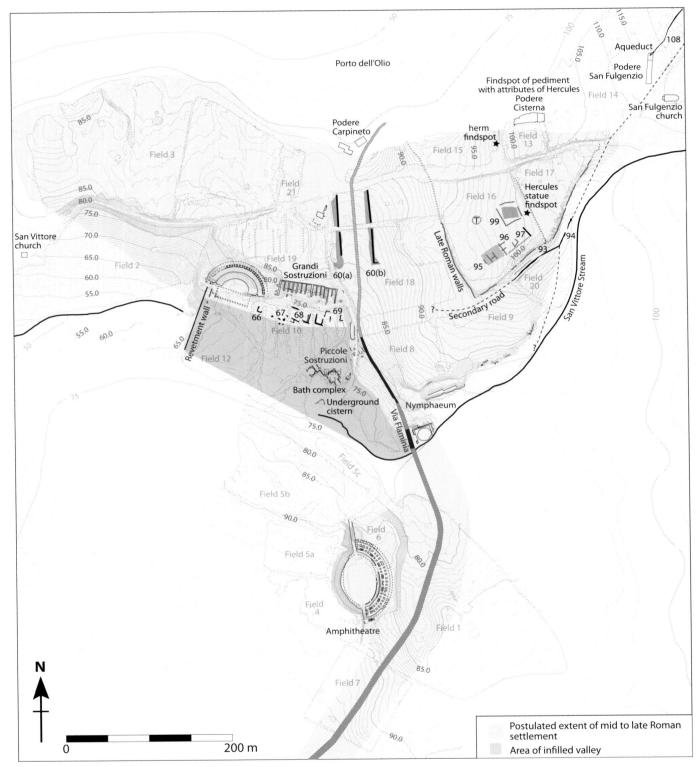

Porto dell'Olio

Aqueduct   108

Podere
San Fulgenzio

Findspot of pediment
with attributes of Hercules
Podere
Cisterna   San Fulgenzio
church

Podere
Carpineto

Field 14

herm
findspot

Field 15   95.0   100.0   Field
13

Field 3

Field
21

Field 17

Hercules
statue
findspot

Field 16

San Vittore
church

Field 2

Field 19   Grandi
Sostruzioni   60(a)   60(b)

Late Roman walls

99

96   97   94

95   93

Field
20

Field 18

Revetment wall

66   67   68   69
Field 10

Field 12

Field 9

San Vittore Stream

Field 8

Secondary road

Piccole
Sostruzioni

Bath complex   Underground
cistern

Nymphaeum

Via Flaminia

Field 5c

Field 5b

Field
6

Field 5a

Field
4

Amphitheatre   Field 1

Field 7

N

0   200 m

★   Postulated extent of mid to late Roman
settlement
Area of infilled valley

FIG. 6.7. The suggested topography of Ocriculum in the mid- to late Imperial period.

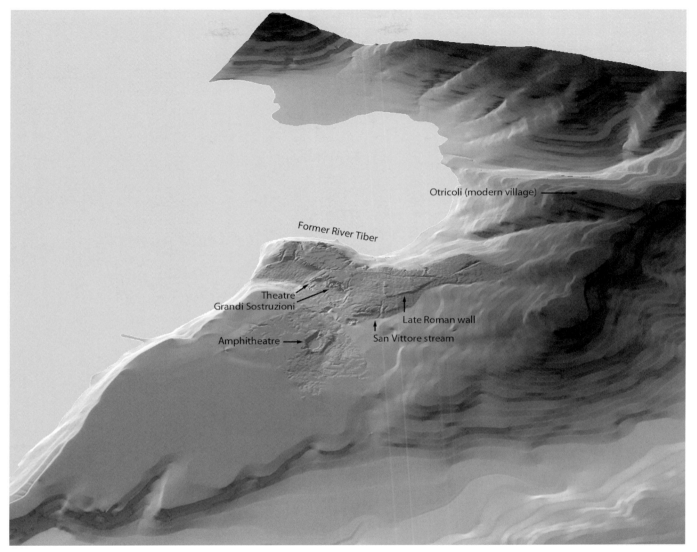

FIG. 6.8. **3-D view of the topography of Ocriculum viewed from the southeast.** *(Image by Elizabeth Richley.)*

above, p. 140). The date of the buildings in this area is unknown, but there are strong grounds for believing that they formed a sanctuary complex. The herm from Field 15 and the statue of Hercules found in Field 16 both date to the early Imperial period (see above, pp. 113–17, S1 and S2), whilst a small pediment found at the Podere Cisterna, decorated with the attributes of Hercules (Pietrangeli 1978: 154, fig. 167), would support the idea that he was one of the deities worshipped.

The presence of this sanctuary to the east and the cliffs on the other three sides constrained settlement on the ridge. It also is clear from the way in which platforms had been created previously around the ridge edges that building land in the town was at a premium. In a remarkable development, this problem

was resolved in the second century AD by the infilling of a substantial section of the San Vittore valley along the southern side of the town. This both radically changed its southern aspect and provided substantial additional building space.

This major development was certainly completed by the date of the construction of a major suite of baths in Field 11 on the newly-made ground in AD 139 (*CIL* XIV 98; see p. 59). The baths were positioned perpendicular to the Via Flaminia so that their façade dominated the new approach to the town. The project clearly involved sophisticated and large-scale engineering work that seems also to have provided a system of cisterns fed by forcing water up from the river as it flowed through a deeply-buried conduit by shutting off the exit. This argues for a functional connection

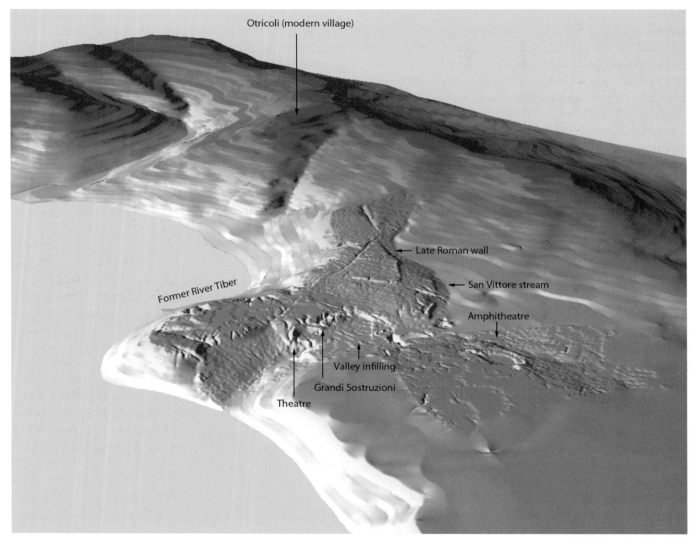

FIG. 6.9. **3-D view of the topography of Ocriculum viewed from the southwest.** *(Image by Elizabeth Richley.)*

between the construction of the baths and the provision of land on which to build them. This postulated connection is supported by the observation that the surviving wall of the major visible cistern was built on the same alignment as the baths (Fig. 3.27). It should be noted, however, that the project was probably completed in a series of phases, so the structures flanking the south side of the theatre and the 'Grandi Sostruzioni' on the northern edge of the valley (Fig. 3.27, [66]–[69]) may be somewhat earlier, a suggestion supported by the fact that these buildings form a line with the *scaenae frons* of the theatre, which is dated by an inscription to the early first century AD (see above, pp. 55, 58; *CIL* XI 7806).

The problem of how the valley filling was engineered has been discussed recently (Bertacchini 2006; Bertacchini and Cenciaioli 2008). Milena Bertacchini

and Luana Cenciaioli have suggested that the infilling was completed in two stages, first with the construction of a dam across the valley to trap sediments (shown as 'Revetment wall' on **Figs 3.13** and **6.7**), then with the addition of a revetment upstream to support these deposits. It appears to us that the upstream revetment is understood better as a large cistern within the infill (shown as 'Underground cistern' on **Figs 3.27** and **6.7**). On this basis, the artificial platform extended further southeast up the valley, to the point where the stream changes direction, and is crossed by the Via Flaminia, and the excavated circular mausoleum. An examination of the present course of the stream in the base of a gorge between the underground cistern and the Via Flaminia crossing shows that it runs within a Roman brick-faced channel. We would interpret this as being a result of the collapse of the conduit and the subsequent erosion of the valley fill to form the present gorge. If we are correct in our interpretation, the infilling extended for *c.* 300 m along the valley, beside the whole southern flank of the city. It is clear that further detailed work is required to understand fully this complex and the important Roman landscaping and hydraulic system, in particular how it was created and how it functioned.

The baths themselves comprised an impressive group of buildings that enhanced the southern façade of Ocriculum. Although extensive, they occupied only a small part of the newly-created level ground, and it seems unlikely that the rest remained unused given the shortage of space for building elsewhere in the town. Our survey was not very successful in defining structures in this area, apart from those immediately in front of the theatre and 'Grandi Sostruzioni' along the northern side of the valley, and the funerary monuments to the south. The layout of the buildings flanking the north side of the valley is consistent with the idea that they opened onto the piazza. The locations of mausolea to the south probably indicate that the *pomerium* of the town followed the line of the stream, which might account for the absence of further buildings along the southern side. The previously excavated remains in this area and the current excavation beside the theatre both indicate that there has been some colluviation since the Roman period (as well as the dumping of spoil from the excavation of adjacent buildings), and it is possible that other major structures remain to be revealed in this area. Indeed, further investigation with GPR might help to resolve whether or not this area was occupied by buildings.

The other feature that deserves mention in the context of the middle Imperial development of the site is the aqueduct and probable *castellum aquae* noted at the Podere San Fulgenzio (**Fig. 3.44**; see above, pp. 73–5). There is no clear evidence for the dating of these, but the exposed remains appear to be early–mid-Imperial. There seems little doubt, given the scale of the cistern here, that they provided a water supply for a significant part of the town.

LATE ANTIQUITY

The only major structures that can be dated to the late antique period are the late Roman walls that formed an enclosure on the terraced slope in the eastern part of the site, and which enclose the sanctuary discussed above (p. 149). Since the only evidence for the date of the walls comes from their construction type, we need to be very circumspect in our interpretation. We also have the evidence of the two early Christian churches of San Fulgenzio and San Vittore, at the eastern and western limits of the ridge-top settlement; and other evidence was taken by Pietrangeli to suggest the identification of early Christian buildings in the centre of the site (see above, pp. 11 and 69). Our survey has done nothing to shed light on this identification or their chronology.

The ceramic evidence from Fields 7 and 9 helps clarify the chronology of the late antique town. Pottery finds diminish from the second century AD onwards, although this pattern is not unusual in the region (cf. Patterson, Di Giuseppe and Witcher 2004: fig. 5). The range of sources of pottery remains diverse, indicating the continued importance of the site's commercial role, although it suggests that the site did not continue in occupation beyond the sixth century (see above, p. 111). Such a gradual decline in the import of pottery provides no evidence to support Pietrangeli's suggestion (1943: 33) of destruction in the 540s. We also must remain aware of the important distinction between a decline in ceramic supply and a cessation in occupation, especially given the difficulty in identifying the earliest medieval pottery in this region (H. Patterson 2008). Given the presence of two late antique churches on the site, future research must focus on attempting to establish for how long there was also a residential population, either on this site or on the hilltop above.

SIZE AND POPULATION

One of the key historical problems we face in understanding Ocriculum, and indeed other Roman cities, is the size of its population. In considering this issue we need to bear in mind the possibility that there was also a significant residential and commercial zone at the Porto dell'Olio, which lay outside the limits of the present survey. Allowing for this, the impression is of a small centre, but one that was not without significance. The core of the settlement on the ridge top is *c.* 12.4 ha. With the construction of the platform in the valley in the second century, the area used for building expanded to *c.* 14.2 ha (excluding the amphitheatre and its surroundings). It is notable that a considerable proportion of this, *c.* 22%, is taken up with public monuments. This emphasizes the fact that Ocriculum, although a modestly-sized settlement, was dominated by élite public display, a characteristic further underlined by the impressive assemblage of sculpture that has been found in the town.

It is difficult to estimate the population size, but given the occupied area we might suggest *c*. 1,480 to 1,860 people in the early Empire, rising to *c*. 1,700 to 2,100 with the infilling of the valley, based on a density range of 120–50 individuals per ha using general comparators (De Ligt 2008: 153–4). Recent work on the plan of Falerii Novi (Millett 2013: 37–9) suggests that a slightly lower range of density (90–110 per ha) might be more appropriate, indicating a population of between *c*. 1,120 and 1,360 in the early Empire to *c*. 1,280 to 1,560 in the mid-second century. These estimates are more uncertain than usual, given both the constrained nature of the site, which may have resulted in a higher than average density of buildings on the ridge, and the fact that there may well have been further settlement at the Porto dell'Olio beside the Tiber, to the north of the ridge.

Even allowing for the uncertainties in such calculations, what is clear is that this was a modestly-sized community. Even at its fullest extent, Ocriculum was only about half the size of Falerii Novi nearby, and well below the size of the smallest centres in northern Italy (De Ligt 2008). Given these comparisons in settlement and population size, the opulence of the architecture and sculpture from the town are all the more remarkable.

OCRICULUM AND THE PATTERN OF ROMAN URBANISM

The urban centre of Ocriculum is very different in scale and layout from the conventional image of the Roman city. Even allowing for the orthogonally-planned core, the overall impression is that of an urban landscape determined fundamentally by its topographic setting. Such city plans were more common in Roman Italy than the archaeological literature might lead one to believe, and Ocriculum thus perhaps should be seen less atypical than the common image of the grid-planned town built on level ground suggests. Nevertheless, it is worth considering further the character of its townscape in relation to a series of factors that have been touched upon above. We need to consider how far the layout was a product of haphazard development, and to what extent it was deliberately conceived to represent an urban ideal that is less familiar to us, and which perhaps may be redolent of earlier settlement in the region (cf. Laurence, Esmonde Cleary and Sears 2011).

It is now clear that the conventional narrative whereby the town beside the Tiber replaced an earlier centre on the hilltop beneath the present village is inadequate, since there is strong evidence that a settlement existed on the ridge overlooking the river from the eighth century BC and that it had reached a substantial extent by the third century BC at the latest. It is within this context that we need to understand the choice of how the urban topography was developed. Certainly, had there been a desire to do so, flat land was available a little to the south, where a new town could have been developed with an extensive Roman-style grid plan (cf. Falerii Novi). Instead, whether because of the significance of the existing site, simple inertia, or a positive choice to build in a particular way, the existing and spatially constrained space on the ridge top was developed as a Roman town. The layout of the early town remains obscure, although the alignments of later buildings suggest that it was developed to follow the natural contours of the ridge.

The construction of the Via Flaminia itself has been discussed by Ray Laurence (1999: 21–3). He emphasized both the role of the road in Rome's strategy of expansion, and the way in which it connected the mother-city with previously established colonies, including Narnia, which lay on the site of the earlier Umbrian settlement of Nequinum. The road's integration of the pre-existing settlement at Ocriculum cannot be without significance, since the other important indigenous centres only a short distance from its route (like Falerii Veteres and Capena) were bypassed. Henceforth, the position of Ocriculum on the *via publica* was of immense significance in its development. This is emphasized not only by the textual sources reviewed in Chapter 2, but also by its consistent appearance not only in the itineraries, but also on the group of four silver goblets from Vicarello (Lago di Bracciano, Lazio). These were shaped as milestones and are inscribed with the itinerary between Rome and Gades, with Ocriculum listed as the second stopping place from Rome, after Ad Vicesumum (*CIL* XI 3281–4; Pietrangeli 1978: 165–6, figs 186–7).

It may be noted that Narnia itself, the next town along the Via Flaminia to the north, shares a similar topographic situation to Ocriculum, situated on the end of a ridge overlooking the river Nera (Monacchi, Nini and Zampolini Faustini 1999; Sisani 2006b: 203–6). Given the superimposition of the later town, it is difficult to see whether there are other parallels in the urban form that might be indicative of common cultural values. Although in 299 BC a Roman *colonia* was superimposed on the indigenous site of Nequinum, which has produced pottery from the seventh century BC onwards (Cifani 2003: 126), the form and location of the Roman town provide a striking parallel with

Ocriculum. However, in contrast with Ocriculum, the Via Flaminia formed the long axis of the *colonia* at Narnia, with a suggestion that its general layout was similar to other colonies like Fregellae (Monacchi, Nini and Zampolini Faustini 1999: 282–90).

After the construction of the Via Flaminia, the development as discussed above shows that both the main approaches to Ocriculum, by road and by river, were developed with architecturally distinctive façades, in order for the town and its patrons to display the status of their community to travellers. In this sense, and in contrast to other late Republican and early Imperial towns in Italy, it had a rather more outward-looking architectural ensemble, perhaps a result of the constrained internal space as well as its key location on the intersection of two major communication systems.

The influence of the road on the development of the town plan of Ocriculum and how it was designed to create an impact on the traveller arriving at or passing through the town has been explored above. Further aspects merit comparison with other towns. Although we can identify only tentatively the forum as lying on the ridge behind the theatre and dating to the replanning of the first century BC/AD (see p. 147), it would appear that it comprised an elongated space that lay perpendicular to the Via Flaminia. Although such an arrangement generally is not understood to have been common in Roman towns, there are significant parallels, both within settlements like Ocriculum where the plan evolved, and in cities planned *de novo*. A little further up the Via Flaminia, the forum at the unplanned settlement of Carsulae lies perpendicular to, and west of, the road, with a further open space continuing to the east in front of the theatre (Morigi 1997: 97–107, figs 75–6). At Pompeii, the forum is set at right angles to the Via Marina–Via dell'Abbondanza, although the Via del Foro exits on its long axis (Gros and Torelli 1994: fig. 109). In colonies, fora set perpendicular to the *via publica* can be seen on the Via Latina at Interamna Lirenas, founded as a *Colonia Latina* in 312 BC (Launaro and Millett 2011), on the Via Appia at the *Colonia Romana* of Minturnae, founded in 296 BC (Sommella 1988: fig. 7; Lackner 2008: 121–5, 358–9) — although here the forum is less elongated —, and at Paestum, a *Colonia Latina* of 273 BC (Gros and Torelli 1994: fig. 100; Lackner 2008: 139–44, 365). Finally, we may note that the same feature occurs at Falerii Novi, where, although set on the ridge following the long axis of the town, the forum is perpendicular to the Via Amerina, and it has been

suggested that it was designed carefully to control travellers' views into it (Keay *et al.* 2000: 86). These examples illustrate how this layout was a recurrent feature of Roman town planning. What is less clear at Ocriculum is the relationship between the forum piazza and the surrounding buildings, which include the so-called Augusteum and the temple that stood above the 'Grandi Sostruzioni', as their arrangement is not suggestive of any coherent planning. However, we should not necessarily expect a neat unity of plan, especially in centres that evolved, rather than being designed *de novo*. This is well illustrated nearby, in the complex and rather 'untidy' development in the civic centre at Carsulae (Morigi 1997: figs 75–6).

Notable at Ocriculum is both the opulence of the surviving sculpture and the apparently large area given over to public buildings and religious space. This confirms the impression given in the texts that Ocriculum was a very significant centre on the Via Flaminia in antiquity. This is all the more remarkable given the small size of the town and since, as John Patterson (2008) has noted, many other towns near Rome seem to have gone into decline in the early Imperial period as their wealth drained towards the metropolis. The explanation must lie in a combination of its economic success as a major intersection of route-ways, the character and aspirations of the social group that controlled it, and its importance for travellers on the Via Flaminia (see pp. 10–11). There can be little doubt that the town was a key economic centre given the importance of the villa estates in the area, the presence of extensive brickyards and the evidence for the timber trade (see above, p. 10). This was enhanced by its role as a hub with a significant river port on the route leading up from Rome into Umbria. We equally may note that its position as a communication centre will have reinforced its regional function as a place where people gathered to market produce.

However, production of wealth is not in itself sufficient, since there also had to be mechanisms and motives for its expenditure on the urban centre, features that were clearly absent at other towns. Small centres like Forum Novum (Laurence 1999; Gaffney, Patterson and Roberts 2004) and Carsulae (Morigi 1997; Sisani 2006b: 181), which may have been the focus of *viritim* colonization, certainly did not see such major expenditure. Equally, towns where military veterans were settled after the Civil Wars and those that lost territory to newly-established colonies seem to have had their development depressed (J. Patterson 2008: 488–91). The suggestion that Ocriculum was linked closely to the Caesarian faction (Bispham 2007: 371–2) may account for the absence of veteran colonization, protecting it from its damaging effects. Such political connections also may provide a background understanding for the presence of the later Augusteum, demonstrating the loyalty of the citizens to the imperial house in the Julio-Claudian period. The only similar complex in the region was a small apsed hall within the forum at Lucus Feroniae (Torelli 1993: 33–4), a sanctuary that had close associations with a senatorial family, the Volusii. The combination of close links to the imperial regime and resident senatorial families, combined with their strong historical and familial links with the locality, may account for the extraordinary flowering of Ocriculum in the early Empire.

CONCLUDING COMMENTS

Much current scholarship lays emphasis on the variability of Roman urbanism, moving away from approaches that have sought common patterns and unifying trends (Laurence, Esmonde Cleary and Sears 2011). Indeed, the research on towns in the middle Tiber valley, within which the work at Otricoli was undertaken, has explored the variation in urban forms within a comparatively small area (Keay and Millett in press). Even against this background, it is clear that the site at Ocriculum is rather different from many of the Roman towns that are cited most frequently in the literature. This is evident most clearly in its unusual wealth of architectural and sculptural material, but is seen also in its small size and topographically determined plan. Whilst not wishing to move back to older patterns of explanation that promote particular type sites, it is worth concluding this discussion by making the point that irregularly organized towns were probably much more common in Roman Italy than the literature on towns might suggest. Archaeological research has tended to be biased towards those sites that are understood easily and are accessible for research, meaning that the many urban sites in the hilly areas of inland Italy, frequently lying beneath modern towns and villages, have been neglected, at least in the context of understanding overall town-plan issues rather than individual buildings. In this sense, Ocriculum is useful in providing an example of a 'hill town' on a major road that was abandoned in the post-Roman period and is thus available for study. Although the disentanglement of its development has proved challenging and there is still work to do, we trust that the ideas offered here

not only carry forward the understanding of this particular site, but also offer perspectives that might help in the understanding of this particular strand of urbanism in Roman Italy more generally. Certainly, the complex interaction between indigenous traditions, Roman influence and topographic constraint has made the study of the site amongst the most challenging we have approached in our research into the Roman towns of the middle and lower Tiber valley.

Note

1. This map, incidentally, shows the course of the Via Flaminia to the south of the town erroneously running southeast from the amphitheatre, not southwest.

REFERENCES

Abbreviations

CIL — *Corpus Inscriptionum Latinarum* (1863–). Berlin, Georg Reimer/Walter de Gruyter.

Ancient sources

Ammianus Marcellinus — Text and translation: J.C. Rolfe (1971) *Ammianus Marcellinus with an English Translation in Three Volumes* I. Cambridge (MA), Harvard University Press.

Cassiodorus, *Variae* — Translation: S.J.B. Barnish (1992) *Cassiodorus Variae Translated with Notes and Introduction.* Liverpool, Liverpool University Press.

Cicero, *Pro Milone* — Text and translation: N.H. Watts (1979) *Cicero in Twenty-eight Volumes* XIV, *Pro Milone.* Cambridge (MA), Harvard University Press.

Florus — Text and translation: E.S. Forster (1966) *Lucius Annaeus Florus Epitome of Roman History.* Cambridge (MA), Harvard University Press.

Hydatius — Text and translation: R.W. Burgess (1993) *The Chronicle of Hydatius and the Consularia Constantinopolitana.* Oxford, Clarendon Press.

Liber Pontificalis — Translation: R. Davis (1992) *The Lives of the Eighth-century Popes (*Liber Pontificalis*).* Liverpool, Liverpool University Press.

Livy — Text and translation: B.O. Foster, *Livy with an English Translation in Fourteen Volumes.* Vol. III *Books V–VII* (1940), Vol. IV *Books VIII–X* (1963), and Vol. V *Books XI–XXII* (1969). Cambridge (MA), Harvard University Press.

Pliny, *Epistulae* — Text and translation: B. Radice (1972) *Pliny Letters and Panegyrics in Two Volumes* I, *Letters, Books I–VII.* Cambridge (MA), Harvard University Press.

Pliny, *Historia Naturalis* — Text and translation: H. Rackham, *Pliny Natural History with an English Translation in Ten Volumes.* Vol. II *Libri III–VII* (1969), Vol. IX *Libri XXXIII–XXXV* (1952). Cambridge (MA), Harvard University Press.

Polybius — Text and translation: W.R. Paton (1960) *Polybius The Histories with an English Translation in Six Volumes* II. Cambridge (MA), Harvard University Press.

Res Gestae — Text and translation: P.A. Brunt and J.M. Moore (1967) *Res Gestae Divi Augusti: the Achievement of the Divine Augustus.* Oxford, Oxford University Press.

Strabo — Text and translation: H.L. Jones (1969) *The Geography of Strabo with an English Translation in Eight Volumes,* Vol. II (1969). Cambridge (MA), Harvard University Press.

Tacitus, *Histories* — Text and translation: C.H. Moore (1996) *Tacitus The Histories Books I–III.* Cambridge (MA), Harvard University Press.

Modern sources

Aldine, T. (1978) Anfore foropopiliensi. *Archeologia Classica* 30: 236–45.

Amedick, R., Bielefeld, D., Grassinger, D., Wölfel, C. and Koch, G. (1998) *Akten des Symposiums "125 Jahre Sarkophag-Corpus" Marburg, 4–7. Oktober 1995.* Mainz am Rhein, von Zabern.

Ashby, T. and Fell, R.A.L. (1921) The Via Flaminia. *Journal of Roman Studies* 11: 125–90.

Bailey, D.M. (1980) *Catalogue of the Lamps in the British Museum. 2. Roman Lamps Made in Italy.* London, British Museum Press.

Ballance, M.H. (1951) The Roman bridges on the Via Flaminia. *Papers of the British School at Rome* 19: 78–117.

Bartman, E. (1992) *Ancient Sculptural Copies in Miniature.* Leiden, Brill.

Bertacchini, M. (2006) Geologica tra passato e presente nel territorio di Otricoli. In L. Cenciaioli, *Un museo per Otricoli: l'antiquarium di Casale San Fulgenzio*: 11–17. Perugia, Fabrizio Fabbri Editore.

Bertacchini, M. and Cenciaioli, L. (2008) The past and present of the Roman town of Ocriculum (Umbria). In F. Coarelli and H. Patterson (eds), *Mercator Placidissimus: the Tiber Valley in Antiquity*: 837–47. Rome, Quasar.

Berti, F., Carandini, A., Fabbricotti, E., Gasparri, C., Giannelli, M., Moriconi, M.P., Palma, B., Panella, C., Picozzi, M.G., Ricci, A. and Tatti, M. (1970) *Ostia* II. *Le Terme del Nuotatore, scavo dell'ambiente IV (Studi miscellanei* 16). Rome, De Luca.

Bignamini, I. and Hornsby, C. (2010) *Digging and Dealing in Eighteenth-century Rome.* New Haven/London, Yale University Press.

Bispham, E. (2007) *From Asculum to Actium: the Municipalization of Italy from the Social War to Augustus.* Oxford, Oxford University Press.

Bloch, H. (1947) The Roman brick-stamps not published in volume XV,1 of the *Corpus Inscriptionum Latinarum. Harvard Studies in Classical Philology* 56–7: 1–128.

Bloch, H. (1948) Indices to the Roman brick-stamps not published in volume XV,1 of the *Corpus Inscriptionum Latinarum* and the LVI–LVII of the *Harvard Studies in Classical Philology. Harvard Studies in Classical Philology* 58–9: 1–104.

Bousquet, A., Felici, F. and Zampini, S. (2008) Produzione e circolazione del materiale ceramico nella media valle del Tevere in epoca imperiale e tardoantica. In F. Coarelli and H. Patterson (eds), *Mercator Placidissimus: the Tiber Valley in Antiquity*: 621–54. Rome, Quasar.

Brecciaroli Taborelli, L. (1978) Contributo alla classificazione di una terra sigillata chiara italica. *Rivista di Studi Marchigiani* 1: 1–38.

Brecciaroli Taborelli, L. (2005) Ceramiche a vernice nera. In D. Gandolfi (ed.), *La ceramica e i materiali di età romana. Classi, produzioni, commerci e consumi (Quaderni della Scuola Interdisciplinare della Metodologie Archeologiche* 2): 59–103. Bordighera, Istituto Internazionale di Studi Liguri.

Broise, H. and Scheid, J. (1987) *Le balneum des frères Arvales.* Rome, École Française de Rome.

Cain, H.-U. (1985) *Römische Marmorkandelaber.* Mainz am Rhein, von Zabern.

Cain, H.-U. and Dräger, O. (1994) Die Marmorkandelaber. In G. Hellenkemper Salies, H.-H. von Prittwitz und Gaffon and G. Bauchheuss, *Das Wrack: der Antike Schiffsfund von Mahdia*: 239–58. Cologne, Rheinland-Verlag.

Cambi, F. (1989) L'anfora di Empoli. In *Amphores romaines et histoire économique: dix ans de recherche* (*Collection de l'École Française de Rome* 114): 564–7. Rome, École Française de Rome.

Caponeri, M.R. and David, E. (eds) *Il Tevere a Otricoli. Vita e fede sulle rive del fiume* (*Bollettino per i beni culturali dell'Umbria* 8). Viterbo, Editore BetaGamma.

Carandini, A. and Panella, C. (1973) (eds) *Ostia* III. *Le Terme del Nuotatore* (*Studi miscellanei* 21). Rome, De Luca.

Carandini, A. and Panella, C. (1977) (eds) *Ostia* IV. *Le Terme del Nuotatore, scavo dell'ambiente XVI* (*Studi miscellanei* 23). Rome, De Luca.

Carandini, A., Fabbricotti, E., Gasparri, C., Gasparri Tatti, M., Giannelli, M., Moriconi, M.P., Palma, B., Panella, C., Polia, M. and Ricci, A. (1968) *Ostia* I. *Le Terme del Nuotatore, scavo dell'ambiente IV* (*Studi miscellanei* 13). Rome, De Luca.

Carlucci, C., De Lucia Brolli, M.A., Keay, S., Millett, M. and Strutt, S. (2007) An archaeological survey of the Faliscan settlement at Vignale, *Falerii Veteres* (province of Viterbo). *Papers of the British School at Rome* 75: 39–121.

Carta, M. (1978) Materiali rinvenuti. In M. Carta, I. Pohl and F. Zevi, *Ostia. La Taberna dell'Invidioso* (*Notizie degli Scavi di Antichità* 32, *Suppl.*): 46–164. Rome, Accademia Nazionale dei Lincei.

Cenciaioli, L. (2000) *Ocriculum: guida ai monumenti della città antica*. Umbertide, Laboratorio Tipografico La Fratta.

Cenciaioli, L. (2006) *Un museo per Otricoli: l'antiquarium di Casale San Fulgenzio*. Perugia, Fabrizio Fabbri Editore.

Cenciaioli, L. (2008) Otricoli: nuove ricerche e recenti acquisizioni della Soprintendenza per i Beni Archeologici dell'Umbria. In F. Coarelli and H. Patterson (eds), *Mercator Placidissimus: the Tiber Valley in Antiquity*: 811–36. Rome, Quasar.

Cenciaioli, L. (2012a) Otricoli (Tr.). Terme di Iulius Iulianus. Nuovi dati per la ricostruzione del mosaico pavimentale della sala ottagonale. In F. Guidobaldi and G. Tozzi (eds), *Atti del XVII colloquio dell'Associazione Italiana per lo Studio e la Conservazione del Mosaico (Teramo, 10–12 marzo 2011)*: 169–77. Tivoli, Scripta Manent Edizioni.

Cenciaioli, L. (2012b) Gli aspetti archeologici. In M.R. Caponeri and E. David (eds), *Il Tevere a Otricoli. Vita e fede sulle rive del fiume* (*Bollettino per i beni culturali dell'Umbria* 8): 21–32. Viterbo, Editore BetaGamma.

Champlin, E. (1983) Figlinae Marcianae. *Athenaeum* 61: 257–64.

Cifani, G. (2003) *Storia di una frontiera: dinamiche territoriali e gruppi etnici nella media valle Tiberina dalla prima età del Ferro alla conquista romana*. Rome, Libreria dello Stato.

Cipollone, M. and Lippolis, E. (1979) Le mura di Otricoli. In M.B. Simoni (ed.), *Studi in onore di F. Magi* (*Nuovi quaderni dell'Istituto di Archeologia dell'Università di Perugia* 1): 58–77. Perugia, EUCOOP.

Dareggi, G. (1978) Una terracotta architettonica da Otricoli. *Mélanges de l'École Française de Rome* 90: 627–35.

Dareggi, G. (1982) Il ciclo statuario della 'Basilica' di Otricoli: la fase Giulio-Claudia. *Bollettino d'Arte* 14: 1–36.

DeLaine, J. (1997) *The Baths of Caracalla in Rome: a Study in the Design, Construction and Economics of Large-scale Building Projects in Imperial Rome* (*Journal of Roman Archaeology Supplementary Series* 25). Portsmouth (RI), Journal of Roman Archaeology.

DeLaine, J. (2002) Building activity in Ostia in the second century AD. In C. Bruun and A. Gallina Zevi (eds), *Ostia e Portus nelle loro relazioni con Roma* (*Acta Instituti Romani Finlandiae* 27): 41–101. Rome, Institutum Romanum Finlandiae.

De Ligt, L. (2008) The population of Cisalpine Gaul in the time of Augustus. In L. de Ligt and S.J. Northwood (eds), *People, Land and Politics: Demographic Developments and the Transformation of Roman Italy 300 B.C.–A.D. 14*: 139–83. Leiden, Brill.

de Rubertis, R. (2012) *Rilievi archeologici in Umbria*. Naples, Edizioni Scientifiche e Artistiche.

Di Giuseppe, H., Bousquet, A. and Zampini, S. (2008) Produzione, circolazione e uso della ceramica lungo il Tevere in epoca repubblicana. In F. Coarelli and H. Patterson (eds), *Mercator Placidissimus: the Tiber Valley in Antiquity*: 587–619. Rome, Quasar.

Diosono, F. (2008) Il commercio del legname sul fiume Tevere. In F. Coarelli and H. Patterson (eds), *Mercator Placidissimus: the Tiber Valley in Antiquity*: 251–77. Rome, Quasar.

Dressel, H. (1899) *Corpus Inscriptionum Latinarum* XV, 2.I. Berlin, Georg Reimer/Walter de Gruyter.

Duncan, G.C. (1965) Roman Republican pottery from the vicinity of Sutri (Sutrium). *Papers of the British School at Rome* 33: 134–76.

Dwyer, E.J. (1982) *Pompeian Domestic Sculpture: a Study of Five Pompeian Houses and their Contents*. Rome, Giorgio Bretschneider.

Dyson, S.L. (1976) *Cosa: the Utilitarian Pottery* (*Memoirs of the American Academy in Rome* 33). Rome, American Academy in Rome.

Ettlinger, E. (1990) (ed.) *Conspectus Formarum Terrae Sigillatae Italico Modo Confectae*. Bonn, R. Habelt.

Farrar, L. (1998) *Ancient Roman Gardens*. Phoenix Mill, Sutton Publishing.

Fontaine, P. (1990) *Cités et enceintes de l'Ombrie antique* (*Études de philologie, d'archéologie et d'histoires anciennes* 27). Brussels/Rome, Institut Historique Belge de Rome.

Fontana, S. (2003) Le anfore. In H. Patterson, A. Bousquet, H. Di Giuseppe, F. Felici, S. Fontana, R.E. Witcher and S. Zampini, Le produzioni ceramiche nella media valle del Tevere tra l'età repubblicana e tardo-antica: 169. *Rei Cretariae Romanae Fautorum Acta* 38: 161–70.

Fontana, S. (2005) Le ceramiche da mensa italiche medio-imperiali e tardo-antiche. In D. Gandolfi (ed.), *La ceramica e i materiali di età romana. Classi, produzioni, commerci e consumi* (*Quaderni della Scuola Interdisciplinare delle Metodologie*

Archeologiche 2): 259–78. Bordighera, Istituto Internazionale di Studi Liguri.

Fontana, S. (2008) South Etruria revisited: le anfore, un tentativo di analisi quantitativa. In F. Coarelli and H. Patterson (eds), *Mercator Placidissimus: the Tiber Valley in Antiquity*: 655–70. Rome, Quasar.

Gaffney, V., Patterson, H. and Roberts, P. (2004) Forum Novum (Vescovio): a new study of the town and bishopric. In H. Patterson (ed.), *Bridging the Tiber. Approaches to Regional Archaeology in the Middle Tiber Valley* (*Archaeological Monographs of the British School at Rome* 12): 237–51. London, British School at Rome.

Gaffney, V., Patterson, H., Piro, S., Goodman, D. and Nishimura, Y. (2004) Multimethodological approach to study and characterize Forum Novum (Vescovio, central Italy). *Archaeological Prospection* 11: 201–12.

Gasperoni, T. (2005) Nuove acquisizioni dai *praeia* dei *Domitii* nella valle del Fosso del Rio. In C. Bruun (ed.), *Interpretare i bolli laterizi di Roma e della valle del Tevere: produzione, storia economica e topografica* (*Acta Instituti Romani Finlandiae* 32): 103–20. Rome, Institutum Romanum Finlandiae.

Giuliano, A. (1987) (ed.) *Museo Nazionale Romano. Le sculture:* I,9. *Magazzini, i ritratti, parte* I. Rome, De Luca Editore.

Golvin, J.-C. (1988) *L'amphithéâtre romain: essai sur la theorizations de sa forme et de ses functions* (*Publications du Centre Pierre Paris* 18). Paris, de Boccard.

Goodman, D., Piro, S., Nishimura, Y., Schneider, K., Hongo, H., Higashi, N., Steinberg, J. and Damiata, B. (2008) GPR archeometry. In H.M. Jol (ed.), *Ground Penetrating Radar Theory and Applications*: 479–508. Amsterdam/Kidlington, Elsevier Science.

Goodman, D. and Piro, S. (2009) Ground penetrating radar (GPR) surveys at Aiali (Grosseto). In S. Campana and S. Piro (eds), *Seeing the Unseen. Geophysics and Landscape Archaeology*: 297–302. London, CRC Press.

Goudineau, C. (1970) Note sur la céramique à engobe interne rouge-pompeién. *Mélanges de l'École Française de Rome. Antiquité* 82: 159–86.

Graham, S. (2006) Ex Figlinis: the Network Dynamics of the Tiber Valley Brick Industry in the Hinterland of Rome (*British Archaeological Reports, International Series* 1,486). Oxford, John and Erica Hedges.

Gros, P. and Torelli, M. (1994) *Storia dell'urbanistica: il mondo romano*. Bari, Laterza.

Guattani, G.A. (1784) *Monumenti antichi inediti ovvero notizie sull antichità e belle arte de Roma per l'anno MDCCLXXXIV.* Rome, Pagiarini.

Guattani, G.A. (1827–32) *Monumenti sabini*. Rome, C. Puccinelli.

Harrison, E.B. (1965) *Archaic and Archaistic Sculpture* (*The Athenian Agora* XI). Princeton, American School of Classical Studies in Athens.

Hawkes, C.F.C. and Hull, M.R. (1947) *Camulodunum. First Report on the Excavations at Colchester, 1930–1939* (*Reports of the Research Committee of the Society of Antiquaries of London* 14). Oxford, Oxford University Press.

Hay, S., Keay, S., Millett, M. and Piro, S. (2005) Otricoli: an integrated geophysical and topographical survey. In *Proccedings of the 6th International Conference on Archaeological Prospection: Extended Abstracts*: 421–6. Rome, Consiglio Nazionale delle Ricerche.

Hay, S., Keay, S., Millett, M. and Sly, T. (2008) Urban field-survey at Ocriculum (Otricoli, Umbria). In F. Coarelli and H. Patterson (eds), *Mercator Placidissimus: the Tiber Valley in Antiquity*: 797–809. Rome, Quasar.

Hay, S., Johnson, P., Keay, S. and Millett, M. (2010) Falerii Novi: further survey of the northern extra-mural area. *Papers of the British School at Rome* 78: 1–38.

Hayes, J. (1972) *Late Roman Pottery*. London, British School at Rome.

Hayes, J.W. (1976) Pottery: stratified groups and typology. In J.H. Humphrey (ed.), *Excavations at Carthage 1975 Conducted by the University of Michigan* I: 116–17. Tunis, Cérès Productions.

Iacopi, G. (1963) *L'antro di Tiberio a Sperlonga*. Rome, Istituto di Studi Romani.

Jashemski, W.F. (1979) *The Gardens of Pompeii*. New Rochelle (NY), Caratzas Brothers.

Johnson, P., Keay, S. and Millett, M. (2004) Lesser urban sites in the Tiber valley: Baccanae, Forum Cassii and Castellum Amerinum. *Papers of the British School at Rome* 72: 69–99.

Kapitän, G. (1961) Schiffsfrachten antiker Baugesteine und Architekturteile vor den Künsten Ostsiziliens. *Klio* 39: 267–318.

Keay, S.J. (1984) *Late Roman Amphorae in the Western Mediterranean. A Typology and Economic Study* (*British Archaeological Reports, International Series* 196). Oxford, British Archaeological Reports.

Keay, S. and Millett, M. (in press) Republican and early Imperial towns in the Tiber valley. In A.E. Cooley (ed.), *A Companion to Roman Italy*. Oxford, Blackwell-Wiley.

Keay, S., Millett, M. and Strutt, K. (2006) An archaeological survey of Capena (La Civitucola, provincia di Roma). *Papers of the British School at Rome* 74: 73–118.

Keay, S., Millett, M., Robinson, J., Taylor, J. and Terrenato, N. (2000) Falerii Novi: a new survey of the walled area. *Papers of the British School at Rome* 68: 1–94.

Keay, S., Millett, M., Poppy, S., Robinson, J., Taylor, J. and Terrenato, N. (2004) New approaches to Roman urbanism in the Tiber valley. In H. Patterson (ed.), *Bridging the Tiber. Approaches to Regional Archaeology in the Middle Tiber Valley* (*Archaeological Monographs of the British School at Rome* 12): 223–36. London, British School at Rome.

Keay, S., Millett, M., Paroli, L. and Strutt, K. (2005) *Portus: an Archaeological Survey of the Port of Imperial Rome* (*Archaeological Monographs of the British School at Rome* 15). London, British School at Rome.

Kleiner, D.E.E. (1992) *Roman Sculpture*. New Haven/London, Yale University Press.

Lackner, E.-M. (2008) *Republikanische Fora*. Munich, Biering and Brinkmann.

Launaro, A. and Millett, M. (2011) Roman Colonial Landscapes: 2011 geophysical survey report. http://www.classics.cam.ac.uk/faculty/research_groups_and_societies/roman_colonial_landscapes/rcl_report_2011/rcl_report_2011_geophys/ [last consulted 23.03.2013].

Laurence, R. (1999) *The Roads of Roman Italy: Mobility and Cultural Change*. London/New York, Routledge.

Laurence, R., Esmonde Cleary, S. and Sears, G. (2011) *The City in the Roman West, c. 250 BC–AD 250*. Cambridge, Cambridge University Press.

Maña, J.M. (1951) Sobre tipologia de ánforas púnicas. In *VI congreso arqueológico del sudeste Español, Alcoy, 1950*: 203–10. Cartagena, Imprenta Papeleria Española.

Marangou Lerat, A. (1995) *Le vin et les amphores de Crète de l'époque classique à l'époque impériale* (*Études crétoise* 30). Athens, École Française.

Martin, A. (1991) Sondages under S. Stefano Rotondo (Rome): the pottery and other finds. *Boreas* 14: 157–78.

Marzano, A. (2007) *Roman Villas in Central Italy: a Social and Economic History*. Leiden, Brill.

Mattusch, C.C. (1994) Bronze herm of Dionysos. In G. Hellenkemper Salies, H.-H. von Prittwitz und Gaffon and G. Bauchheuss, *Das Wrack: der Antike Schiffsfund von Mahdia*: 431–50. Cologne, Rheinland-Verlag.

Mau, A. (1898) *Corpus Inscriptionum Latinarum* IV, 2. Berlin, Georg Reimer.

McCann, A.M. (1978) *Roman Sarcophagi in the Metropolitan Museum of Art*. New York, Metropolitan Museum of Art.

Millett, M. (2000) Dating, quantifying and utilizing pottery assemblages from surface survey. In R. Francovich, H. Patterson and G. Barker (eds), *Extracting Meaning from Ploughsoil Assemblages*: 53–9. Oxford, Oxbow Books.

Millett, M. (2013) Understanding Roman towns in Italy: reflections on the role of geophysical survey. In P. Johnson and M. Millett (eds), *Archaeological Survey and the City*: 24–44. Oxford, Oxbow Books.

Ministero per i Beni Culturali e Ambientale (1990) *Rediscovering Pompeii*. Rome, 'L'Erma' di Bretschneider.

Monacchi, D. (1999) La sigillata chiara italica. In D. Soren and A. Soren (eds), *A Roman Villa and a Late Roman Infant Cemetery. Excavations at Poggio Gramignano, Lugnano in Teverina*: 259–76. Rome, 'L'Erma' di Bretschneider.

Monacchi, D., Nini, R. and Zampolini Faustini, S. (1999) *Forma* e urbanistica di Narni romana. *Journal of Ancient Topography* 9: 237–98 (= G. Uggeri (ed.), *Proceedings of the Third Congress of Ancient Topography: Roman Roads in Italy*).

Morel, J.-P. (1981) *Céramique campanienne: les formes*. Rome, École Française de Rome.

Moreno, P. (1995) (ed.) *Lisippo: l'arte e la fortuna*. Milan, Fabbri.

Morigi, A. (1997) *Carsulae: topografia e monumenti* (*Atlante tematico di topografia antica, III supplemento*). Rome, 'L'Erma' di Bretschneider.

Morselli, C. and Tortorici, E. (1989) (eds) *Curia, Forum Iulium, Forum Transitorium* (*Lavori e studi di archeologia* 14, II). Rome, De Luca.

Oakley, S.P. (2005) *A Commentary on Livy Books VI–X. Vol.* III: *Book IX*. Oxford, Clarendon Press.

Panella, C. (2001) Le anfore di età imperiale del Mediterraneo occidentale. In É. Geny, *Céramiques hellénistiques et romaines* III (*Travaux du Centre Camille Jullian* 28): 177–275. Paris, Les Belles Lettres.

Pascual Guasch, R. (1962) Centros de producción y difusión geográfica de un tipo de ánfora. In *VII congreso nacional de arqueología, Barcelona, 1960*: 334–45. Zaragoza, Secretaria General de los Congresos Arqueológicas Nacionales Seminario de Arqueología Universidad de Zaragoza.

Patterson, H. (2004) (ed.) *Bridging the Tiber: Approaches to Regional Archaeology in the Middle Tiber Valley* (*Archaeological Monographs of the British School at Rome* 12). London, British School at Rome.

Patterson, H. (2008) The middle Tiber valley in the late antique and early medieval periods: some observations. In F. Coarelli and H. Patterson (eds), *Mercator Placidissimus: the Tiber Valley in Antiquity*: 499–532. Rome, Quasar.

Patterson, H. and Millett, M. (1998) The Tiber Valley Project. *Papers of the British School at Rome* 66: 1–20.

Patterson, H., Di Gennaro, F., Di Giuseppe, H., Fontana, S., Gaffney, V., Harrison, A., Keay, S.J., Millett, M., Rendeli, M., Stoddart, S., Roberts, P. and Witcher, R. (2000) The Tiber Valley Project: the Tiber and Rome through two millennia. *Antiquity* 284: 395–403.

Patterson, H., Di Giuseppe, H. and Witcher, R. (2004) Three South Etrurian 'crises': first results of the Tiber Valley Project. *Papers of the British School at Rome* 72: 1–36.

Patterson, J.R. (2006) *Landscapes and Cities: Rural Settlement and Civic Transformation in Early Imperial Italy*. Oxford, Oxford University Press.

Patterson, J.R. (2008) Modelling the urban history of the Tiber valley in the Imperial period. In F. Coarelli and H. Patterson (eds), *Mercator Placidissimus: the Tiber Valley in Antiquity*: 487–98. Rome, Quasar.

Pélichet, E. (1946) À propos des amphores romaines trouvées à Nyon. *Zeitschrift für Schweizerische Archäologie und Kunstgeschichte* 9: 189–202.

Pietrangeli, C. (1943) *Ocriculum (Otricoli)*. Rome, Reale Istituto di Studi Romani – Editore.

Pietrangeli, C. (1978) *Otricoli: un lembo dell'Umbria alle porte di Roma*. Rome, Ugo Bozzi Editore.

Pineschi, I. (1997) (ed.) *L'antica via Flaminia in Umbria*. Rome, Editalia.

Piro, S., Goodman, D. and Nishimura, Y. (2003) The study and characterisation of Emperor Traiano's villa (Altopiani di Arcinazzo, Roma) using high-resolution integrated geophysical surveys. *Archaeological Prospection* 10: 1–25.

Piro, S., Peloso, D. and Gabrielli, R. (2007) Integrated geophysical and topographical investigations in the territory of ancient Tarquinia (Viterbo, central Italy). *Archaeological Prospection* 14: 191–201.

Piro, S., Ceraudo, G. and Zamuner, D. (2011) Integrated geophysical and archaeological investigations of Aquinum in Frosinone, Italy. *Archaeological Prospection* 18: 127–38.

Pohl, I. (1970) Materiali rinvenuti. In F. Zevi and I. Pohl, Ostia (Roma). Casa delle Pareti Gialle, salone centrale. Scavo sotto il pavimento a mosaico: 75–234. *Notizie degli Scavi di Antichità* 24, Suppl. I: 43–234. Rome, Accademia Nazionale dei Lincei.

Pohl, I. (1978) Materiali rinvenuti. In M. Carta, I. Pohl and F. Zevi, *Ostia. Piazzale delle Corporazioni, Portico Ovest: saggi sotto i mosaici* (*Notizie degli Scavi di Antichità* 32, Suppl.): 216–443. Rome, Accademia Nazionale dei Lincei.

Pugliese Carratelli, G. (1981) (ed.) *Enciclopedia dell'arte antica classica e orientale — atlante delle forme ceramiche* I. *Ceramica fine romana nel bacino mediterraneo (medio e tardo impero)*. Rome, Istituto della Enciclopedia Italiana.

Ricci, A. (1987) Ceramica a pareti sottili. In G. Pugliese Carratelli (ed.), *Enciclopedia dell'arte antica classica e orientale — atlante delle forme ceramiche* II. *Ceramica fine romana nel bacino mediterraneo (tardo ellenismo e primo impero)*: 231–357. Rome, Istituto della Enciclopedia Italiana.

Rizzo, G. (2003) *Instrumenta Urbis* I. *Ceramiche fini da mensa, lucerne ed anfore a Roma nei primi due secoli dell'impero* (*Collection de l'École Française de Rome* 307). Rome, École Française de Rome.

Roberts, P. (1997) The Roman pottery. In T.W. Potter and A.C. King (eds), *Excavations at the Mola di Monte Gelato. A Roman and Medieval Settlement in South Etruria* (*Archaeological Monographs of the British School at Rome* 11): 316–63. London, British School at Rome.

Robinson, H.S. (1959) *The Athenian Agora* V. *Pottery of the Roman Period. Chronology.* Princeton, American School of Classical Studies at Athens.

Sear, F. (2006) *Roman Theatres: an Archaeological Study.* Oxford, Oxford University Press.

Sisani, S. (2006a) Ceramica a vernice nera. In L. Cenciaioli (ed.), *Un museo per Otricoli. L'antiquarium di Casale San Fulgenzio*: 69–70. Perugia, Fabrizio Fabbri Editore.

Sisani, S. (2006b) *Umbria, Marche* (*Guide archeologiche Laterza*). Rome/Bari, Laterza.

Sommella, P. (1988) *Italia antica: l'urbanistica romana.* Rome, Jouvence.

Spinazzola, V. (1928) *Le arti decorative in Pompei e nel Museo Nazionale di Napoli.* Milan, Bestelli and Tumminelli.

Staffa, A.R. (1986) Località Rebibbia, via San Cannizzaro. Un punto di sosta lungo la via Tiburtina antica fra l'età di Augusto e la tarda antichità. *Bullettino della Commissione Archeologica Comunale di Roma* 91: 642–78.

Stefani, E. (1909) Regione VI (Umbria). XIX. Otricoli. *Notizie degli Scavi di Antichità*: 278–91.

Stefani, E. (1929) Regione VI (Umbria). V. Otricoli. *Notizie degli Scavi di Antichità*: 259–60.

Steinby, E.M. (1974) La cronologia delle 'figlinae' doliari urbane dalla fine dell'età repubblicana fino all'inizio del III secolo. *Bullettino della Commissione Archeologica Comunale di Roma* 84: 7–132.

Steinby, E.M. (1981) La diffusione dell'opus doliare urbano. In A. Giardina and A. Schiavone (eds), *Società romana e produzione schiavistica* II*: merci, mercatori e scambi nel Mediterraneo*: 237–45. Bari, Editori Laterza.

Stopponi, S. (2006) Terrecotte architettoniche. In L. Cenciaioli, *Un museo per Otricoli: l'antiquarium di Casale San Fulgenzio:* 55–68. Perugia, Fabrizio Fabbri Editore.

Torelli, M. (1993) *Etruria* (*Guide archeologiche Laterza*). Rome/Bari, Laterza.

Ungaro, L. (2007) The memory of antiquity. In L. Ungaro (ed.), *The Museum of the Imperial Forums in Trajan's Market*: 130–69. Milan, Electa.

Visconti, G.B. and Visconti, E.Q. (1782–1807) *Il Museo Pio-Clementino*, 7 vols. Milan, N. Bettoni.

Wallace-Hadrill, A. (2011) The monumental centre of Herculaneum: in search of the identities of the public buildings. *Journal of Roman Archaeology* 24: 121–60.

Welch, K.E. (2007) *The Roman Amphitheatre: from its Origins to the Colosseum.* Cambridge, Cambridge University Press.

Werner, K.E. (1998) *Die Sammlung Antiker Mosaiken in den Vatikanischen Museen.* Vatican City, Monumenti, Musei e Gallerie Pontificie.

Yerkes, S.R. (2005) 'Living architecture': living column and vegetal urn. Shared motifs in Roman wall painting and 'neo-Attic' furnishings. In J. Pollini (ed.), *Terra Marique: Studies in Art History and Marine Archaeology in Honor of Anna Marguerite McCann*: 149–70. Oxford, Oxbow Books.

CONTRIBUTORS' ADDRESSES

LUANA CENCIAIOLI
Soprintendenza per i Beni Archeologici dell'Umbria,
Piazza Partigiani 9, 06121 Perugia, Italy.
luana.cenciaioli@beniculturali.it

SOPHY DOWNES
Institute of Archaeology, University College London,
31–4 Gordon Square, London, WC1H 0PY, UK.
sophydownes@gmail.com

ROSE FERRABY
Department of Geography, College of Life and
Environmental Science, University of Exeter,
Amory Building, Rennes Drive, Exeter, EX4 4RJ, UK.
roseferraby@hotmail.com

ENRICO FLORIDI
Via Mazzini 1, 05030 Otricoli (TR), Italy.
enricofloridi@tiscali.it

SHAWN GRAHAM
Department of History, 400 Paterson Hall,
Carleton University, 1125 Colonel By Drive, Ottawa,
Ontario, K1S 5B6, Canada.
Shawn_Graham@carleton.ca

SOPHIE HAY
APSS, Archaeology, University of Southampton,
Highfield, Southampton, S017 1BF, UK.
S.A.Hay@soton.ac.uk

SIMON KEAY
Archaeology, University of Southampton, Highfield,
Southampton, S017 1BF, UK.
sjk1@soton.ac.uk

MARTIN MILLETT
Faculty of Classics, University of Cambridge,
Sidgwick Avenue, Cambridge, CB3 9DA, UK.
mjm62@cam.ac.uk

LEONIE PETT
Museum of London Archaeology, Mortimer Wheeler
House, 46 Eagle Wharf Road, London, N1 7ED, UK.
leoniepett@me.com

SALVATORE PIRO
Istituto per le Tecnologie Applicate ai Beni Culturali
ITABC-CNR, c.p. 10,00016 Monterotondo Sc. (Roma),
Italy.
Salvatore.Piro@itabc.cnr.it

TIM SLY
Archaeology, University of Southampton, Highfield,
Southampton, S017 1BF, UK.
tjts@soton.ac.uk

LACEY M. WALLACE
Faculty of Classics, University of Cambridge,
Sidgwick Avenue, Cambridge, CB3 9DA, UK.
lmw36@cam.ac.uk

ANDREW WALLACE-HADRILL
Faculty of Classics, University of Cambridge,
Sidgwick Avenue, Cambridge, CB3 9DA, UK.
aw479@cam.ac.uk

SABRINA ZAMPINI
Parsifal Cooperativa di Archeologia, via Gaba 40,
00183 Rome, Italy.
sabrinazampini@yahoo.it

INDEX

compiled by Martin Millett